Joanna Lumley

Tim Ewbank and Stafford Hildred, both well-known show business journalists, are the authors of best-selling biographies of John Thaw, David Jason and Rod Stewart.

Joanna Lumley

The Biography

Tim Ewbank and Stafford Hildred

André Deutsch

First published in 1999
by Andre Deutsch Limited

This paperback edition first published
by Andre Deutsch Limited, 2002
20 Mortimer Street
London
W1T 3JW

A catalogue record for this book is available from the British Library

ISBN 0 233 05092 2

10 9 8 7 6 5 4 3 2 1

Typeset by Derek Doyle & Associates, Liverpool
Printed in Great Britain

Dedication

Tim: To Emma, Oliver, my mother Joy, and Carole Anne, and in special loving memory of my father Harry. And to Bailey, Rupert, Kali and Sammy, and to The Old Parsonage, Rolvenden.

Stafford: To Janet, Claire, Rebecca, and my mother Rosemary.

Acknowledgements

The authors would like to record their thanks and appreciation to all of the many people who have helped in the writing of this biography. We are particularly grateful, of course, to Joanna Lumley herself for living such a remarkable life and for giving her time so generously to us for interviews over the years.

Fellow actors, writers, directors, producers and film and television executives also helped enormously but some of them would prefer to remain anonymous, so we would simply like to thank them all collectively.

For their encouragement, practical assistance, support, friendship and inspiration, we would also like to thank: Brenda Barton, Sue and Guy Batchelor, Ruth Berry, John Blake, Roger Boar, Norma and Cecil Booker, Kim Booker, Rachael Booker, Day Bowman, Paul Bradley, Mary Chapin Carpenter, Brian Clemens, Tom and Mags Condon, Commander Rod Craig, Juliet Dakers, John and Wendy Dickinson, Kenneth Eastaugh, Kathy Ferris, Peter and Janet Garner, Rod and Joy Gilchrist, Grimsby Town FC, Richard Hall, Kate Henderson, Jerry Johns, Piers and Hilary Johnston, Alan Kingston, Simon Kinnersley, Robert Kirby, David Knight, Fiona Knight, Ray and Janet Lewis, Sarita Martin, Geoff Mayor, George and Bonnie Muir, Garth and Davina Pearce, Jean Platts, Celia Rebuffa, the remarkable Walter Robson, Kathy Ritchie, Andrew Sinclair, Rev Clive Tomkins, the late Michael Nixon, Gordon Webb, Gilly and Jeremy Webster, George and Lottie Wood. And finally a big thank you to Tim Forrester, Deborah Waight, Louise Dixon and Claire Richardson and all at André Deutsch for their co-operation and kindness.

Contents

Introduction
First Lady

Even fast asleep Joanna Lamond Lumley is restless. Ever since she was born, the first lady of British entertainment has been in an almighty hurry to cram a kaleidoscope of different experiences into just the one life. She usually wakes very early, in her stylish but deliberately unostentatious five-storey home in Stockwell, south London, frequently with the vivid memory of a nightmare fresh in her mind.

The horror of the River Thames flooding is a regular scenario, where Joanna finds herself rushing frantically along the Embankment screaming to warn people sitting in the meadows of the historic London of medieval times that they are about to be washed away. They fail to take notice and then Joanna is left starting the day feeling guilty that she had been unable to save them.

However much she achieves in life, Joanna always wants to do more. Dazzling the nation as Purdey in *The New Avengers* in the 1970s and doubling audiences up with laughter as Patsy in *Absolutely Fabulous* in the 1990s is only a small part of her whole high-speed world. She is an award-winning actress, a best-selling writer, a devoted mother, a supportive and loving wife, a gifted artist, a highly active supporter to some thirty charities and assorted good causes, and much, much more. She has become an icon for the oppressed because she always, always listens.

Instead of complaining about the restrictions and irritations of five-star celebrity status her screen success has provided, like so many of her contemporaries, Joanna chooses to use her fame for positive ends. Joanna has been voted everything from Britain's most stylish scarf wearer to the owner of the toes men would most like to tickle. She has been selected as everything from the sexiest body to the new Dr Who. But instead of bridling at the mindless intrusion of it all, Joanna has given time and money most selflessly to support countless campaigns she believes in.

She has taken a pig to Parliament and even locked herself in a cage like a battery hen to lend publicity to Compassion in World Farming. She has battled for the homeless. She journeyed to Eritrea for a heartening Comic Relief report and she stripped for Children in Need. She has given thousands and thousands of pounds of her own money to support worthy causes. Much of the earnings from endless voice-overs and adverts for which she is forever in demand goes in secret donations to the needy. When she heard an under-funded inventor in despair on the radio she rang up and rescued his wonderful new way of combating oil slicks with her own money. She has raged at conferences of businessmen and raved at busy prime ministers in her determination to fight for a gentler, kinder way of life.

Sometimes of course it becomes too much. For Britain's most in demand actress, time is now the most precious commodity. At her lowest she feels, 'Every day now, I wake up and there is somebody tugging at me and I think, "Oh God, please just leave me alone!" It is very difficult to get people to understand. For them it might be only one little charity but for me it might be the 43rd that week.' But because Joanna hates to hurt or disappoint, she fights to find a way of helping. As she puts it, 'It's really only when you're tired that everything seems too much trouble. When you're full of energy you think, "Well, actually, I can do it all."'

It seems almost unfair that along with looks most women would die for and a personality that occasionally verges on the saintly, Joanna also has one of the best brains in the land. When celebrities were persuaded to take the Common Entrance exam by a newspa-per, Joanna excelled herself and came close to equalling eminent historian A.J.P. Taylor in his own subject. When Joanna was persuaded to appear on the esoteric television game show *Call My Bluff* in the 1970s, Frank Muir was so taken with her combination of brains and beauty that he shamelessly campaigned for her to reappear as often as possible. 'She is like a shaft of sunlight in a grey world,' said Frank.

Yet however willowy and feminine she might appear, Joanna is no soft touch and has a strength of will that can take men's breath away. While filming the science fiction series *Sapphire and Steel* with David McCallum she clashed with director Shaun O'Riordan who recalls, 'She didn't want to obey rules, didn't Jo. We filmed a scene on the top of ATV House in Great Cumberland Place where there was supposed to be a flat belonging to aliens. Joanna and David were both right on the edge of this high building. They seemed to be without any fear of vertigo. I had to lie down because I couldn't take it.

'The episode was about animals which had been killed or eaten and because of the sorrow of all the creatures, we wanted Sapphire to shed a tear. But we could not get Joanna to agree that Sapphire would be so saddened by what had happened that she would weep. David McCallum and I were saying "Sapphire's got to have a heart, she's got to be able to feel." "Not at all," Joanna said. "She is an element sent down to function." You couldn't beat her down – she's an educated girl and will match you argument for argument in metaphysical subjects or anything else. She wouldn't have it and that was the end of that.'

Joanna might have been born in exotic Kashmir but she has the typically English passion for supporting the underdog very much at her heart. Her inspirational mother Beatrice taught her as a young child that every living creature deserves love and respect and that belief is at the centre of Joanna's philosophy. She might look and sound as though she was born with several canteens of silver cutlery in her mouth but there was no vast family wealth or privilege to enable her to leapfrog over others to success. As a young woman struggling alone in the ultra-competitive worlds of modelling and acting, she carved out a remarkable career with energy and talent while all the time caring wonderfully for her son, whom she cheerfully brought up without the benefit of a husband to help out. She protected Jamie fiercely from the start by keeping the identity of his father secret and worked like a Trojan to earn the money to send him to Harrow.

There were plenty of setbacks along the way, a rare medical

complaint that had a succession of doctors monstrously mis-diagnosing her, a disastrous first marriage, and the endless fight to be accepted as much more than a pretty face and a beautiful body. She was cruelly exploited in a film that required her to strip off and parade her young body. Other movies frustratingly failed even to appear.

She has experienced life and learned as much from her difficul-ties as from her delights. Former lovers and her charismatic but highly unsuitable first husband, Jeremy Lloyd, are still among her closest friends.

Joanna most definitely does not want to be richer and richer and has an icy contempt for the excesses of materialism. She firmly believes that less materialism and more spiritualism would benefit the West. 'I've been to very poor countries and I'm convinced that happiness is not connected with wealth. It's how you count yourself lucky.' Joanna insists she is as 'shallow as a puddle' but is always very aware of the spiritual side of life and is very sensitive to different locations. 'There are journeys I don't like and will always go a different way, given the chance. There are some roads in East Kent that have a strangely menacing feel-ing even on hot summer days. When I first saw Stonehenge I couldn't get out of the car, I was so afraid. There is a hilly mount in Italy where a gory battle took place and when I went there all I could sense was shrieking and death and hatred, even though there were butterflies on the scratchy meadow grasses and high clouds in the blue sky. There are evil places and it is important to know good from bad.'

Fame and fortune do not mean that much to Joanna. She works hard and spreads her net wide because you have to unless, as she put it, 'You are a genius like David Jason who can flit effortlessly from top job to top job.' For her the more she gets the more she wants to give. 'One of the great pressures in our life is that people always want to be first or top or the biggest seller or very very rich. Real life is not like that. Always having to be the most is rather a bore. I don't want to be the highest paid performer or the most popular – who wants that? Actually the more you give away, the more comes back.' And if you dare to suggest that all sounds rather worthy, Joanna says, 'I'm a sinner. I only do this out of sheer desperation that I'm nearly the devil! I just try my hardest to be good. I realized quite a long time ago that unless I tried to be terribly good, I wouldn't even keep up to the norm.'

Joanna was greatly inspired by a close friend who died of Friedrich's Ataxia, a disease which leaves the brain operating but eats up the body. 'The last four years of his life were awful,' she said. 'Except that he married, he continued to invent crosswords, he went to New Orleans to listen to jazz, and he was a fabulous letter writer. I also know people with a new Mercedes, Armani clothes and a nice family and they're as miserable as sin. It's not what you've got, it's what you think and believe that is important.'

The love of her life arrived when she was old enough to really appreciate it. Now Joanna is devoted to her musician husband Stephen Barlow, but she is still very much her own woman. He has his own busy schedule so their time together is at a real premium. Joanna prefers to work while he is touring. 'If he is doing an opera in Australia for five weeks, it is pointless for me to sit in an hotel room all day.' But they make time for each other and for their marriage. This summer they walked from Sienna to Rome together, fifteen miles a day along the ancient roads, in a 'golden' experience for Joanna. 'Marriage is more than just falling in love. It is managing to live happily together,' says Joanna.

The heir to the British throne has certainly spotted something special in Joanna. She was invited to not one but three of the parties to celebrate his fiftieth birthday. Joanna was flattered and thoroughly enjoyed the experience but she was a great deal more impressed by Prince Charles's forward-thinking views on the environment than ever she was by the occasion.

For his part Prince Charles surely recognizes the warmth and goodness of an exceptional human being and loves the Lumley sense of humour. She is relaxed and self-assured enough now to laugh at some of her past. In early interviews she was almost always head over heels in love with the actor Michael Kitchen or with pop singer Rod Stewart, and she almost always said, 'I love him more than life itself.' It was true at the time of course but now that she has found her husband Stephen Barlow it seems that although she is rather less effusive about her feelings and restricts herself to public observations like, 'I am terribly lucky to be happily married,' she is in fact happier than ever.

Growing old has never bothered Joanna. 'When I was eighteen I couldn't wait until I was thirty – I thought that was the age I would really be together. But when I got to thirty I still thought I was a bit young and now I'm waiting till I get to about seventy-four before I hit my prime. That's not when I'm going to die, that's when I am really going to start living. All this now is just checking it out. I'm going to be outrageous when I grow old. I am going to be one of those old ladies who sit in church with their knees open letting it all hang out and doing all those things you've longed to do.'

It sounds as though the next twenty years are going to be absolutely fabulous fun for Joanna Lumley.

1
Early Childhood

In May 1946 the British government was preparing to ration bread for the first time as western nations mobilized against the growing threat of world famine, British boxer Freddie Mills was training for his world light heavyweight title fight against American Gus Lesnevich, and Prime Minister Clement Attlee was preparing to announce plans for an independent, united India.

At the start of that same month, the Attorney-General Mr Hartley Shawcross was preparing to announce new measures to deal with a major post-war social problem – nearly 50,000 British servicemen, fresh from fighting and winning the war but losing their marriages, were queuing up for a divorce.

But for one close-knit British service family thousands of miles away in Kashmir, high up in the Himalayas, there was much cause for rejoicing with the arrival of their second child, a baby girl. On the evening of 1 May 1946, Joanna Lamond, a sister for two-year-old Ælene, was born to Beatrice Lumley and her husband James who was in India serving with the 2nd 6th Gurkha Rifles.

The birth of Joanna in Srinagar, Kashmir, represented a continuation of a strong family connection with the Middle and Far East, which stretched back for generations. Joanna's grandfather had been a banker in India and she says: 'My parents lived out there, were married out there, had a honeymoon on the Dal lake in a houseboat and often conversed in Hindustani.'

But the initial joy of a new baby quickly gave way to some alarm for the Lumley family when Joanna contracted whooping cough. 'I had to be quickly brought down from the mountains,' says Joanna.

'They were so high up and I had to be brought down away from the mountain air to recover.

'We left India a year after I was born in 1947, after the partition of India, and went on to Hong Kong for two years, nipped back to England, then went out to Malaya when I was five and lived there till I was eight.'

In Hong Kong at the age of two, Joanna experienced sad loss for the first time when the little roo of her cuddly toy kangaroo tumbled forlornly from its mother's pouch from the balcony of their high-rise flat to the bustling street below never to be seen again.

'We always had tremendous amahs and ayas,' Joanna recalls. 'I used to cry at night because there was this water tank that used to crank at night – I called it the Gudda Gudda because of the noise it made. It made me howl at night when I was two and when my parents had gone out for the evening the amahs would take me into the kitchen in this high block of flats in Hong Kong and feed me dried melon seeds and rock me about and scream with laughter till my parents came back.'

Apart from the unfortunate loss of roo it was an early childhood of which Joanna has clear and fond memories and one about which she always talks with enthusiasm. 'It was a terribly happy time,' she says. 'Once your senses have been exposed to the Far East you yearn for the night noise of the Tropics, for hot dusty roads, monsoons, flowers that blossom and die in a night, trees that grow four feet in a week, great ships that put into port and are gone just as suddenly, the slums, movements.'

Joanna's father was given a new posting every three years which allowed for a few weeks' leave back in England in between. 'I remember that the Army sailing dates were always on my birthday, 1 May,' says Joanna, 'and on my fifth birthday we sailed for Malaya.

'It took a month in those days on those old troop ships. They had this extraordinary class system on the ship – officers and, awful words, other ranks. Other ranks had wonderful decks out in the sunlight and officer class had shields from the sun and so we were hidden away like white worms on sunless decks for the whole journey.

'But it was a particularly magical time. There was something terribly exciting about being at sea for two weeks and then seeing land. I understand sailors having a thing about the sea – waking up in the morning in completely different ports and everything is weird and the light is different and then you are off again, and the intense boredom and monotony and trappedness of a ship.

'When I first came to England I missed the storms, the smell of the dust with rain falling on it. I longed for the scent of spices and the night noises of insects.

'My father first went off to the jungle to fight when I was about six. When he came back with a beard six months later, my elder sister and I were shy, even wary of him. My mother then had to weave us and him gently back together again. Then he was off again. It must have been agony for him as he loved us more than life itself. As I got older it worried me a bit. I looked so much like he did as a boy and identified with him so. Those separations broke his heart and eventually made him leave Army life.'

Right from her earliest childhood Joanna learned from her father and her mother, especially, to love and respect animals and all living creatures. It was a lesson lovingly taught, one which Joanna was never to forget and which in years to come was to benefit all manner of animal charities which Joanna would fervently support.

'My mother has always loved animals,' says Joanna, 'but she also loves the lowest of the low and everything that creeps because, as a child, she was brought up in India and when she came to school in England she was brought up by a godmother who had dogs and parrots, birds, mice and rats.

'She always liked things that other people don't, like snakes and spiders. She wouldn't let people be unkind to lizards, snakes or spiders and I was always made to feel these were our friends and that we must help them.

'In Malaya she once found this beautiful iguana and she asked me: "What's the biggest lizard you've ever seen?" and I lied through my teeth and said I'd seen a really big one. So then she took me out the back of the house and there was this huge iguana. We had ducks at the time and the iguana went and ate the duck eggs and my mother thought that's good, the ducks can feed the iguana.

'But we had a Chinese cook at that time and one day he said

"Iguana eat duck eggs" and killed it. Mummy was livid. She sacked him on the spot and put the iguana in a sack and took it down to the jungle and buried it.

'Occasionally we'd see big snakes and I remember mummy once even tried to save a cobra that had got stuck in a monsoon drain. She was trying to coax it out.

'We always had cats and dogs, guinea pigs and odd animals around us when I was growing up. In Malaya we had a dog and a cat and went out for walks with the dog on a long lead because of rabies. One day we passed a huge sewage tank and heard mewing coming from inside and found that the Malays had got a litter of kittens and chucked them in. All had drowned except one and we pulled it out and it was our cat for three years. She was called Kinky because she had a kink in her tail. Then my father found a dog that was just wandering around the mess. It would have been put down so we took it in and loved it. We also had three ducks and took them for train rides carefully sitting them in dishes of water.

'I also remember the Gully-Gully men would come along at birthday parties and bring their snakes and they'd come to the ships in port and do tricks like produce eggs out of their ears and paper out of people's mouths. They also had lots of tricks with baby chicks. One chick, I remember, fell over the edge of the ship and landed light as thistledown in the water and paddled away. And, it being a British ship, a lifeboat was lowered and matelots rowed out to save this tiny chick.'

Joanna's memories of Malaya are vivid. 'I loved it out there,' she says, 'and I forgot England completely. I listened to stories of England, of green fields and fat sheep but in Malaya I saw only three sheep while we were out there and they were thin and spiky little creatures. In Malaya it was hot and the seasons never changed, the grass was green and very cutting and flowers opened for a day then dropped and trees grew in a month and it was so harsh and fierce. I remember the night noises, the birds, the sunsets, the smells, the vividness of it all. I remember houses on stilts and a rabid dog underneath when I came back from Mrs Calvert's dancing class where we always curtsied and the last dance was always a gallop round the room.

'I acted in school plays out there. I was a queen in one with a crown and a blue satin dress and I had to dance with a teddy bear for some Army stage show. My front teeth had just fallen out and my mother told me not to smile for the cameras.'

Joanna's first acting part was in a dramatization of the A. A. Milne poem 'The King's Breakfast', at the age of six. 'I can remember very clearly wearing a blue satin dress and walking down a flight of steps playing the Queen. They all clapped. I was the centre of attention.' Joanna told one of the authors years later she was always a great show-off and clown and loved to make people laugh.

'When I was seven I decided to be an actress, not only an actress but a movie star because I had seen a marvellous advertisement for cigarettes with two people, a man and a woman, and he was in a white tuxedo and she was in a strapless evening gown and they were leaning over some high balcony in Manhattan and there were the lights of New York and there were drinks and they had this incredible elegance and I thought: somewhere in this world it's going to be like that.

'In Malaya my parents would go out to dinner parties and my father was ADC to the High Commissioner so they'd go to King's House a lot and in those days you really dressed up – you wore beautiful long frocks and gloves and my mother would come in to kiss me goodnight and say, "Don't muss my hair, darling." And I thought: That's beautiful, that's what beautiful people look like dressed up in the evening with my father in his full dress uniform, white with the sword by his side and the Sam Browne. Marvellous! That's where I think I got the smell of how lovely it is to have lovely clothes.

'But in the Middle East it wasn't all grand and snob, it was a way of life. I learned a lot about the British Raj from my parents and my parents' friends and they were kind and good people. They were friends with their servants, true friends and treated them with the greatest courtesy and respect on both sides. It's a shame some people see the Raj like a distortion of history. My parents always impressed upon me that race, class, religion mean nothing.'

When Joanna was eight her father was posted to the War Office and the family packed up their belongings and made ready to leave the bungalow which had been their home in Malaya for the past three years. Reluctantly the Lumleys left their pets behind but bequeathed them to the incoming family of Brits replacing them, and prepared to return to England. 'My last memory of that time,' says Joanna, 'was getting on to a train for Singapore in my pyjamas and waving goodbye to everyone in my pyjamas. Then the train took us all the way through the night and finally we sailed for England.'

It was 2 June 1954 by the time the ship taking Joanna and her family nosed its way into Southampton waters. That day Lester Piggott was, at the tender age of eighteen, to become the youngest jockey ever to win the Derby at Epsom on Never Say Die, Maureen Connolly was on her way to winning her third successive women's singles Wimbledon title and Doris Day was top of the 'hit parade' with 'Secret Love', the Oscar-winning song from the film *Calamity Jane*.

'I was stunned at my first glimpse of England,' Joanna remembers, 'my storybooks showed neat fat hills, crisp little fences and apple-cheeked people and we were sallow and brown, lean with yellow hair.

'We arrived at Southampton at four in the morning and we were allowed to get up early and ran with great excitement to the decks and there was this sea of concrete and cranes and ships and trains and railway lines and overhead wires. It was horrifying. I wept for England. My England of my storybooks had been taken away. But it was high June and as we jogged across England in a train to Ashford and there were roses, I realized it was staggeringly beautiful.

'At first we lived on an aunt's pig farm at Woodchurch, near Tenterden, and then we moved to a house in Epsom we called Pokey Hole because we thought it was a terrible place. Pokey Hole claimed us for two years. Father would take us up to the Epsom Downs very early in the morning and out of the mist we'd hear the drumming of hooves which was very exciting and then we'd see the horses galloping past at 5 a.m. My father loved riding, he was a good horseman and he'd had polo ponies in the Far East – that wasn't grand, it was just the way of life out there.'

The Lumleys finally chose to settle in the Kent village of Rolvenden and Joanna's parents could hardly have chosen a more delightfully olde English village in which to raise her and her sister Ælene. Tucked away in a glorious, unspoilt area of rural Kent,

Rolvenden was a village where time had seemingly stood still for centuries and it remains very largely untouched by the march of time to this very day.

At first the family stayed in temporary accommodation for a year in a nearby hamlet, Rolvenden Layne, at picturesque Walnut Tree Cottage situated on the fringe of the delightfully named Pixies Lane, a sleepy narrow road where clusters of wild bluebells and primroses sprang up each spring and formed colourful carpets at the foot of the hedgerows lining the lane.

Outings on foot from Walnut Tree Cottage to Rolvenden village took on the form of adventure walks tinged with history for they took a wide-eyed Joanna past Frensham Manor, the magnificent mansion owned by the First Baron of Rolvenden, Lord Geddes, and his wife Lady Isabel, into a right turning past Frog Lane, past wild blackberry bushes bowing low under the weight of unusually huge, succulent berries, past horses lazily grazing in fields on the estate of Colonel Wood, and past the turreted coach house entrance to Great Maytham Hall.

At Great Maytham, one of the last great English houses to be designed and built by Sir Edwin Lutyens in 1910 on the site of its predecessor, there was a fairy story come to life for Joanna. She quickly learned that contained within Great Maytham's majestic grounds was an ancient and beautiful walled garden of some historical note.

This was the garden which was thought to have become the inspiration for Frances Hodgson Burnett's magical story of *The Secret Garden* in 1911. Frances Burnett, who wrote *Little Lord Fauntleroy* in 1886, had come over to England from America in the 1890s and rented Great Maytham where she had become enchanted by the garden. A small brass tablet commemorating Frances Burnett can to this day be found in Rolvenden church on the wall by the screen dividing the south aisle from the south chapel.

On the last leg of Joanna's short walks from Walnut Tree Cottage to the heart of Rolvenden village, she passed Sparkeswood, the house which was soon to become the Lumley family's permanent home. Situated on the other side of Pixies Lane from Walnut Tree Cottage, Sparkeswood was just a stone's throw from

Rolvenden's parish church dedicated to St Mary the Virgin which dates back to 1470. The church tower, built from dark coloured ironstone with white ragstone corners surmounted by a crocketed spirelet, boasted a distinctive blue clock and made for a highly visible landmark for Joanna on her frequent country rambles, often with the family's black Labrador, Hugo.

As a small girl Joanna had no trouble taking to Rolvenden as her new home and as she grew up she came to adore Rolvenden with its picture postcard charm of village green and white weather-boarded cottages cosily nestling together under Kent peg tile roofs. The Lumleys and their two little girls were warmly welcomed by the villagers and they soon became popular and valued members of the community. 'They were lovely people, real sweeties,' says Norma Booker who still lives there. 'The family were often to be seen together at church and Joanna's mother became a staunch member of the British Legion, making and organizing all the poppies for Remembrance Sunday. She later became a governor of the primary school and was very sweet with the little ones. She never passed anyone by in the village, she always stopped to say hello. And if she was in a car, she'd slow down to say hello or stop to admire any dogs being taken out for a walk.'

Joanna's parents always taught her good manners and to be polite. She curtsied to grown-ups until she was eleven. Her parents taught her never to give up and never to believe herself worse or better than anyone else.

Rolvenden provided an idyllic country childhood for Joanna for which she has always remained profoundly grateful. It was a childhood of a bygone age lived with an innocence that is hard to imagine in today's multi-TV-channel, computerized world of the young. 'I saw only three films before I was nine,' Joanna remembers. 'One was *Cinderella*. The witch queen in *Snow White*, wasn't she beautiful with her high collars, black pointed nails and blood-red lips and green eyes? That was wonderful. I've never seen anybody to touch her on the screen. Such imagination – Disney can make trees four miles high, valleys can go on and on, chasms can go on the earth's core, flowers can open, animals can talk. That's magic and that I love. My happiest films will always be cartoons. Where else can Sylvester be dropped by Tweety one thousand feet on to his face and get up and walk away, no bruises, nothing.'

Joanna's great screen idol for a long time was Dirk Bogarde after she had been taken to see *A Tale of Two Cities* at the cinema in Sevenoaks when she was nine. 'I adored him,' she says. 'I saw him in *The Spanish Gardener* and later in *A Tale of Two Cities* and I cried for hours and hours. Even now I get tears in my eyes thinking of "It is a far, far better thing that I do" and the way he let her go first so she wouldn't have to see him having his head cut off. The guillotine stuck in my mind as a nightmare instrument for years afterwards. The inhuman things we do!'

Apart from sporadic trips to the cinema, Joanna's was a childhood of bracing country walks in gumboots across rolling fields, of vaulting stiles, of climbing trees to peer into vacated birds' nests, of riding horses, of learning the names of flowers she picked and pressed and how to distinguish a Peacock butterfly from a Red Admiral.

It was tea and tennis parties, tombola at the annual village fête, gymkhanas, talk of sporting declarations and a brave half century on the village green, and reading books under a chestnut tree in the tranquil setting of the Lumleys' walled garden where often the only sound to be heard was the call of a wood pigeon, the drone of a distant threshing machine, or the laboured puffing of Rolvenden's steam train as it began its journey up the hill to Tenterden. Regular trips to a friend's fruit farm were eagerly looked forward to with the opportunity to ride once Joanna had learned to groom a horse. Many a happy summer day was spent at the farm riding or talking incessantly about horses while drawing and painting.

Like many small rural English villages in the 1950s, Rolvenden offered Joanna and the Lumley family an unhurried, peacefully undisturbed, simple, self-contained country way of life where even the village doctor, Brendan Wyllie, ran his surgery from home, The Old Parsonage. An appointment with Dr Wyllie was worth it just to walk up the tree-lined drive to his glorious family house set in five acres with two large ponds, a tennis court and marvellous views of fields, woods and orchards rolling gently away down towards Rye. While he listened to the ailments of his patients Dr

Wyllie would sit them down in the gentle setting of a beamed front room with a log fire roaring away in the inglenook.

The village had two pubs, The Star and The Bull, a primary school, a post office, a garage run by kindly Derek Tonbridge, a newsagent's, and a clutch of other shops. Mr Playfoot's general store in the high street stocked everything from Wellington boots to pots and pans to groceries, and Fred Porter's Falstaff Fish Shop thrived on its sale of wet fish while his wife Vi ran the Bon Bon.

Even Joanna's first school, Mickledene, had a distinct country feel to it. Situated about one mile outside Rolvenden, it was converted from two oast houses and for lessons Joanna sat at a desk in a classroom set out in the roundels. Mickledene, where Joanna eventually became a boarder, gave her an early love of poetry and a first appreciation of Shakespeare. She says: 'Because my sister and I had been to a very good Army school, we had been taught so well and when we came back we were a year ahead of our age group which made us appear frightfully bright.'

When Joanna first arrived at the school some of the other pupils regarded her with a little suspicion. After years spent in the far east, she looked so brown compared with them. But she soon settled in and made friends.

At Mickledene Joanna appeared in school plays, including a role as Will Scarlet in Robin Hood, walked in a two-by-two crocodile to Rolvenden church on Sundays and, at the age of eleven, showed enough promise at ballet to be taken up to London for a ballet exam. She was subsequently offered a place at Sadler's Wells Ballet School but by now Joanna was in the full grip of her horsey phase and she turned the opportunity down preferring to ride instead.

'I had to choose between ballet and riding,' she recalls, 'but my first passion was horses. I was mad about them and the dream was to ride at the White City. I danced until I was eleven but by then there was a lack of interest at school. There were only two pupils and the woman who taught us wore high heels and wouldn't get into ballet shoes. So I knew it was time to give up which was a shame as I wasn't bad at it.'

But Joanna had plenty to look forward to, including a letter in the post from the then Chancellor of the Exchequer, Selwyn Lloyd. She says: 'When I was eleven I'd written to him and said that if you just say £1 is worth £2 we would all be twice as rich. I got a charming letter back from Selwyn Lloyd at No. 11 Downing Street which said: "The Chancellor has received your letter and is giving it his due consideration and much thought." '

Best of all, Joanna had a new school to look forward to. At the end of the summer term in 1957 Joanna left Mickledene to join Ælene at St Mary's, an Anglican convent at Hastings.

2

St Mary's

In 1957 Paul Anka's paean to young love 'Diana' became one of the biggest selling singles of all time, Elvis Presley was packing the cinemas with *Jailhouse Rock*, Harold Macmillan replaced Anthony Eden as Prime Minister and the Russians put a dog, Laika, into space in Sputnik II.

In September of that year, Joanna Lumley joined her elder sister Ælene at school in Sussex at St Mary's Anglican Convent at 731 The Ridge, Hastings, a grey stone establishment set in walled grounds on a hill on the fringe of the historic seaside town.

St Mary's was an altogether more imposing seat of learning than Mickledene with its spacious grounds and playing fields fronting on to the main road which led in one direction to Battle and thence to London and in the other to the Hastings seafront some three miles away and on to Rye and to Dover. It had originally been built in the 1860s as a private residence by Victorian writer and traveller, Augustus Hare, but twelve years after his death in 1903 it was converted into a school by the Sisters of the Community of the Holy Family.

Joanna joined St Mary's as a boarder. 'I didn't start solidly boarding at school till I was eleven,' she says. 'I'd had a year of weekly boarding when I was about nine but I was terribly upset by it because you were neither one thing nor the other. You missed out on all the boarders' fun and then you cried on Monday morning when you had to leave home to go back to school. But I liked St Mary's with its old stone corridors, gas lamps, uneven floors and creaking rooms and clattery desks and generally I was very happy there and it was bliss because it seemed to me the whole school had been set up for me to be cheeky in and break the rules.

'I was extremely bad. There was a web of rules to be broken and I adored it. There were places out of bounds and I was out of bounds beyond measure. I was always out of bounds or late for everything. I was always terribly bad. I kept mice at school as the rest of my naughty friends did. They stayed in our pockets during the day and they'd run under your sleeves. At night we kept them in a drawer with our socks and pants and you can imagine what the smell was like.'

It was here at St Mary's in her teenage years that Joanna first tried out a bouffant hairstyle which was famously to become one of Patsy's TV trademarks some thirty years later in *Absolutely Fabulous*. 'There was one pretty girl called Patricia Somerfield who had lovely floppy yellow hair,' Joanna remembers, 'but the rest of us were gross. Before I discovered hairspray and kirbigrips I had hair from hell. It was a sort of beige, English mouse colour and was quite long. It was just bloody awful, frizzy and unbiddable. I first tried to change it at fourteen when I poured ink on it and I had it a plum colour when I was eighteen. The only time Mummy put her foot down was when I dyed my hair pillar-box red.

'The bouffant came in when I was about fifteen. For years we had been told to brush our hair one hundred times a night and now here was the chance to do the complete opposite. It was called back-combing then and it looked so sinful I couldn't wait to start. As I was still at school I used to construct the look myself. I used to razz up my hair with a comb until this sort of nightmare lozenge appeared on top of my head with a few bits hanging down around the sides. Then I secured it back with some kirbigrips at the back. It was not what you could call pretty, but god I thought I looked good.

'Really we looked ghastly. Unlike these glamorous schoolchildren who wander about with lovely long hair and pretty shoes, we were laced up in these ghastly brown shoes and dreary skirts and blazers and I looked like a lump in everything. Filthy blazer, ink everywhere on my fingers. I was a pig. Men have this secret idea that girls are wonderful at school. But we were dogs. We had fun, but god we were dodgy lookers. In my teens my face was plump and squidgy. I was also covered in spots. I just hated *me*. I used to pray "Dear God, I'll do anything if you'll only take my spots away." '

Despite this self-deprecation, Joanna's bouffant muffin of hair was in fact either much admired or regarded with insane jealousy by her friends who were also keen to vary their hairstyles as a way of breaking up school routine and of making themselves more glamorous in their plain school uniforms. 'We were all at it at school,' she says. 'But I could comb my hair up and it would stay there while others' dropped down. There was no secret to mine. I had the right hair and just backcombed it like mad. And if you could get some hairspray you could make it into a great brittle nightmare that no comb would get through.'

Big hair was in vogue at the time thanks to singer Dusty Springfield and to French screen sex symbol Brigitte Bardot who had taken to piling her blonde locks high on top of her head. Joanna says: 'I used to look in the mirror after I had done my bouffant and pout and talk to myself in this little French accent and convince myself I was like Brigitte Bardot. Hardly! My hair was a different colour, my face was completely different and I had spots. To this day I remain dissatisfied with my hair and I have changed it as radically and as often as possible. I haven't been blonde since I was a very little girl living in the Tropics. My hair is naturally a mousy brown.'

As with many boarding schools in the 1950s, St Mary's offered an insular life. Once girls had been delivered through the gates by their parents at the start of each term, their lives revolved around only what went on within the buildings, on the playing fields and in the gardens and extensive grounds bordered by stone walls. There was no television, no newspapers and just a screening of a film in the gym every fortnight and a dance in the gym on Saturday nights to lighten the routine.

At times it was a life to test all but the stoutest young hearts and those of the hardiest constitution. There were no radiators in the spartan dormitories and when the school was in the icy grip of winter and a chill wind was blowing in from the sea it would quite literally feel freezing. Joanna eventually graduated to the lacrosse, tennis and netball teams but the games kit also came in handy to pull on over pyjamas on winter nights as the cold air swirled in from the Sussex coast.

Religion, inevitably, played a key part in the daily running of St Mary's. School rules required Joanna and the other pupils to don little chapel veils to attend chapel twice a day and the Convent gave her a Christian upbringing and an appreciation of choral music which has had a profound effect on her life and still does. 'I cry if I go into a church and anybody starts singing anything,' Joanna says today.

'We went to chapel once before breakfast and once in the evening and we also had prayers after breakfast. The nuns were very holy, very good people and there was no whipping to go off to church. It was pleasant unforced religion, very high church, a lot of bells ringing and incense which I don't mind at all.

'I have very strong religious feelings even now because otherwise I would despair. It has actually helped me a lot. At the best of times I pray and at the blackest times in my life I pray like mad. I pray a lot. It's like when your mother says take this tonic it will work and you don't want to but then you do and you find it does work. I'm sure it's a good format acknowledging a greater force no matter what religion it is or how it takes over.

'What disturbs me a lot as you grow older is the cant, the schisms and the rifts in the church and you can't believe the Christian Church has been divided into so many splinters. It can't be right. When you study what the whole of Christianity is about or Buddhism or Mohammedanism you go back to very basic Christian rules: the Sermon on the Mount, the Lord's Prayer and the Ten Commandments and that's all. Forget all the Sundays before Septuagesima and what colour a bishop's mitre should be. Christ must be spinning in his grave – luckily he's not in one – but it's good and I'm glad people like it but that's not the most important thing.

'Not a lot of girls at St Mary's went on to be nuns but we played games against Catholic convents and I was upset to see a lot of them were small Irish girls who were over here in England and stayed over here for the holidays, presumably because they could not afford to be sent back to Ireland. They were being groomed for the nunnery and I thought that was sinister, very sinister, because they were only little girls and it's very easy when your parents are in a distant country to hang on to religion when they tell you your father, your true father, is the Father in Heaven. Well, we all know that but you can't restrict their thinking so much that that's the only home they've got.

'There were nuns, but sensible nuns. We didn't have to keep dropping curtsies or crossing ourselves. They were good teachers, nice people – very sweet and jolly and good-natured. I know nuns are good and wonderful people because I've met a lot of them and enjoy them enormously and I know a lot of them teach and nurse and I think that's splendid. But I don't remember Christ saying you should lock yourself up and not sleep with men and not have a good time. I don't remember him saying that. But if that's a good way of living for them, that's good.

'The nuns certainly did not force religion upon us at St Mary's at all. One goes through more religious phases just as you go through horsey phases, falling in love with film stars phases and crushes on other girls. It's a part of growing up and girls more than boys tend to get very religious probably around twelve and thirteen.

'I can remember when I was confirmed going to Confession and I suddenly didn't know what to confess. I was in fact a naughty little tyke but I couldn't truly think of that as a sin. I know I am a sinner but I didn't sin. I made mistakes. It wasn't evil.

'I don't like the guilt of the Church. We're not guilty. You have got to try to be good but you are not guilty just because you are human. I always felt a bit uncomfortable about making twelve-year-olds go down on their knees to God apologizing for being criminal. It didn't seem right, not at twelve.'

As well as readily embracing the unforced religion at St Mary's, Joanna showed an early glimpse of her charitable nature by sending Oxfam a silver bracelet she particularly treasured. But in class her mischievous nature still managed to get the better of her at times. 'They wouldn't let me take Religious Knowledge because I had been cheeky about St Paul,' she says. 'Only a few subjects interested me. I liked languages so I did French, Latin, German, English Literature and Art which I loved. I also did Italian and jammed that in a year and found it very easy to learn if you'd done

French and Latin. Latin is always good for *The Times* crossword.

'In History and Geography I used to sit at the back of the class and laugh until I cried. It was the confinement of a classroom, the same confinement you sometimes get on film sets or plays or rehearsals that's very dull and you get hysterics. I was very, very lazy but I could do the exams so they couldn't be too angry with me and in fact they even jumped me up a year.'

Joanna showed such talent and promise in Art that she was permitted to take Art O level one year earlier than scheduled. 'I loved painting. In the exam we had to do a picture of a statue in an overgrown garden and in *The Secret Garden* there were some glorious illustrations of that little girl. But there was one picture of her holding her hat and looking into the water of the pool where she had wandered down to and this flashed through my brain. Seeing it in my brain I painted something jolly like it and they were terribly impressed and gave me very high marks. But I always felt a bit of a fraud because I'd copied it out of my head.'

Just one year after she had begun boarding at St Mary's Joanna was quite unexpectedly given the part of Aaron in the school play *The Firstborn* by Christopher Fry. She was thrilled but it turned out to be a terrifying experience. 'I was then just twelve,' she recalls, 'and the Head Girl, Imogen Newbatt, was playing Moses and I was so frightened because I was the squit, the worm and you didn't even talk to someone one form above you let alone to the Head Girl. It simply wasn't done. So conversing with her was a nightmare.

'I've never had stage fright like that since. Nobody has held for me the awe of that Head Girl, at my having to speak lines to her and she would answer me back again. Always in my mind I knew that as soon as the play was over I would have to hold the door open for her or clean her shoes because I had been naughty or something.

'To add to my nerves I didn't understand the play. I had to say a line with the word "pregnant" in it and they wondered if I was old enough to know what the word meant. I had to say: "One hundred pregnant women had to dig their graves" and there were long discussions about it until finally they took me aside and asked me if I knew what the word pregnant meant. I said I did, but I don't know if I really did. I was quite old enough to know but in those days one was a child. I wore sandals and climbed trees till I was fourteen or fifteen and we had vows that we would not kiss boys or wear lipstick or stockings and that we'd be the tough guys and we'd be up in the trees like Tarzan. At fifteen! It's difficult to believe now. But back then I was lazy, had spots and thought boys were disgusting until I was sixteen.'

Joanna's performance in *The Firstborn* showed potential enough for her to become regarded as an automatic choice for future school stage productions. She played Jo in *Little Women* and featured in various nativity plays. But as she grew in stature Joanna's height often led to her playing the male roles. One of her most notable was when she played Petruchio in *The Taming of the Shrew* with a false moustache glued to her upper lip. It was a defining experience because, thanks to the expertise of her broad-bosomed drama teacher Mrs Curran, it also opened Joanna's eyes to the endless possibilities of acting and drama.

In rehearsals Mrs Curran, although nudging late middle age, took it upon herself to play Katharina to Joanna's Petruchio. Joanna was enthralled by the way her teacher effortlessly slipped into the role. 'Suddenly she changed into a petulant twenty-two-year-old with no make-up, no props, no tricks with false noses, nothing,' Joanna remembers, 'and I thought: "Now that's what it's all about." I remember thinking: "I believe it."' Mrs Curran equally sensed that Joanna had grasped the moment and stopped the rehearsal in mid flow. 'Look everybody,' she said, 'watch Jo do this. You'll be an actress, Jo, you know how to move.'

The school production of *The Taming of the Shrew* was comple-mented a few days later by a trip to London for Joanna and other pupils involved in the play to see the Royal Shakespeare's own production starring Diana Rigg, Vanessa Redgrave and Derek Godfrey. When the curtain came down Joanna went backstage and was breathless with excitement when she was able to obtain Diana Rigg's autograph. It was something the two of them were able to joke about years later when Joanna gained a small role in the James Bond film *On Her Majesty's Secret Service*, in which Diana Rigg took the female lead, and later still when Joanna followed Diana as an Avengers girl.

After *The Taming of the Shrew*, Joanna, by now thoroughly stage-struck, was given roles in Wilde and Shaw plays at St Mary's and went on to excel in her drama exams. She came out top not only of the school with extra honours but top of the South of England to boot. She even received a special award because she was also excellent when it came to reciting a poem although the award came as a total surprise to Joanna because she felt she had delivered it simply, without any great energy.

The nuns generally regarded Joanna as an exceptionally bright girl and it was no surprise when she comfortably achieved passes in nine subjects at O level. But Joanna disappointed everyone including herself by gaining just French at A level. She failed Latin and German and says she has only herself to blame.

Whereas her photographic memory had served her well at O level, A levels required more than just memorizing Latin ablative absolutes the night before. 'I took French, Latin and German at A level and S level in French but I was such an idle sod I never opened a book,' she says. 'It was only after I'd left school that I realized the delights of learning.

'Until A levels I could go into the lavatory the night before an exam and read and hold everything in my brain. I could read it off the page into my head and then I could go into the exam and pass although two days later I'd no idea what it was all about.

'But you can't pass A levels like that. You have to have read the books and to have done the work. So although I passed French and they gave me German O level again, I didn't get French S level or Latin A level but I retained a great love for them and I still keep Latin books about which I read through now and again. As soon as I got into Virgil I was mad about Latin. It's a beautiful language. I adore words and grammar and Latin teaches you English. For example, if you know your Latin you don't get problems about saying something is "different to". You know it's "different from".'

It was Sister Dilys's ability to make French accessible and exciting which got Joanna through at A level, she says, but it was having to read Cicero's speeches, which she disliked, rather than the Latin poetry she adored which did for her in the Latin exam. And Joanna had got off on the wrong foot with German because she had been forced to take it at A level when really she would have preferred to take English instead. Joanna reckons this enforced switch to German rather than English at A level marked the end of her childhood. It was, she reflects, the very first time in her life she had been forced to do something much against her will.

But by the time Joanna was seventeen and in her last term at St Mary's, she had shown such promise in the school drama productions that she was encouraged to audition for the Royal Academy of Dramatic Art. Mrs Curran gave her special training to prepare her for the audition and Joanna travelled up to London to take her place in the queue of would-be students at Britain's most prestigious drama college. Joanna remembers it vividly. 'As we queued up waiting our turn, I saw there were a lot of boys there smiting their chests and going: "Blood, blood, blood!" My goodness, I thought, they've gone right over the top. But I did notice that they were the ones who all got called back.

'This was my first audition ever and I was trembling at the knees when my turn came and they asked what's your name and why are you here. I had to do a piece from *St Joan* which I hated because she was carping away in prison about no daylight and I couldn't identify with Joan then.

'At one point in the audition I was pausing for some electric effect and I was prompted very loudly and that threw me completely because they then just wanted me to say my piece and get off. They were not interested in me. I was failed dismally and I thought: Never! I'm not going to any of these drama schools, it's not for me. They don't want what I am and I don't admire what they want – which may have been pig-headed but that's how I felt.

'They turned me down so smartly my feet had hardly touched the stage long enough for me to open my plummy mouth. I did the audition awfully. I was oppressed and afraid and appalled, quite clearly not the kind of material they were looking for, but I terribly wanted to act.'

Joanna's jaundiced view of drama schools had also been coloured by her participation in the Hastings Music Festival, an event which encapsulated poetry as well as the usual violin and piano. Joanna was entered at the festival to recite several poems and she was astonished at the over-the-top histrionics of some of her rivals as they recited their poems.

'I can remember cringing at some of these girls reading their poems,' she says. 'They were terribly twee and bright and gay and perky and stage-schoolly. I didn't like that at all. I thought that I'd get up and do a rather subtle, under-played delivery – even back then I was doing film-acting instead of doing the play to the audience. But the other girls did just that and I thought they were awful. Yet they won. So I'm glad I didn't go to stage school. I think I'd have been bad.'

Joanna's last year at St Mary's was clouded by a humiliating demotion when she was stripped of her prefect's badge for smoking. The punishment was announced publicly once she had finished reading the lesson in chapel. Joanna was standing behind the Head Nun as she announced to a hushed school that she had the very unpleasant task to perform of demoting Joanna. Then Joanna and other girls who had also been caught smoking were told to attend the headmistress for their punishment. Joanna remembers the shame as the Head whispered 'Judas' at her as she turned on her heel and swept past.

Joanna has always maintained that her time at St Mary's was very largely a happy one. But right throughout her teenage schooldays there was something which worried her intensely, a nagging anxiety which cast a frightening shadow over her teenage years and which ultimately was to have momentous repercussions.

While all her schoolfriends began having their monthly periods, Joanna was puzzled and then alarmed to find that she did not. She was growing and fast developing the body of a young woman but, her periods remained mystifyingly absent.

At first Joanna was unconcerned, fully aware that some girls developed faster than others. But as time went on without any sign of the problem righting itself, it gradually became more of a worry to her that her body was not functioning in a way that should have been. 'I wasn't the same as the others and that was terrible,' she says. 'I hated it. I felt lousy.'

The problem was so personal and intimate that Joanna felt quite isolated, unable to share her fears with her friends and peers and certainly not with the nuns. She was too embarrassed even to raise the subject with her mother, although Mrs Lumley's heart would have undoubtedly gone out to her younger daughter if she had but known the anguish Joanna was going through.

In hindsight, Joanna knows that her mother would have willingly talked the matter through with her and would have taken immediate steps to try to sort out the problem if she had but known and if Joanna had plucked up the courage to tell her. But as a highly self-conscious teenager, Joanna felt unable to turn to her for advice on this matter.

There were occasions when Joanna was going through puberty when the subject of sex was introduced at home. But Joanna felt that any discussion with her parents to do with sex would somehow contaminate her and them and their relationship. So Joanna wretchedly suffered in silence and kept her secret totally to herself.

Such was her inner torture about what might be wrong with her and what she should do about it that Joanna went to great lengths at school to pretend that nothing was amiss. 'I used to fib,' she says. 'There were things called Doctor White's sanitary towels and every month girls would go to matron and ask for a pack. I used to go and ask for them and store them up even though I had no need for them.'

Finally, Joanna summoned the courage to go and see the school doctor, who happened to be a man. He listened intently to what Joanna had to say then sent her on her way with what he must have imagined were the comforting words she was anxious to hear. He assured Joanna that everything was all right and went on to vouch that when she was happily married she would have babies. But Joanna walked away anything but convinced. Instinct told her everything was far from right and this nagging anxiety and fear that something was very wrong almost certainly took its toll on Joanna's final years at St Mary's.

During her last year she felt she had outgrown the school. She says, 'I didn't enjoy my last year there. At St Mary's you were expelled if you talked to boys or if you smoked and at seventeen I was finding that a bitter pill to take. I was head prefect and I kept having to write lists or tick little girls off which bored me to death.

'I left St Mary's with only one A level, no wish to go to drama school and no hopes of going to university which was all rather a disappointment to everybody except me because the thought of going to university appalled me having just got free of school.'

If anyone had suggested to Joanna that within a couple of years she would be emerging as one of Britain's top ten working models, she would have laughed them to scorn.

3

Modelling

The year 1964 saw the launch of the BBC's new TV channel BBC-2 and on ITV actress Jane Rossington threw open the doors of a mythical Midlands motel to millions of soap opera viewers with the words: 'Crossroads Motel. Can I help you?'

It was also the year Harold Wilson took Labour to power but for eighteen-year-old girls like Joanna Lumley, 1964 was the year when British youth was holding sway. Beatlemania was reaching a peak with the release of the Fab Four's first film, *A Hard Day's Night*. It was the year the BBC bowed to the demands of teenagers and launched *Top of the Pops*, a TV show which reflected the hit records youngsters were buying as fast as they could be pressed. Not so welcome for the BBC, but greeted with glee by British teens, were the pirate radio ships like Radio Caroline and Radio London which had begun to rule the airwaves with their diet of non-stop pop hits broadcast from off the British coast outside territorial waters.

It was the year Manfred Mann's Paul Jones sang 'Doo Wah Diddy Diddy', which became a popular chorus at teenage summer parties, and Diana Ross and the Supremes hit number one with the Motown classic 'Baby Love'. It was also the year when a short-sighted girl from Dagenham calling herself Sandie Shaw topped the charts in her bare feet with a Bacharach–David song 'There's Always Something There To Remind Me', and an ex-convent girl with the face of an angel called Marianne Faithful had teenage boys in raptures over her look of lustful purity while she sang 'As Tears Go By'.

Although at this time ex-convent girl Joanna was relieved to be out of school at last, her delight was soon replaced by a realization that she really ought to get out in the world and do something. At school she had harboured four ambitions – to become Prime Minister, a brain surgeon, a pilot, or an actress.

Having been turned down by RADA, Joanna had decided not to try for any other drama colleges, a decision which almost certainly was to delay her being regarded as a serious actress later on in life but one which at least prevented her from possible further rejection in her teens. That, she feels, might have been very hard to take. But now the prospect of finding herself some sort of employment, although somewhat daunting, was a moral, almost puritanical, imperative for Joanna and soon she had landed herself a job working for family friends in a shop in nearby Tenterden.

Situated just three miles away, Tenterden was the nearest town to Joanna's home at Rolvenden. With its thirteenth-century beginnings, its hop-picking heritage and its famous association with the Cinque Ports, Tenterden is steeped in history. At Smallhythe Place, about one mile outside the town, is the sixteenth-century half-timbered house which was home to Shakespearian actress Dame Ellen Terry from 1899 to her death in 1928.

As a shopping centre, Tenterden has always been much patronized by Kent's county set. The High Street is a former turnpike road constructed in 1761 and by the 1950s when Joanna was setting off on the number ninety-seven bus from Rolvenden for shopping expeditions as a teenager, several of the eighteenth-century timber-framed buildings which lined the north side of the High Street had been turned into fashionable shops selling upmarket goods.

It was at just such a shop, called Argosy, that Joanna found employment as a general assistant earning £5 a week. Argosy sold very beautiful furniture and rather expensive Swedish glass and Joanna was conscious that she hardly fitted in with the goods on display.

'In the shop I'd wear my nice home-knitted jerseys and my tweed skirt,' Joanna recalls. 'At school, as you played games every day and you ate like a horse, you became a rather large person. And since my mother also used to give me building-up sandwiches, at seventeen rising eighteen I had indeed become a rather large person.

'But I can remember the change in me when one Saturday afternoon a sylph-like creature floated into the shop wearing a vast fox-fur coat. She was pale as snow with white lily legs and, with pale little hands with scarlet nails, she picked out a few things to go. Then she wrote a cheque and drifted out and I thought "How wonderful! But here am I, all clod-hopping in gum boots getting on the bus to go home." '

Once again, just as the elegance of the woman in the cigarette advertisement had so captivated Joanna when she was a child, so now the wealthy elegance and sophistication of the young woman she had just served in Argosy had similarly entranced her.

On the way home Joanna was deep in thought as the bus wound its way down the hill from Tenterden, juddered over the old steam railway crossing at the foot of the incline and meandered up the country road dividing the Kent meadows which surround rural Rolvenden. By the time the bus was slowing to drop Joanna off in the centre of the village, her mind was made up. She too was going to be thin and elegant. She was heading home to announce to her mother and father that she was going to become a model.

'I told my parents that I thought I'd like to go to London,' Joanna remembers, 'and mummy and daddy, who'd never bat an eyelid, said: "Why, what do you want to do?" I said, "I want to be a model." Now this was just after the Christine Keeler–Profumo affair and that's what Christine Keeler was called – a model. Daddy fell silently to the floor but then stood up again and said: "Fine!" '

The most reliable and reputable route to modelling was through grooming courses and one London organization in particular, the Lucie Clayton Modelling Agency and Training School, had built itself an impressive reputation offering young ladies a sound grounding in decorum, deportment, poise, grooming and etiquette in its Charm Course, as well as providing the rudimentary requisites for modelling on its Modelling Course.

Lucie Clayton's had started up in 1928 and its long established standing over a period of more than thirty years appealed not just to Joanna's parents but to Joanna herself. It was the top modelling agency in the country and just four years earlier, in 1960, two coltish teenage girls called Jean Shrimpton and Celia Hammond had emerged on the same day having completed the same Lucie

Clayton course to embark on modelling careers – and look what had happened to them. They had both become hugely successful. Celia was on her way to becoming revered photographer Norman Parkinson's favourite model and Jean 'The Shrimp' Shrimpton was now the reigning monarch of modelling, her gamine face adorning the cover of every fashion magazine in both Britain and America.

Jean Shrimpton held the admiration and the envy of teenage girls everywhere, Joanna included. It wasn't just Jean's extraordinary beauty they all envied, it was also the fact that Jean was a model who seemed to have it all, not least the love of actor Terence Stamp, voted in one classroom poll at Joanna's school, St Mary's, 'the world's most beautiful man'.

Models, it seemed to teenage girls like Joanna, had the time of their lives. They earned good money, travelled to exotic locations, wore wonderful clothes and had famous boyfriends. Mention the name of a pop star, a rising young actor, or a thrusting young fashion photographer and the odds were that his girlfriend was a model. There was Jean Shrimpton and first David Bailey then Terence Stamp, Patti Boyd and Beatle George Harrison, Suzy Kendall and Dudley Moore, Judy Huxtable and Peter Cook. Michael Caine also fell in love with another Lucie Clayton model, Shakira.

But when Joanna plucked up the courage to travel to London and walked into the Bond Street headquarters of Lucie Clayton for an interview, what she was told was not at all what she was hoping to hear. They informed her that she was considerably overweight for modelling and her back was too hollow. They also told her that her mouth was too large, but she had heard that before. Joanna's father had once teased her that her mouth was like a hammerhead shark's.

At least at five feet eight inches, Joanna had the height for a model. 'When I said: "Can I be a model?" they said, "Ugly, fat lady, no – unless you take our course", which was a month of mornings and only £12. So I took it.

'We learned to get in and out of E-Type Jaguars with our knees together so that nobody could see our knickers, and how to put on make-up. We learned to say "Thank you" and wear blue eye shadow. It wasn't really a great help.'

Walking around with books on their heads, improving their posture by imagining they had a steel rod running up their backs, learning how to cover their faces in pancake make-up, how to eat asparagus without dribbling butter down their chins and how to leave a room by pausing at the door and throwing a dazzling smile over the shoulder, may have seemed tedious for Joanna and the other aspiring models but it nevertheless gave them the confidence and poise which young girls were expected to exude whether they were strutting down the catwalk or making conversation at a cocktail party. 'Women perform better if they think they look good,' was the Lucie Clayton principal's tenet, and the course was designed to enhance the confidence of her young charges.

It must have done wonders for Joanna. 'One afternoon, just for a lark, I borrowed a friend's suit and went off to the Jack Barclay car showroom in Berkeley Square and pretended I wanted to buy a Rolls-Royce,' Joanna remembers. 'What gall! I had fourpence in my purse to get me home to Earls Court.'

The Lucie Clayton courses were calculated to make the girls feel important and glamorous even if the exaggerated model walk they were taught did appear awkward and faintly absurd – shoulders back, hips thrust well forward and one foot crossing over in front of the other each step. But it was a walk which Joanna was expected to learn and she would regularly practise it down the Earl's Court Road on her short walk home from the tube station to her aunt's flat in Bramham Gardens where she was temporarily staying while she worked out whether she really was cut out for modelling and London life.

The Charm Course lasted for one month and, for those girls with real modelling potential, the course held the promise of propelling them straight on to the books of Lucie Clayton's own modelling agency attached to the school.

Disappointingly for Joanna, her first chance to model after completing the course was not on some exotic location in some far-flung land but in the Model Suit department at Debenham and Freebody, a store barely a stone's throw from Lucie Clayton's, in London's Wigmore Street. There Joanna was required to clock in every morning and she earned £8 a week. She says: 'I had to show the clothes when the buyers came in – people from America or from the grand shops. Sometimes I had to get sandwiches for other people's lunch or run errands or deliver clothes. Once I remember having to work the switchboard when one of the girls was away on holiday. It was awful – I kept cutting people off. Rows of little switches and lights: beep! "Yes, hello? One moment I'll put you through." Click!'

Confined to the rigid clock-in routines and strictures of Debenham and Freebody, it was far from the life Joanna had envisaged for herself as a model. 'I just wanted to be free, I wanted to race about doing loony things and travel for which modelling was ideal,' Joanna explained. Debenham and Freebody was a foot on the first rung of the modelling ladder but the only regular trips she was able to look forward to each day were those to the store's restaurant at lunchtime.

Unexpectedly the chance to escape from Debenham's was indirectly presented to her by Jean Muir who was then in her early thirties and operating as a dressmaker under the banner Jane and Jane but who went on to become a revered designer with a name synonymous with elegance. One of Jean Muir's clothes buyers had spotted Joanna on a buying expedition to Debenham and Freebody and had been impressed by the palpable air of class which Joanna exuded. Joanna's unmistakable breeding would reflect Jean Muir's designs perfectly, she felt, and at a discreet moment she asked Joanna whether she would consider joining Jane and Jane as a house model. Joanna duly presented herself for an interview and after a brief inspection by Jean Muir herself she leaped at the chance to move on to Jane and Jane's from Debenham and Freebody and with it the opportunity to increase her wages to £10 a week.

By now Joanna could just about afford to move out of her aunt's flat and rent somewhere to live. She soon settled into a flat with her sister Ælene, a schoolfriend from St Mary's who worked in an art gallery and a fourth girl, a dancer, whom Joanna had met through her aunt. The flat was just a few hundred yards away from her aunt's in Earls Court, then popularly known as Kangaroo Valley due to the number of Australians who seemed to descend on the area when arriving in London from Down Under.

Joanna's flat at 24 Trebovir Road comprised three rooms on the third floor of a grand looking terraced house entered through a portico of two white pillars in a tree-lined street, which ran between the bustling Earl's Court Road at one end and Warwick Road at the other.

When the girls moved into the flat, it needed completely redecorating and they cajoled friends into coming round to help give the place a lick of paint. In deference to the trendy pop art explosion which was accompanying the Beatles-inspired revolution in pop music, the flat rapidly became a blaze of colour, especially the kitchen where the gas stove was given a garish coat of purple and green and the walls were painted a glossy yellow. 'It's like walking straight into a pat of butter,' Joanna would enthuse as she showed guests into the kitchen for the first time.

The hall, which was almost square, boasted sophisticated dark red wallpaper with rush matting on the floor, Charles Kean posters on the walls and a striking art nouveau hallstand in pink and green. Suspended high up on one wall on a hanger was Joanna's father's striped cricket blazer.

On the floor of the large, white-walled sitting room was a yellow carpet which Joanna had managed to get cheap in a nearby sale and had staggered back with on her shoulder. Against one wall stood an apricot couch while another wall was dominated by a long, mustard-coloured, tobacco advertisement proclaiming 'Smoke Boar's Head'. On another was a sheet of aluminium and a big Mark Lancaster abstract. As Joanna's modelling career progressed and staying thin was ever more of a requisite, an exercise bike hired for a guinea a week became a key feature of the sitting room and Joanna would pedal away the calories to keep her 34-24-35 figure in trim.

Most of the furniture was provided by the girls' parents and three beds, including one for Joanna and one for Ælene, were squeezed into one room which the girls nicknamed 'The Dorm'. It rapidly filled up untidily with piles of dresses, skirts and tops, mountains of coloured patent shoes and Joanna's growing collection of wigs. The second bedroom appeared far more civilized with its brass bed and a rainbow design stencilled on to one of its blue walls.

Handily the flat was just around the corner from Earls Court tube station which meant an easy journey to work for Joanna.

Oxford Circus was but a few stops away on the underground and from there it was just a short walk to Jane and Jane's premises at Great Portland Street.

At lunchtime Joanna would regularly go to a nearby snack bar for a saveloy sausage washed down with a cup of coffee which cost all of five old pence. But since money was not exactly plentiful either for her or her flatmates, Joanna kept an eagle eye out for left-over sandwiches at the snack bar every lunchtime and when no one was looking she would scoop them up and hastily shove them in her pocket to take back to the flat to share around.

There were times when she could not afford a decent meal. 'I set my eyes on a fellow, flashed him a radiant smile and when he invited me out to dinner I accepted. Once I was satisfied that he could afford it, I'd eat as much as I could to keep me going for at least three days. And when he wasn't looking, I'd slip a few rolls or whatever else remained on the table into my bag.'

However, there were times when Joanna's trusting nature exposed her to potentially dangerous situations. On one occasion she got caught in the rain near Hyde Park and found herself shel-tering near the Round Pond. She fell into conversation with a tall Chinese youth who told her that he was called Jerome and came from Singapore. He said that he was a keen artist and Joanna felt an instant affinity, agreeing to look at his sketches at his Bayswater flat. He said that this would mean a great deal to him because his family was so far away. Joanna was sure afterwards that he did not say etchings! When they reached his building she climbed five flights of stairs behind him to his attic flat. It was not until the very last minute that Joanna panicked.

There was no sign of any paintings in the flat and something in the look on his face frightened her. As Jerome opened the door to his den Joanna slipped free from his arm and raced down the stairs. She ran into the street, over the road and across the park and when she finally turned to look back was horrified to see Jerome chasing her.

She sprinted on round the pond and past the Broadwalk to Kensington High Street and dived on to a bus that was just pulling away. Unfortunately the bus then became stuck in traffic and Joanna looked back to see Jerome still following. Eventually she leapt from the bus in Earl's Court Road and ran into her flat with

Jerome watching her every move. He was seen hanging around several times after this and Joanna's flatmates used to tease her by pretending that they had asked him for supper. Fortunately this incident was soon eclipsed by happier memories and she looks back on her time with Jane and Jane as invaluable. 'Being a house model for the great designer Jean Muir was a wonderful foundation,' she remembers, 'because she was so meticulous. I had to stand and have the clothes made on me and just when I thought they looked wonderful, she'd go *rrrrrrrrip* and snatch a whole sleeve off because she wasn't happy with it.' Joanna always listened and watched and learned and years later she was able to say: 'Jean Muir taught me that you can get away with anything as long as you have black legs and feet.'

After a few months Joanna felt ready to leave Jane and Jane to try her luck in the competitive world of photographic modelling. The usual procedure was for a set of Lucie Clayton passing-out pictures to be taken to make up a portfolio and a composite sheet of photographs to prove how different a girl could look, thus enhancing her chances of picking up modelling assignments. Then it was up to the fledgling models to do the rounds of London's photographers, to call on a list of photographic studios supplied by Lucie Clayton's and generally to tout themselves for bookings by hawking around their glossy photos in black albums.

'I paid to have some photographs taken and I thought they were smashing,' says Joanna, 'but they were a mouldy little selection really because I couldn't afford to have them done properly. I took them round to people and I touted my pictures everywhere for six months. But it was so very depressing. They asked who I'd worked for and when I said: "Nobody" they then said, "Well we can't use you, you're not experienced." It was the chicken and the egg situation. So I began to lie and I'd drop names like David Bailey and I said I'd worked for all sorts of people. When they said: "Where are the pictures?" I'd say, "They haven't come out yet." '

So desperate was Joanna to impress photographers and possible employers that she was not averse to augmenting her portfolio occasionally with pictures from magazines of other models in the hope no one would scrutinize them too closely to notice the model posing in the photos was not Joanna Lumley.

Rapidly Joanna came to realize that competition for modelling jobs was becoming fiercer by the week but then this was the Day of the Model. Up and down the country pretty girls aspired to be models on the strength of a couple of rolls of film shot by a local photographer or a boyfriend, followed by the encouragement of a photo printed in the local paper. The more enterprising and ambitious among them headed for London to swell the ranks of 'dolly birds' queuing up to try to make their mark on the vibrantly youthful London scene, not just in modelling but in other areas of fashion, art and design as well as in the movies and the world of pop music.

Once America's *Time* magazine had branded it 'Swinging London' in 1964, the capital was viewed with growing fascination by America and the rest of Europe and the era of the English Girl in her Mary Quant-inspired mini-skirts had well and truly dawned. Jean Shrimpton and Celia Hammond in modelling, Julie Christie, Susannah York, Shirley Anne Field, Susan Hampshire and Charlotte Rampling in movies, Marianne Faithfull, Dusty Springfield, Cilla Black and Sandie Shaw in the pop charts – all had shown that the moment was there for a girl to seize. Every teenage girl, it seemed, could be famous, even lowly £10 a week secretaries from Streatham like Cathy McGowan who suddenly found herself presenting a 'smashing, terrific' new pop show called *Ready, Steady, Go*, or Samantha Juste whose pretty face landed her the job of 'flipping the discs' on *Top of the Pops*.

For many girls, modelling appeared to offer the quick and easy route to fame and fortune – no need for three-year drama courses or months of painstaking exercises at a dance school. So there was no shortage of teenage girls prepared to give it a try and for six months Joanna was just one of dozens of budding young models making little headway, trudging round the metropolis with her photographs and spending hours hanging around the studios of unresponsive photographers.

Drawing a depressing blank so frequently on her foot-sore rounds of the photographic studios did, however, afford Joanna the chance to pick up the tricks of the model girl's trade and to observe all the procedures. She had to learn that once she landed a job, photographers would expect her to arrive on time with her hair done properly and pancake make-up in place. She would also be expected to take her own accessories with her which meant she would frequently be laden down with bags full of clothes, wigs and hairpieces, gloves, belts, shoes, hair rollers, nail varnish and make-up.

False eyelashes, it was impressed on Joanna, were very definitely de rigueur and she learned that most models bought them in long strips then snipped off the required length before sticking the strips above their own eyelashes. The trick was never to leave a white line of glue gleaming on the eyelid because, she was told, it would be total agony to remove.

'I also learned the trick of changing eye colour,' she says. 'It used to be a great pose to clamber on to an aircraft to fly off on a modelling assignment in Hawaii looking as if one had just got out of bed, and I once sat next to a girl who gradually transformed herself into a slinky sex bomb, finally clapping in a pair of cobalt blue contact lenses. They were sensational.' Years later Joanna was to follow this example to give her TV character Sapphire an out-of-this-world look in the sci-fi series *Sapphire and Steel*.

'Miniskirts were the thing,' Joanna says, 'and we girls all had chalk-white faces and sometimes three or four layers of eyelashes. So by this time I'd got on all the false eyelashes and stuff and was experimenting with everything under the sun. At twelve I'd often been taken for sixteen. When covered in layers of make-up and spiky eyelashes at eighteen I was taken for twenty-five.

'We also had to be so thin. I tried one fad diet after another. Steak and salad or grapefruit or nothing but bananas. Eventually I realized starvation was the only thing which got the pounds off. Sitting up all night with gin and tonics helped kill the hunger pangs. But a cup of coffee and a cigarette had the same effect.

'In those days, the thickest part of your leg was the knee bone, so all our time was spent trying to be thin and trying not to be spotty. Unfortunately I was still a bit spotty and I also had rotten finger nails which were always breaking so I glued them on. I used to glue them on while I was on the tube going to work. That was OK, people watched with interest. But coming back, when I took them off, men would nearly be sick because it looked so real.'

Eventually a trickle of modelling work started to come Joanna's way and she was always a popular model on assignments. Unlike other models who were simply pretty faces and slim figures, Joanna endeared herself to almost everyone with her warm personality and lively mind. She would call people 'Baby doll', offer to read their palms and more than held her own in intelligent conversation on a wide range of topics. She also had a commendable appreciation of what was required of her as a model. She took the view that anyone could look good in a Dior dress photographed by David Bailey and so the bread and butter jobs for catalogues often presented the real challenge. If you could model a Crimplene two-piece well enough for the pictures to sell the garment then you could consider your-self a good model, Joanna reasoned.

No one could question Joanna's professional approach but it was not uncommon on assignments to hear Joanna surprisingly putting herself down in the most self-critical manner. During one fashion shoot for a popular woman's magazine she went off to Moscow to be photographed in five fur coats in six days and then moved on to other European locations for further fashion photos where she surprised her travelling companions by dissecting and denigrating herself from head to toe.

On this particular fashion shoot everyone found Joanna to be good company and a thorough pro as she stomped for the camera-man up the ruined, rocky Phoenician city of Solunto in Sicily in thick leather brogues with a huge lizard portmanteau wearing a Persian print trouser suit and then swung through the jam-packed streets of Palermo in a Mexican smock, headscarf and hat. The photographs were just what the magazine required but the fashion editor was amazed at the way Joanna belittled her own attributes by reciting a long list of her physical imperfections: fat head, spotty face, prize-fighter shoulders, deformed ribcage, huge hips, bottle legs and tiny flipper feet – this was Joanna's extraordinary, damn-ing assessment of herself.

Models were infamous for their confident, look-at-me attitude and a self-belief bordering on arrogance but, astonishing to relate, here was Joanna putting herself down with the most unexpected candour. On another assignment, this time for hats, Joanna was just as uncomplimentary about herself: 'I have a grade three jaw which means even Henry Cooper stands aside and I have no back to my head and small ears,' she said apologetically.

Fortunately for Joanna the inadequacies she perceived in herself did not appear detectable to the majority of photographers who peered at her through their lenses and her fortunes as a model took a dramatic upswing the day she was photographed for what turned out to be six pages in the glossy, stylish, upmarket weekly magazine of the moment, *Queen*. It was the breakthrough she so desperately needed and from that point work snowballed to such an extent that Joanna went on to become one of the top ten most booked models of the post-Shrimpton wave and her earnings rocketed to an average of £120 a week. 'I was paid £4 and 5 shillings an hour, and that was good money,' she says. Joanna was never in the Jean Shrimpton or Twiggy league and never made the cover of *Vogue* but over a period of three years she was always in great demand.

'It was a magical time,' she says. 'I was paying £3 a week rent with another £1 a week for food. The world was my oyster. It was 1964, it was the Swinging Sixties and one worked every day, three, four, five jobs a day and earned a fortune. They'd ring me up and say: "Can you go to Portugal tomorrow morning?" and I'd just drop everything and go off. I went to virtually every European country there is, to Russia and to north Africa and I loved it. Some girls said: "Oh there's no hot water and I can't find anywhere to plug in my hair-dryer", but I'd say: "Bullshit, we're in Tunisia. It's magic!" I'd travelled, I was used to travelling and I was thirsting for more travel.

'My main memory is of fun and excitement. I'd buy a dress and if I didn't like it I'd chuck it away or give it to a friend. I'd buy dinner for fourteen people. It was spend, spend, spend and I never thought of stopping or settling down or having children, or not working. I didn't think of any of that. It was just get what you can and spend it all.'

As her modelling career gathered pace Joanna spent a fortune frivolously following the fashion for hot pants, mini-skirts and flares and bowing to a penchant for new shoes. Among her most outrageous buys was a pair of eight-inch stilettos from Biba. 'I had difficulty getting through doorways, it was like walking on stilts,' she says. Her most extravagant moment was when she spent £100 in 1965 on a James Wedge knitted bathing hat with silver sequins. But, like the Mini she acquired to get around in, she could afford it.

With the modelling success came a new-found confidence and an aura of glamour especially noticeable when she returned to the tranquillity of Rolvenden. The transformation in Major Lumley's younger daughter was there for all to see.

'I remember a midnight service at Rolvenden church one Christmas Eve,' says villager Norma Booker. 'The service was just about to start when in came Joanna in a fur coat and a fur Davy Crockett hat. She looked so glamorous and the congregation went into a hushed silence at her entrance.'

In many ways Joanna had been uniquely placed to take advantage of the changing world of modelling. She was a thoroughly modern mini-skirted model but she had undeniable class and a strong, magnetic personality. 'She was very cool, very independent and had an IQ of a million and something,' remembers Evelyn Kark who ran Lucie Clayton's during Joanna's time there.

Until the Swinging Sixties energized the capital, London models tended to be grand, well bred, well brought-up young ladies and the glossiest upmarket magazines like *Vogue*, *Harper's* and *Vanity Fair* were unlikely to hire a girl who did not possess a cut-glass accent and that positive stamp of breeding that the nanny-trained always have. Joanna had that breeding but a modern outlook as well.

The 1960s was also witnessing a change in fashion photography as a profession. Until then John French, Cecil Beaton, Angus McBean and Norman Parkinson were the grand photographers, and working-class fashion photographers were almost unheard of. But mainly due to French, the East End boys started battering their way through into what was a rarefied and elite profession. Ambitiously aspiring to join it were cockney lads of the day like David Bailey, Terence Donovan and Brian Duffy. They learned from their masters and they were talented and determined enough not to be denied the chance to carve a niche for themselves in the world of fashion photography.

This new wave of streetwise cockney photographers held an intriguing fascination for the naive, well-bred model girls up from the country like Jean Shrimpton and Joanna Lumley, even if at times it seemed they appeared to be insufferably rude. At one photo session Duffy famously made 'The Shrimp' repeat the

Humpty Dumpty nursery rhyme over and over five times to make her relax, and another photographer took one look at Joanna as she arrived for an early modelling assignment and crushingly remarked: 'You look like a pig, but I suppose we can use you.' It might in part have been joshing of an unsubtle nature but for a young girl like Joanna who was anxious about her height and the possibility of yet another spot beginning to show, such a derogatory rebuke did nothing to bolster her confidence and self-esteem.

One crisp morning in 1966 Joanna hurried off to a studio in King's Road, Chelsea to prepare herself for a swimwear photo shoot for a brash tabloid newspaper called the *Sun* which had been launched two years earlier. After changing into a skimpy two-piece and taking a last check in the mirror Joanna stepped from the dressing room into the studio where the photographer and his twenty-six-year-old assistant Michael Claydon were waiting for her. It was an entrance which took Claydon's breath clean away. 'When Joanna walked in, my eyes nearly popped out,' Claydon recalls. 'She was in this tiny red bikini and I thought "Wow!" I wanted to ask her out but I didn't have the courage.'

On the fashion photography circuit there always seemed to be something happening at the studios once the day's work was done and, even though it was a competitive business, rival photographers would materialize at each other's studios when the sun went down and together they would plan their evenings out with their friends. Usually it meant a few drinks, a meal and then on to a nightclub.

The model girls were expected to be the accessory when required and dodging passes from the photographers became an occupational hazard of modelling. That is to say, models learned to dodge them – if they wanted to. Claydon was too much in awe of Joanna to make a pass and it took him two weeks before he was finally brave enough to telephone Joanna to ask her for a date. When he did he was overjoyed by her answer. 'I rang and asked her out to the pictures,' he says. 'When she agreed, I couldn't believe it.'

The date at the cinema never materialized, however, because Joanna decided instead that they should drive down to Rolvenden where she introduced the would-be photographer to her parents at the family home. Even though it was a first date with Joanna,

Claydon remembers that it did not appear unusual to be taken to Sparkeswood to meet Major and Mrs Lumley. 'It didn't seem a heavy thing to do,' he says. 'We just enjoyed ourselves.' It was the start of an affair which was to change Joanna's, and Claydon's, lives for ever.

4

James

By the time Joanna Lumley had embarked on her passionate affair with Michael Claydon, she was firmly resigned to the belief that she could never have children. She had been told emphatically, not by just one doctor but by several, that she did not need to take contraceptive precautions because she was infertile. Faced with what was ostensibly expert medical opinion, she had no reason to disbelieve it.

It must have been shattering for Joanna as a young woman to be informed that she would never be a mother, but that was the conclusion doctors had reached after Joanna had decided she must determine once and for all why she had not been menstruating.

The school doctor at St Mary's may have waved her away with the reassurance she had nothing to worry about, but Joanna wanted a second medical opinion and at the age of eighteen she had gone into hospital for the problem to be checked out. Naturally she was anxious to discover if there really was anything seriously wrong with her and, if so, whether she might need an operation.

It transpired that Joanna was in fact suffering from amenorrhoea, which is the medical term for the temporary or permanent absence of periods. In itself, amenorrhoea presents no risk to health except in rare cases when it is symptomatic of a more serious disorder, but medical prognosis indicates that a woman with amenorrhoea may find it difficult or impossible to have a child.

'Aren't you lucky not to be troubled by that time of the month?' was the almost flippant response Joanna was given from another male doctor . 'No,' she remembers replying, 'because it's not right, there's something wrong.' The advice she was given once more was 'Don't worry.'

Of course Joanna was worried but it was the attitude of her doctors which really appalled her. 'Stupid men doctors saying "You won't have all the troubles,"' was Joanna's understandably angry reaction. 'It was gross negligence on their part because I became pregnant at twenty-one having asked should I take any precautions and they'd said: "No, you cannot have babies. You are sterile." '

The doctors had been so insistent that she would be unable to have children that it was difficult for Joanna to imagine that she could possibly be pregnant when she discovered she had begun putting on a little weight around her midriff. Yet she was at a loss to explain why.

The pressure on models to be wafer-thin was not quite so severe back in the 1960s as it is today but model girls like Joanna were still expected to watch their diets closely and the gaining of an unwanted pound was always greeted with a groan.

Joanna at that time modelled with an enviably trim 24-inch waist. Now, inexplicably, in 1967 around the time spring was nudging towards summer, she found her waistline expanding and, irritatingly, she even had to endure teasing from those who started to notice her figure was becoming a little more rounded. 'Who's a fatty then?' was one of the more charitable jibes Joanna remembered being aimed at her as she attempted to continue with her modelling assignments. Having worked so hard at her career and having so successfully shed her puppy fat, Joanna was not best pleased at this sudden surprising change in one vital statistic.

When she started to feel very nauseous in the mornings, all the signs were that Joanna must be pregnant. But, incredibly, medical opinion continued to say otherwise – not just once but on several separate occasions. Over a period of a few months Joanna consulted three or four doctors and every single one concluded she was not expecting a baby. 'When I thought I might be pregnant the doctors asked: "When was your last period?" and I said: "I don't have periods." So they said: "Then you can't be pregnant." ' The doctors were all so adamant about it that some of them gave her slimming injections while others gave her pills to counter water retention.

Privately Joanna still had nagging doubts, but even she was beginning to be convinced she couldn't possibly be pregnant, as she said: 'I even had a urine test which came back negative so it was a bit of a freak.'

Yet still she seemed unable to control her weight around her tummy and, in a desperate attempt to cut back on her intake of food, Joanna restricted herself to eating little more than one tomato a day. As she starved herself ever more strictly, her arms, her legs and her face subsequently became progressively thinner but her waist stubbornly refused to follow suit.

Still unaware she was indeed pregnant, Joanna was not only a long way short of eating for two, she was far from eating even for one, and inevitably the lack of any sort of regular nourishment eventually took its toll. Without sustenance she began to feel strangely weak, easily tired and lacking in energy. And, at a time when the Beatles were proclaiming 'All You Need Is Love', Joanna was perversely becoming uncharacteristically irritable even with her closest friends.

For Joanna it was not the best of times to be feeling so uncomfortable, so worryingly unwell and seemingly so out of harmony with herself and the world. It was the great Summer of Love of 1967 and while Joanna was feeling so out of sorts, the many millions of other young people her age across Britain were looking fondly at life through their trendy, granny-style dark glasses, with psychedelic smiles on their faces and embracing the gospel of LSD guru Timothy Leary of 'Turn on, tune in, and drop out.' Garlanded that summer in flowers, beads, bells, and a kaleidoscope of multi-coloured clothing, they were living in a world where they made the rules and being a hippie was 'where it's at'.

Their flower-filled world may have been frequently viewed through an illegal haze but for the young it was a world positively brimming with vibrant optimism because they were convinced they could change it. It was an extraordinarily uplifting period to be young and free, a time of great youthful rejoicing – and achievement.

It was a summer when the Beatles released their LP masterpiece

Sergeant Pepper's Lonely Hearts Club Band, when Procul Harum were skipping a light fandango to 'A Whiter Shade of Pale', when Sandie Shaw was winning the Eurovision Song Contest with 'Puppet on a String'. It was a summer when a young actor called Dustin Hoffman spoke the line 'Mrs Robinson, you're trying to seduce me' and became a star overnight in *The Graduate*, when the Duke of Bedford was playing host at Woburn Abbey to a three-day Festival of the Flower Children, when the BBC's new pop channel Radio One began broadcasting with the Move's 'Flowers in the Rain', when the king of rock 'n' roll, Elvis Presley, married his sweetheart Priscilla and the Kinks were being acclaimed for their outstanding pop classic 'Waterloo Sunset'. It was a summer which faded abruptly into pain and uncertainty for Joanna Lumley: 'I was dreadfully ill trying so hard to lose weight and finally I collapsed.'

Mercifully for Joanna, Colin Turner, the local family doctor based at Tenterden, was on hand to diagnose at once that Joanna was expecting a baby and she was whisked off to the Kent and Canterbury Hospital on the outskirts of the historic cathedral town where it was confirmed that she was indeed six months pregnant.

It's not hard to guess the extraordinary range of emotions Joanna must have gone through on being given the news that she was to be a mother after all that she had endured. She had suffered three worrying years in which she had repeatedly been told she was unable to have children, and the sudden revelation that she was six months pregnant must have come as an extraordinary mixture of shock, elation, anger and fear. But, she says, apart from being poleaxed by the news, her initial feelings were of excitement: 'It was absolutely thrilling in a world-turning-upside-down way.'

But any sense of joy Joanna can have felt that she was, after all, very much a normal child-bearing woman must inevitably have been clouded by anger that the doctors had all been so very wrong. Not only had their gloomy and off-hand predictions about Joanna's child-bearing capability been proved to be totally unfounded, they had also failed in the past few months to diagnose correctly such glaringly obvious pointers to pregnancy such as her morning sickness and expanding waistline. Their misinterpretation also raised a very real fear that the injections they had given her and the pills they had administered to help her slim might have done irreparable harm to her unborn baby.

There was also one other vitally important matter for Joanna to consider once the reality sank in that she was soon to give birth. Her two-year affair with Michael Claydon, the father of the child she was carrying, was now over. What was she to do? Should she marry? Or have an abortion, perhaps? – it was probably already too late for that. Or have the baby adopted, or be a single mum?

There was much for Joanna to ponder upon but of two things she was absolutely certain: she knew that having the baby was right but marriage to Claydon was not. She had loved Claydon enormously but if the marriage might fail there was no point in going through with it for some cosmetic purpose. 'I knew it would be wrong to run back and say let's get married for the child's sake,' Joanna reasoned. 'Jamie's father and I hadn't discussed marriage and it seemed to me it wasn't something to be entered into just to stop gossip.'

If Major and Mrs Lumley ever had any feelings other than pride, joy and excitement about what was for their younger daughter a most vulnerable point in her life, they never let Joanna know. They backed and supported Joanna's decision unconditionally.

When Joanna's parents took her into the maternity ward of Kent and Canterbury Hospital they were told by staff that they could safely leave their daughter at the hospital and go back home to Rolvenden. Joanna was so small, they were advised, that there was no chance of her baby being born that night. But once again Joanna was to confound medical opinion. On that evening of 16 October 1967, Joanna Lumley gave birth to a son, James, named after her own father.

Strapped up in that hospital bed giving birth to a tiny, premature baby boy, Joanna had never felt so helpless. Her parents had been sent off home to Rolvenden some forty-five minutes drive away and she had chosen not to tell Michael Claydon that she was about to give birth to his child. Joanna was so very alone and felt desperately in need of someone, someone who knew her story, someone who could just tell her that they were there for her.

'It was one of those dreadfully lonely births,' Joanna confided afterwards. 'Jamie was nearly dead when he was born, he was blue and weighed four pounds and he stayed in hospital for six weeks. So the whole thing was an appalling trauma.' But as she gazed daily at Jamie in his incubator during those first six weeks of his life she realized what a wonderful gift to her he was and how terribly much she wanted her son to live.

Even in the Swinging Sixties when the sexual revolution was hip and happening, in an era of Flower Power, so-called free love, and the preaching of a freewheeling do-your-own-thing lifestyle, having a baby and taking the decision to stand alone and manage on her own was still an extraordinarily brave thing for Joanna to do. Even though the 1960s was a period of great liberation, there was still a considerable stigma attached to being an unmarried mother.

Other girls in Joanna's circumstances might have been tempted, or persuaded, to have their baby adopted but Joanna courageously made up her mind she would cope with bringing up her son on her own and never ask Jamie's father for anything or pressure him financially so that they could remain friends. Years later she was able to say of Claydon: 'I still see his parents. My parents and his still stay in touch. I'm sure it's because money hasn't come into it.'

As it was, Joanna's own parents set about creating a structure of security for Joanna and Jamie. Their unflagging support is something for which Joanna has remained eternally grateful.

After Jamie's birth it took Joanna some six months to recover her own health during which Major and Mrs Lumley rallied round to give her as much practical and financial help as they could as well as their time to help look after her boy. Joanna resolved that she would tell Claydon she had given birth to his son when the time was right. She wanted to keep Claydon's name a secret to protect his family from the inevitable publicity which would follow. 'It was quite a scandal at the time and would have been difficult for them,' she later explained. 'Why should they be paraded around?'

In Rolvenden gossip of the most specious nature could have been made of the Major's daughter being in the family way with no sign of a father being around, particularly as Joanna was seeking to keep the father's identity a secret. But, on the contrary, Joanna found that in the village there was jubilation rather than any hint of condemnation – 'sort of thank God, now she's one of us,' is how Joanna gauged local Kent reaction.

'At that time, girls who found themselves pregnant often ran away from home or gave their babies away because it was such a scandal to have an illegitimate child. Lots of people since have said to me how brave I must have been to ignore convention, but it wasn't done deliberately. I didn't set out to thumb my nose at the standards of the time.'

But not everyone looked so kindly upon her status as a single mother. There were many occasions when Joanna wished she had a ring on her wedding finger. 'It was harrowing,' Joanna admitted. 'People on a train would say: "Oh what a lovely baby." But when they saw I had no wedding ring they moved away as though I were a leper. I didn't want to kid anybody by wearing a ring.

'I've never had any regrets, not even for a second. I can't think of anything nicer than babies. For all the rules we put upon these things, there's nothing to beat the wonder of babies.'

At weekends Joanna would regularly return to Rolvenden taking her washing with her. She was always keen that Jamie should be very much part of the village and encouraged him to make friends with other village children. Jane Booker, daughter of kind Norma and Cecil Booker, still remembers with affection Joanna coming to pick her up and taking her and Jamie off to the seaside and to Bodiam Castle with Joanna recounting exciting children's stories on the way.

By the time Jamie was grown up she had doubts that she had been a good mother. She says she sent Jamie to private school because of practical difficulties of being a single parent. 'But when I was at a celebrity lunch I was told I should have given up acting and gone to work in a corner shop so I would have had the time to look after James. Now I wonder if that was right. Did I do the right thing by sending him away? I don't know.'

Later, as her fame grew through the 1970s, Joanna became a much respected and eloquent contributor to one-parent debates. 'What one-parent families need is help,' she once went on TV to say. 'Quite often they are people who have had somebody run away from them. They all need help and I don't think sneering or weepy stuff works at all.'

With her parents providing such solid back-up for Jamie, especially during the first two years of his life, Joanna was able to return
to London to pick up her modelling career.

Now there was a reason for it all – Jamie. Before Jamie's arrival,
modelling had been lucrative fun for Joanna but financially she had
very little to show for it. She had barely saved a penny, frittering
her money away on clothes, shoes, friends and fun times. Now
there was another mouth to feed and someone to think of other
than herself. Jamie gave her a purpose in life and every time she felt
she might be wilting, Jamie's very existence gave her the will to
carry on. The bills had to be paid.

In her more reflective moments during the first heady days of
real success as a model when she was earning around £120 a
week, Joanna was almost ashamed of the trivial way she was
making such an extraordinarily good living. She was always
faultlessly professional in her approach to her work but at times
it did not seem right to be making quite so much money for
doing something which, deep down, she considered so massively
unimportant.

After three years of posing for the cameras, she began to find the
model girl's life had started to pall. The work had become repeti-
tious, constantly having to dress and undress had become irksome,
and sitting in front of a mirror for hours making herself up had
become tedious. Not for the first time Joanna was coming round to
the view that 'If you look at an immaculately made-up woman
you'll often find a bore beneath.'

'By that stage it was really beginning to bore me,' Joanna said. 'I
had also smoked a bit of grass and got to that disillusion state. It
had all dropped into my lap. I kept looking for more mountains to
climb and it seemed I could work at anything. I'd never really
considered myself a model. I always thought I was going to do
something else and so I made the great decision to try to be an
actress.' But it proved to be a far tougher goal than Joanna had ever
imagined.

Most would-be actresses do not look like Joanna Lumley did at
twenty-two. Most actresses are of normal build and height, they
are not show-stoppers and they do not automatically turn heads.
But when Joanna walked into an audition or a casting session, or

even just entered a room, she could not help but make a formidable impression. At five feet eight and more in high heels, she was often, quite literally, head and shoulders above other girls and with her endless legs, dyed blonde hair and track record as a model, Joanna Lumley oozed glamour and sex appeal. But it was an identity which she was now desperate to pull away from if she was to be regarded seriously as an actress, and it turned out to be a long, painful eight years before she was able to do so.

Instead of finding modelling to be a natural stepping stone to an acting career, Joanna was mortified to discover it was anything but. Whereas her looks and figure had been her passport to modelling, now the very word model on her CV was a handicap. 'The penalty of it was absolutely colossal,' she says, 'because in those days you just didn't do that. It was frowned upon. You could be a waitress and an actress. That was all right. But a model and an actress was really bad. It was not until later that I realized it was the worst setback I could have started with.

'While I was modelling, niggling away at the back of my mind was that feeling that somehow I could make the breakthrough into acting and I was desperately keen. I became a member of the Royal Shakespeare Company's cheap student tickets scheme and I'd flog round on trains earnestly sitting in the gods, staring at plays and thinking "Ah, it could be me." To me at that time, acting was doing Shakespeare. I was appalled to find that one didn't, one just played ordinary little secretaries saying "Thank you, sir." That wasn't acting at all.

'There was an awful lot of prejudice. If you had been a model it meant you could not learn your lines because you did not have a head and probably couldn't read.'

Joanna's first venture into films owed more to luck and timing than to any latent talent. 'When I was twenty-two I was at a party and I met Richard Johnson and I knew he was an actor and so I told him I'd like to get into films,' she recalls. 'It was a naive, clichéd thing to say, I know, but he said: "I just happen to be making one at the moment. Perhaps you'd like to say something in that?" '

The film was *Some Girls Do*, a British spoof melodrama in the Swinging Sixties mould, produced by Betty Box and directed by Ralph Thomas, in which Bulldog Drummond traces the sabotage

Joanna as Samantha
Ryder-Ross and Jeremy
Lloyd as Bobby Dutton
in the BBC comedy
*It's Awfully Bad For Your
Eyes, Darling.*

Joanna met her first
husband, Jeremy Lloyd,
in costume for
Games That Lovers Play.

A passionate moment with
Richard Warwick in
The Breaking of Bumbo.
(CANAL+)

Joanna with Andrew Sinclair
who wrote and directed
The Breaking of Bumbo.
(CANAL+)

Joanna trying hard to smile in a publicity photograph.

Joanna with Bill Roache in her role as *Coronation Street*'s Elaine Perkins, the headmaster's daughter. Ken proposed marriage, but she turned down her chance to be Mrs Barlow.
(Scope Features)

Joanna with Brian Rix and Leslie Phillips in *Don't Just Lie There, Say Something*.
(Scope Features)

Joanna with son Jamie, aged two.

Joanna in her Holland Park
flat with a poster of
Michael Kitchen

(Scope Features)

Joanna displaying Purdey's essential stockings at her launch as the *New Avengers* girl.

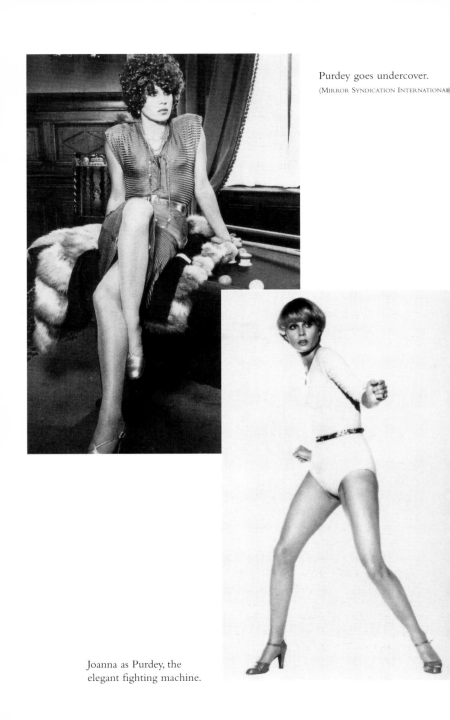

Purdey goes undercover.

Joanna as Purdey, the
elegant fighting machine.

of a supersonic airliner to a gang of murderous women. In addition to its star Richard Johnson, who duly managed to arrange for Joanna to play a tiny role, the film featured several highly competent British actors including Robert Morley, Maurice Denham and James Villiers, and the stunning Israeli actress Dahlia Lavi who was cast as the leading lady.

'My first ever scene was with Dahlia Lavi,' Joanna remembers, 'a beautiful woman, so lovely and looking immaculate. She'd had her own make-up people and her own specially tailored leather suit to make her look like a goddess and she was very beautiful anyway and then there was this shrivelled dog which was me in a pair of overalls because I was playing a mechanic.'

When it came to filming her scene, Joanna was thrown in at the deep end and she found it an unnerving and disorientating experience. 'I was dumped into it and oh, the horror of the film jargon! I didn't understand it and I thought: I can't do this. I hate being bad at anything and I hate not knowing what I'm doing and suddenly to be shown up to be a fool. I was only on screen for a few seconds, I had one line "Yes, Mr Robinson" and I was blown up before the credits!'

It was the most inauspicious of film debuts but at least it helped Joanna towards that all-important membership card from the actors' union Equity, without which she would be unable to work as an actress. And, however meaningless and minuscule her role in *Some Girls Do*, at least it was a start and soon there would be a helping hand up the next rung of the ladder from a certain Mr Bond.

His name was Bond, James Bond. And from that moment in 1962 when Sean Connery as Bond watched totally unknown actress Ursula Andress emerge from the Jamaican surf and stride languidly across a sun-kissed beach in a white bikini in the film *Dr. No*, the myth of the 'Bond girl' was born.

Ursula Andress not only made $1000 a week, no mean wage back in 1962, but she also made her name in *Dr. No* and set the mould for a 'Bond girl' image which was destined to become legendary in the series of films which followed.

In Ian Fleming's books, secret agent 007, James Bond, ate danger for breakfast, lunch and dinner but he also loved women and they always found him irresistible. Fleming and the movie moguls surrounded the writer's hero with girls with names like Fatima Blush, Pussy Galore, Plenty O'Toole and Holly Goodhead and there was no doubting Fleming's frank sexual innuendoes.

Following Ursula Andress's lead, beautiful girls became as essential an ingredient of Bond films as the exotic locations and the tightly edited special effects. Over the years a plethora of pulchritude paraded across the screen even if not all of the girls were to find their way into the industrial-strength bed of the world's sexiest secret agent.

By the time Joanna Lumley found herself up for consideration as a Bond girl in *On Her Majesty's Secret Service* in 1967, five Bond films had already been made with unqualified success. Joanna had seen unknowns like Daniela Bianchi and Martine Beswick in *From Russia With Love* quickly discover what wonders the Bond girl status could do for a career. They had rapidly become internationally famous and were showered with scripts. Joanna had seen, too, the impact British actress Shirley Eaton could make as a Bond girl in *Goldfinger* by doing little more than suffer an unlikely celluloid demise by having her entire body covered in gold paint.

As the Bond bandwagon rolled triumphantly onwards and ever upwards, any actress or model who could attach the words 'Bond girl' to her name found it an instant passport to fame. The words 'Bond girl' were synonymous with glamour and those girls lucky enough to gain even a blink-and-you-miss-me walk-on role in a Bond film were the envy of their peers. Never mind that they were in a crowd scene or fleetingly seen in the distance in a swimsuit, they could call themselves 'Bond girls'. That tag had a ring to it and carried a cachet which said you were beautiful, sexy, desirable and an actress or model going places. What's more, Bond girls were proud to call themselves Bond girls. It was even totally acceptable in the 1960s for any pretty girl with half an eye on a showbiz career to express the aspiration 'I want to be a Bond girl.'

Swiss miss Ursula Andress was astute enough not to bridle at being billed by tub-thumping movie men as 'Ursula Un-dress, Switzerland's most perfect creation since the Alps,' when she unexpectedly found herself cast as the very first Bond girl. As Ursula was to be constantly reminded ever afterwards, she should be so lucky.

Cubby Broccoli, co-producer of *Dr No*, had picked the little-known Ursula after spotting a photograph of her among a pile of hopefuls, following a long search for just the right girl for his movie. The photograph showed Ursula in clichéd starlet pose, wearing a man's T-shirt and soaked to the skin so that her nipples jutted prominently. But aside from Ursula's obvious assets, Broccoli was struck by her extraordinarily beautiful face.

There were protestations that she couldn't act and talked like a 'Dutch comic' but Ursula was nonetheless signed up as the first Bond girl, the gorgeous beauty whom James Bond first encounters almost naked on a beach. 'Botticelli's Venus seen from behind,' is how Fleming described her.

Spectacular as Ursula's figure and screen entrance in *Dr No* later turned out to be, it's fair to say that the honey blonde starlet was not to be unduly cerebrally challenged when she was unveiled as the first female to be fed to girl-hungry James Bond on the big screen.

Initially Ursula, playing the suggestively named Honeychile Ryder, simply had to rise from the waves like Aphrodite and stand there lissom, golden and glistening. Thereafter she was largely called upon to spend the remainder of the movie in her bikini looking decorative and eagerly submissive to Sean Connery's mischievous grin, puppydog eyes, and virile sex appeal as James Bond. But *Dr No* made her a star.

Such was the alluring mystique surrounding Bond girls that when any new Bond film was announced there was always feverish speculation about who would play the hero's love interest and who would be the lucky beauties to be chosen as subsidiary Bond girls. Of course it made for marvellous publicity and in turn generated heated competition among starlets and models.

It was in that climate that Joanna Lumley found herself excitedly hurrying to the offices of producer Harry Saltzman to be considered for a role as a Bond girl in *On Her Majesty's Secret Service*.

'It must have been the shortest interview on record,' Joanna remembers. 'I arrived for the interview at Harry Saltzman's office in South Audley Square and this huge, massive Rolls-Royce drew up just as I got there and out he stepped. I walked up and said: "I think I've come to see you." He said: "Ah yes. You must be Joanna Lumley" and I nodded.

'We then proceeded to walk up four flights of stairs to his office by which time he was completely out of breath. He then walked slowly across the wooden floor of his leather studded office, sat down and told me: "You have the part." That was that. I thanked him and then walked all the way back down four flights of stairs again. I was going to be a Bond girl and I was ecstatic.'

Widely regarded as the best of Fleming's later novels, *On Her Majesty's Secret Service* had been postponed as a movie project several times since it was originally published in 1963. It had been earmarked to follow *Goldfinger* as the fourth Bond film but had been shelved when the *Thunderball* project emerged. When *Thunderball* was completed it was felt that *On Her Majesty's Secret Service* was too similar and, with its snowy setting, might look like 'a Thunderball on skis' so again it was put back.

Now, in 1967, the project was very much back on again although it looked increasingly likely that it would go ahead without Sean Connery as James Bond. After protracted negotiations, Connery's threats to walk away from the role became fact in June of that year. Reluctantly Harry Saltzman and Cubby Broccoli had to resign themselves to losing the 007 who had served them so well for five box office blockbusters.

Connery, anxious to branch out from Bond, instead flew off to Spain to begin filming a western, *Shalako*, with Brigitte Bardot. That was adding salt to the producers' wounds for Peter Hunt, the director Saltzman and Broccoli had chosen to take the helm of *On Her Majesty's Secret Service*, had put the name of Brigitte Bardot top of his list for the role of Bond's love interest, Tracy. Neither would now be available.

Saltzman and Broccoli, however, decided to move quickly to allay fears that Connery's departure would signal the end for James Bond on screen. The legend of 007, they insisted, was bigger than any actor who might embody the hero. Of course losing Connery was a blow and he would be a very hard act to follow but they would launch a search for a new Bond and *On Her Majesty's Secret Service* would go ahead.

The 007 mantle eventually fell on the broad Australian shoulders of George Lazenby who had arrived in England in 1964 after spending two years in his own country earning £30 a week selling cars. Tipped off by fashion photographer Chard Jenkins that his masculine good looks could earn him ten times that amount, Lazenby soon found himself in demand as a model.

With the search for a new Bond intensifying, Lazenby's agent suggested to Saltzman that he might fit the bill. Saltzman was indeed impressed with Lazenby's physique and added his name to his list of possibles. Despite his lack of acting experience, Lazenby surprisingly proceeded to snatch the role from four other hopefuls by virtue of his athletic performance in an action test.

Before they finally made up their minds, United Artists wanted to see fighting footage of the would-be Bonds, and Lazenby was the one who came through with flying colours after an energetic and physically imposing test fight with former wrestler Uri Borienko playing a would-be assassin who surprises Bond in a hotel room.

Lazenby at the age of twenty-five was duly signed to play James Bond and the go-ahead was given for filming of *On Her Majesty's Secret Service* to begin in the autumn of 1968. Telly Savalas was chosen to play Ernst Stavro Blofeld, Bond's arch enemy and head of the sinister organization SPECTRE which stood for Special Executive for Terrorism, Revolution and Espionage.

For Joanna there was a certain piquancy about the signing of Diana Rigg, then a highly popular TV star thanks to her role as Emma Peel in the spy spoof *The Avengers*, to play Bond's main love interest, Tracy. As previously noted, Joanna had briefly met Diana when she'd been among a school party which had travelled up to London from Hastings to see the Royal Shakespeare production of *The Taming of the Shrew* at the Aldwych. 'Diana was playing Bianca,' Joanna remembers, 'and after the performance I went backstage and asked her for her autograph. I remember how thrilled I was to meet her but she hated me reminding her of that!'

Joanna's excitement at becoming a Bond girl was tempered by the ever-growing awareness that she would be little more than background decoration although it transpired that Richard

Maibaum's screenplay would at least give her one line to say. Joanna was luckier than most. It proved to be one line more than that accorded to the majority of the other beautiful Bond girls assembled for the movie and flown to Switzerland to film key scenes.

For once, the girls really were an integral part of the storyline which unfolded in *On Her Majesty's Secret Service*. The plot had Bond continuing his frustrating search for the elusive Blofeld after the evil megalomaniac had survived the destruction of his Japanese rocket base in *You Only Live Twice*. Bond finds the head of SPEC-TRE holed up in the Alps where he is plotting germ warfare against the UK. Blofeld's HQ is a Swiss mountain fortress dubbed Piz Gloria from where he plans to wage biological warfare against the agricultural and livestock producers of the world.

His agents are ten beautiful girls from different parts of the world who sincerely believe that Blofeld is a famous allergist and have travelled to his 'sanatorium' to be cured of their personal allergies. Then, brainwashed by Blofeld and believing they are cured, the girls are each secretly equipped with a deadly atomizer in their make-up kits. Now they are ready to be sent back to their respective countries where they will receive radio communications from Blofeld who will then order them to spread their cargo of disease throughout the world. The scheme is about to be put into operation when Bond arrives to scupper the plan.

For many of the major scenes, including those which briefly involved Joanna, Broccoli and Saltzman went scouting for a mountain retreat accessible only by cable car and situated above a small village. After some fruitless reconnaissance, they eventually learned that a new revolving five-storey restaurant complex was being built 9,712 feet up above the picturesque town of Murren on top of the Schilthorn mountain and was approaching completion. They agreed this Swiss location was ideal and that it would be perfect for Blofeld's snow-capped lair.

Joanna was told that she would be required in Switzerland for two months in her role as 'English girl', one of evil Blofeld's unwitting agents of death, and she took Jamie to stay with her parents in Rolvenden before setting out for the location with the other girls.

Some, like Jenny Hanley (Italian girl), Angela Scoular (Ruby),

Catherina von Schell (Nancy) and Anoushka Hempel (Australian girl), were familiar to her. Like Joanna, they were young actresses forging a career for themselves in England. Others, like Julie Ege (Scandinavian girl), Mona Chong (Chinese girl), Ingrid Black (German girl), Zara (Indian girl), Sylvana Henriques (Jamaican girl) and Helena Ronee (Israeli girl), quickly became friends. 'And they really were all so beautiful,' says Joanna. 'When I think back, they were an extraordinary, breathtaking array of girls.'

Playboy magazine quickly latched on to the fact that there were twelve beautiful Bond starlets in the movie and rubbed their hands with glee. They wanted to fly to Switzerland to photograph each one in the nude, one for each calendar month. But Jenny Hanley, Joanna and one or two others put their foot down and said no.

Tiny though her role was, *On Her Majesty's Secret Service* gave Joanna a first real glimpse of big-time movie-making and the big money behind a success story like the Bond films. A cool £60,000 was spent just on transforming the restaurant into Blofeld's HQ, and in return for being allowed to film there, Saltzman's and Broccoli's company Eon Productions agreed to build a heliport near the building.

Some of the filming literally took Joanna's breath away. At nearly 10,000 feet, lack of oxygen on the Schilthorn peak took some getting used to when having to do anything remotely energetic. Worryingly for everyone, the snow levels on the edge of Piz Gloria also had to be frequently checked to ensure film units did not stray over a crevice that might split open and send them plunging to almost certain death.

Joanna resolved to make the most of it all. 'Two months up a mountain filming in Switzerland? It was marvellous,' she says. 'It was fun and I loved being up in those mountains although some of the filming was pretty boring. But the location was magical. There were no cars in Murren, just pony traps and ski lifts. The pay was fantastic – £100 a week and £25 expenses – and it was first-class everything and all the food you could possibly want. All our clothes were beautifully designed and the boots handmade. I also learned a lot and I was intrigued to find that Telly Savalas, who had his earlobes taped back, shaved his bald head every day. And so did his double.'

Joanna's great moment in *On Her Majesty's Secret Service* arrived in a scene where Bond, dubiously impersonating a British genealogist, turns up dressed in a kilt to sit down to dinner with the girls at Piz Gloria. The camera pans round the room to show the girls lounging in armchairs and sofas and then it suddenly focuses on Joanna dressed in a sparkling black evening gown, with spidery eyelashes which look a foot long, and with her hair scraped tightly back off her face into a bejewelled bun-cum-ponytail. The camera lingers just long enough on Joanna's face for her to give Bond a meaningful, rather longing look.

Later, after a dinner in which Bond has ostensibly bored the girls to death with details of British heraldry and equally ostensibly has shown no signs of addressing their problem of male starvation, he gets up to leave and departs remarking: 'May all your allergies be swiftly cured.' Then, with the camera in close-up on Joanna doing her best to look wistful gazing after the fast disappearing Bond, she says in a frightfully posh English accent: 'Of course I know what he's allergic to.'

That line was hardly a scene-stopper but at least it gave Joanna the dubious distinction of being the only Bond girl ever to insinuate that perhaps James Bond wasn't really as virile as he's always been made out to be.

By December 1968 Joanna and the other girls were no longer required in Switzerland. Joanna was able to return home for Christmas taking with her the blanket she had knitted for Jamie during the seemingly interminable pauses during filming when nothing appeared to be happening. To some of the crew, Joanna's knitting seemed strangely untypical of a Bond girl but they were not to know that her most frequent thoughts were of Jamie. And while the other Bond girls occasionally let their hair down and talked of boyfriends and sex, Joanna enthused about her son and couldn't wait for letters from home for news of him.

It was another six months before *On Her Majesty's Secret Service* was finally completed. The movie came in at just under three hours and, alarmingly for the producers, that was more than one hour longer than any of the previous Bond films. Editor John Glen had to cut thirty minutes from the movie. Although her mini appearance remained intact, Bond girl Joanna Lumley was never going to get carried away with her cameo. 'Really I was just a blur,' she said after the film came out.

5

The Breaking of Bumbo

In 1969 Neil Armstrong, the commander of Apollo XI, took a first small step for man and a giant leap for mankind after landing on the moon, colour television came to the BBC and ITV, British golfer Tony Jacklin won the British Open, and Concorde made its maiden flight. The trial of the Kray twins lasted nine months, English actress Jane Birkin was admonished by the Pope for her blatantly sexual chart-topping banned record 'Je t'aime' with her Gallic lover Serge Gainsbourg, and the youth of Britain were flocking to the cinema to peer through a haze of dubious-smelling smoke at the hippie film *Easy Rider*, a cult movie starring Peter Fonda and Dennis Hopper heading east on Harleys and using expressions like 'I'm getting my thing together' and 'do your own thing in your own time' which have taken their place as part of our cultural history.

Made for the unbelievably small budget of £300,000, shot in seven weeks and with a minimal script, *Easy Rider* went on to make a staggering £30 million. It was an encouragement for film-makers everywhere and that same year an ailing British film industry decided it was time to get its act together and evoke the ghosts of movie moguls long dead by appointing Bryan Forbes to the position of head of production at Elstree Film Studios. It was an appointment that was to have significant, but ultimately deeply depressing, repercussions for the acting aspirations of Joanna Lumley.

During his two-year tenure at Elstree, Forbes set the cameras rolling on a production programme of, incredibly, no fewer than ten movies. One of these, *The Breaking of Bumbo*, was to give

Joanna the longed-for, priceless opportunity of a first starring role in a major movie at the age of twenty-three. Yet, just as she was poised to be launched as a sparkling new British film star in *The Breaking of Bumbo*, Joanna's hopes were dashed in the most bewildering manner leaving her frustrated and bitterly disappointed.

It had all started so promisingly. *The Breaking of Bumbo* was to be a film based on a largely autobiographical 1959 best-seller of the same name by Old Etonian, Andrew Sinclair. While up at Cambridge University he had written his book about a British officer in the elite Brigade of Guards called Bumbo Bailey whose life and career are plunged into turmoil when he falls helplessly under the alluring spell of a rich model girl who turns out to be a revolutionary. They become lovers, she incites Bumbo to rebel, he starts a riot, faints on parade and is threatened with court martial when he refuses to go to Suez after the canal zone crisis of 1956 erupts.

Sinclair, a former colleger at Eton, was a man who had paid his own way from the age of thirteen – 'a poor boy in rich circumstances', is how he puts it – who on leaving Eton then served for two years in the Coldstream Guards as a National Service officer. 'All I did was public duties in London,' Sinclair now recalls. 'I then got a scholarship to Trinity College, Cambridge, and then this great moral crisis happened. I was called up as a reservist to go to Suez during the Suez crisis and I decided it was immoral and wrong and, anyway, that the Government was lying to us, which turned out to be true. When you can write and you are faced with a moral crisis like that, what do you do? You write about it. I decided to write about it all when I was twenty-one in my long vac term. I wrote *The Breaking of Bumbo* as a tragedy but everyone fell about laughing. The publishers Faber and Faber took it and it was a great best-seller.'

Bryan Forbes had enjoyed Sinclair's novel when it had first become a hugely popular though controversial best-seller some ten years before and he saw great potential in *The Breaking of Bumbo* as a movie project when it was brought to him by Andrew Sinclair himself and American producer L. Jeffrey Selznick who had together formed a company called Timon Films. The timing for bringing *The Breaking of Bumbo* to the screen looked to be perfect, too, as Sinclair's story of rebellion mirrored the tidal wave of revolt and insurrection by the young which had swept through Europe and the United States the year before in 1968.

To Bryan Forbes, the movie project had a sound pedigree. Jeffrey Selznick was steeped in the world of film-making. He was the son of David O. Selznick, one of Hollywood's most distinguished and prolific film-makers and his grandfather was the legendary Hollywood movie mogul Louis B. Mayer, co-founder of MGM. After graduating from Yale university, Jeffrey Selznick had worked his way through many different jobs in the film industry, including the post of assistant director on films like *Giant*, which had starred Elizabeth Taylor, Rock Hudson, James Dean and Carroll Baker, and *The Ten Commandments* starring Charlton Heston, Yul Brynner, Edward G. Robinson and Yvonne De Carlo. He had also co-produced two European films and was the producer of another major movie in France called *The Long March*.

Andrew Sinclair had gone on to become a top writer of screenplays in Hollywood following the success of his book and Forbes was therefore not overly concerned when the director everyone had in mind for the movie dropped out and Sinclair declared himself ready and willing to direct the film himself. Like Sinclair, Forbes had also been a writer before progressing to the director's chair so he trusted Sinclair would do a good professional job.

First choice to play the hero-martyr-mutineer-debs' delight Guards Officer Bumbo Bailey was Malcolm McDowell who had just enjoyed a notable success in Lindsay Anderson's 1968 movie *If. . .* McDowell had played Travis, the leader of a trio of rebellious public schoolboys who sealed their brotherhood in a blood oath and then took up machine guns to create violent mayhem in the quad on school speechday. *If. . .* was a superbly detailed picture of that ambivalent love–hate relationship which a public school rebel has with his alma mater and McDowell's performance had been highly impressive.

The opportunity to build on McDowell's screen image as a rebel would have been ideal for Selznick and Sinclair but they discovered to their immense disappointment that the rising young actor had been snaffled by Bryan Forbes himself for his own film *The Raging Moon* and was therefore unavailable.

Instead they turned to Richard Warwick, another young British actor who had also caught the eye in *If...* as the keen schoolboy gymnast and least troubled of McDowell's two youthful partners in classroom crime. Warwick had trained at the Royal Academy of Dramatic Art, spent a year with the National Theatre under Laurence Olivier and then appeared in Franco Zeffirelli's *Romeo and Juliet* playing the young servant who starts a brawl between the Montagues and the Capulets.

Although Richard Warwick's face and name were not as readily recognizable as McDowell's, Warwick's own rebellious public schoolboy image from *If...* was something on which *The Breaking of Bumbo* could capitalize, and he came with the highest recommendation from John Schlesinger who described him as 'without a touch of vanity, completely natural and always concentrated'. Warwick was duly signed as the good looking, intelligent, well educated young Bumbo who enlists in the Brigade of Guards.

The choice of Warwick's co-star to play Bumbo's beautiful revolutionary girlfriend Susie eventually narrowed down to just two young actresses and Joanna Lumley could barely contain her excitement to find herself one of them. Although she wasn't to know it at the time, Joanna was facing stiff opposition in the lissom shape of Anoushka Hempel.

Like Joanna, Anoushka was exceptionally beautiful and, like Joanna, intelligent too. She was some four years older than Joanna and, with her large eyes and blonde hair, Anoushka's striking sex appeal elicited comparisons in some quarters with Brigitte Bardot. Of Russian-German ancestry, Anoushka had arrived in England from the Antipodes in 1962 with a degree in psychology and had turned to acting seven years later. Now, here she was, on the brink of a starring role in a major British movie.

At this point in their young lives, both Joanna and Anoushka were hardly known at all as actresses. Their names meant nothing to cinema-goers but Sinclair and Selznick were not unduly concerned by the girls' anonymity. 'That didn't matter,' says Sinclair. 'We had a small budget and after the success of *If...* the fashion was to go for unknowns.'

When producer and director came to assess Joanna's and Anoushka's credentials there was really very little to choose between them. Since neither had undergone formal training as an actress, both girls were compensating with their looks. Each girl was clearly much more than a pretty face but Joanna had the edge, if anything, because of her very British breeding.

Looking back, Andrew Sinclair says: 'I could have taken either Joanna or Anoushka. The one I didn't take was Anoushka Hempel and she has never, I think, quite forgiven me for it. But Joanna was just perfect. She fitted the role perfectly and the great thing about Joanna was, and is, that she's exactly as she seems to be.

'At that point Joanna was no actress but she was exactly as she appeared to be. She was incredibly beautiful and exactly the character she played. I thought she was absolutely wonderful. Joanna was a model and this was a major acting role but I took her without any reservations and I didn't even screen test her.'

For the ambitious Anoushka Hempel, losing out to Joanna was heartbreaking. Her acute disappointment at having fallen at the final hurdle was, however, somewhat softened by Selznick and Sinclair offering her a small role in *The Breaking of Bumbo* as a pretty debutante. It was a generous gesture by the two movie men but, having come so close to landing the starring role, Anoushka had to swallow the bitter pill of finding that her name would ultimately appear at the very bottom of the thirty-strong cast list: 'Debutante – Anoushka Hempel'. The name Joanna Lumley was to be second in prominence only to that of Richard Warwick.

The significance of clinching the leading female role was not lost on Joanna. It represented a tremendous breakthrough for her as an actress, a chance to prove that she was so much more than just a model. At last she was the star of a major movie with all that entailed. 'It was going to be such a movie,' she says. 'It was cars everywhere and press receptions and my name just below the title. They told me they were going to give the role to Julie Christie if I behaved badly. I promised I wouldn't behave badly.'

Gradually the remaining cast fell into place. John Bird was signed to play a London School of Economics lecturer who combines his college duties with inciting students to rebel, and among those recruited to play Bumbo's colleagues in the Guards were several actors who were to go on to become familiar names on TV and at the cinema, such as Simon Williams, Edward Fox,

Donald Pickering, Jeremy Child and Warren Clarke. Around eighty ex-Guardsmen were also recruited from newspaper advertisements ready to be drilled rigorously for three weeks by ex-Gurkha officer Graham Campbell.

While the cast were being assembled, Joanna began familiarizing herself with the role of Susie, the attractive young girl who is perpetually involved in some form of protest demonstration or student revolt. It was not difficult to see why Joanna had been chosen. In Sinclair's book Susie was described as a red-haired model girl with a beautiful body and a face which changed like a chameleon from the pert to the pleasing to the pleasurable. Physically Joanna might have stepped straight from the pages of Sinclair's book and the more she got to know Susie the more she relished taking on the role.

Sinclair's screenplay remained fairly faithful to his book but he updated key scenarios to capture the flavour of the Swinging Sixties and youthful rebellion and included a flower power scene where Joanna, as Susie, turns up outside Wellington Barracks to inflame a demonstration and pop a flower down the muzzle of a Guardsman's rifle.

Otherwise Sinclair's characterization of Susie remained largely as originally written, a gorgeous-looking girl who lived on her own in a plush bedsitter in London, was frequently to be seen down the King's Road buying eye-catching clothes such as shocking pink Italian blouses but was equally at home munching on a hot dog while watching the greyhounds at Harringay racetrack. Susie was a girl who had gained a first at Reading University, a girl who lived for the moment and whose past included two brief lovers before meeting Bumbo. But she had never really enjoyed the flings. As a model she had been out with a different celebrity every night to get her name known. When out with other men she told them about her relationship with Bumbo but decided that if they still wanted to spend their money on taking her out to dinner then that was fine because, after all, a girl had to eat.

While Joanna spent time working on fleshing out Susie's character, she also made regular journeys to Maida Vale in north London to sit for a large portrait painting which *The Breaking of Bumbo*'s set dresser required for scenes in Susie's flat. The plan was that the cartoon-style, figurative portrait of a lounging Joanna as Susie would dominate one wall above Susie's trendy, pop-art, leopard-print sofa.

Unsurprisingly, given the controversy his book had caused in military circles, Sinclair was granted no co-operation whatsoever from the Guards when it came to filming *The Breaking of Bumbo*. As Sinclair's film would later point out in its pre-release marketing blurb: 'Of all the forces who wear the military uniform of Her Majesty the Queen in Great Britain, probably none is more efficient, strict, proud or colourful than the Brigade of Guards. For over three hundred years the Guards have been synonymous with the highest standards of the British Army.' It was little wonder then that they had been distinctly underwhelmed by Sinclair's tale of a subversive officer inciting his comrades to mutiny.

Sinclair found the top brass were still smarting from his book and they were alarmed at the prospect of further adverse impact now it was being adapted for a movie. They even refused to give Sinclair permission to shoot scenes in the forecourt of Wellington Barracks which fronts St James's Park in London so the bold decision was taken to construct an authentic replica on the back lot at Pinewood.

With the aid of detailed maps, plans and photographs, art director Ray Simm and construction manager Leon Davis set about recreating a duplicate of the famous barracks and square. It took sixty-five men six weeks to build the replica at a cost of £25,000 using twenty-five tons of plaster and 20,000 feet of tubular scaffolding. By the time the construction of the barracks was completed, even an experienced military eye could not tell the difference.

Although Andrew Sinclair was totally inexperienced as a director, it was noticeable to Joanna and the production team when it came to filming that he nevertheless approached each scene with great conviction. A very tall, eloquent and imposing man, Sinclair had little difficulty in winning the confidence and respect of cast and crew and the many scenes involving the Guards on and off the parade ground were filmed with an eye for scrupulous detail for which two years of National Service now proved invaluable. 'I had to drill a squad of thirty ex-Guardsmen myself – and I knew how to do it,' he says.

'I knew nothing about film directing but I had become a top screenwriter in Hollywood and I also ran a little publishing firm producing classic screenplays in book form. We'd published eighty of them so I did know a lot about the grammar of the cinema. I was an experienced screenwriter and I knew how a film sequence should be put together.'

Sinclair emphatically ensured that Joanna Lumley's first screen entrance was dramatic. Bumbo Bailey, having become heavily involved in the London social season of Lord's, Ascot and Henley with a succession of different debutantes but with an increasing sense of boredom, turns up as a guest one night at a wild party being thrown at London's famous Madame Tussaud's waxwork museum.

He is surveying the scene on his own in the museum's Conquerors' Room when an old schoolfriend Billy, played by Jeremy Child, and a pretty young deb Sheila Veyne-Browne, played by Natasha Pyne, enter without seeing him and start to make love on the floor beneath the disapproving eyes of the waxwork dummies of Hitler, Napoleon, the Kaiser and Genghis Khan.

Suddenly a large coloured actor carrying a pot of red paint enters with a plump fortyish man and Joanna, looking striking in a pair of tight, flared, red snakeskin trousers with a matching waistcoat over a red chiffon blouse. Around her waist is an ornate belt with an Oriental-style curved knife tucked into a sheath at her hip.

After an impromptu show by the trio watched by the party guests, Joanna as Susie provocatively wraps herself around the Genghis Khan waxwork and starts to smooch with the figure before joining her two comrades in destroying several wax figures, including that of Sir Winston Churchill, and spraying their audience of party guests with paint.

Mayhem ensues and when security arrive the trio escape with Bumbo in tow and go back to Susie's bedsit where it transpires the demonstration she had just staged was just one of her ongoing protests against the futility of war. 'I'm a dropout from the affluent society,' says Joanna by way of explanation for Susie's comfortable surroundings and expensive clothes. With Bumbo clearly intent on staying the night, Susie regards him as something of a catch, hoping he might be persuaded to subvert the Brigade of Guards. But first she must take him to bed. They must become lovers.

From the very start of filming Joanna knew that this was the point in the script when she would be required to play for the camera a nude love scene with Richard Warwick. Disrobing in the cause of cinematic art has always been an occupational hazard for young actresses and Joanna was not to be an exception but *The Breaking of Bumbo* at least presented something of a rarity for a budding starlet, a love scene that was genuinely important to the script.

In truth, it's only after Susie takes Bumbo to bed for a torrid night of passion that he falls helplessly in love with her and is subsequently swayed by her revolutionary views. Later, just when he is ready to bring about a full-scale mutiny of his men to please and impress her, he finds her in a passionate embrace with a strapping blond man at a party, 'a Swede with a need' as she calls him, and she proceeds to tell Bumbo that she no longer wants to sleep with him because she needs a more mature man.

Joanna got on well with Richard Warwick and thought he was a sweet young man. Like Joanna, Warwick was well educated and could swap reminiscences about early years spent growing up in a Kent country village because his family had lived at Longfield near Gravesend until they all moved to a rambling old vicarage in Gloucestershire. There he revelled in a country area steeped in history and delighted in telling Joanna and others how when he sat in the dentist's chair at Tewkesbury he sat in the same room where Queen Margaret had looked out over Bloody Meadow in 1471 during the War of the Roses.

But the generally affable rapport between Joanna and Warwick did not guarantee that their love scenes were going to be easy. It wasn't simply a case of the couple falling into bed. Under Sinclair's direction, Joanna and Warwick first needed to be filmed naked from the back, slowly climbing five stairs on either side of Susie's bed before turning to face each other then plunging on to the bed in unison for a passionate embrace.

Other essential shots included Joanna sitting up in bed naked, first writing 'Make Love Not War' in lipstick on Warwick's torso then tracing circles on his chest with the point of his military sword. A further shot required Joanna to stand nonchalantly naked to the waist beside a painting. The closing scene of Bumbo's sexual tryst with Susie was to end with Joanna stretched out naked face down on the bed filmed from above.

When the day appointed for filming these sex scenes finally arrived, it was noticeable to some of the crew that, of the two would-be screen lovers, Richard Warwick appeared to be far more anxious. He seemed much more apprehensive, flustered even, about it all whereas Joanna, if she had any nerves, was hiding all trace of them.

In deference to his two young stars, however, Sinclair thoughtfully ordered that Joanna's love scenes with Warwick would be shot on a closed set which meant that only those members of the film crew crucial to the scene were allowed to remain. He was determined it would be an intimate setting and not a general peepshow for the crew and production team.

Joanna and Richard Warwick were due to be called to the set for their screen tryst after their lunch break and to give them Dutch courage and to help them relax a little, Sinclair presented Joanna and Warwick with a bottle of champagne each with the suggestion that they should be consumed over lunch. 'They told us not to appear until we had drunk the lot!' Joanna recalls.

The bubbly clearly had the desired effect on Joanna even if, as Sinclair laments: 'It didn't do much for Richard Warwick.' The finished film shows Joanna appearing to be very much at ease without her clothes on and convincing in her passionate clinches with her co-star. As Sinclair directed the couple he couldn't help but admire Joanna's professional approach and, particularly, her composure.

Sinclair says: 'One had to be discreet in this love scene with Richard Warwick when Joanna lay on her back as she didn't have any clothes on. But I remember she said to me: "Andrew, if you are doing a side shot of me, always do it when I breathe out because otherwise I will appear to have two pairs of breasts. The other pair will be my ribs." What wonderful self-possession! So I did exactly that.'

Interspersed with the shots of the couple's love-making are scenes of Joanna playfully clowning around in Bumbo's busby and tunic and the whole episode is given an added tender, romantic air with the voices of Joanna and Richard Warwick singing a recorded duet in the background of a specially written love song called 'I Never Knew'.

Upon looking at the rushes Sinclair found he could hardly fault Joanna in these crucial love scenes. Joanna herself later expressed the view that she very happy about them too. 'It was beautifully lit, beautifully shot,' she commented. But Sinclair was desperately disappointed with Richard Warwick's performance. 'These remarkable love scenes were a bit of a damp squib,' he says ruefully.

As the film bears testimony all too clearly, Warwick failed to project the kind of crackling, electric intensity expected of a young man who finds himself lucky enough to be plied with champagne and paid to roll around on salmon pink sheets with a naked girl as delectable as Joanna Lumley.

'Frankly, as we now know, Richard was gay,' says Sinclair of the actor who died from AIDS in December 1998, 'and there was really no sexual chemistry between him and Joanna whatsoever. I didn't know he was gay at the time – it wasn't a thing you thought about in those days. Richard had appeared very sort of rough and tough in *If. . .* so I never suspected it.'

Richard Warwick's obvious lack of passion for Joanna in the clinches was a real setback for *The Breaking of Bumbo*. 'Of any ten films you make, only one actually works,' says Andrew Sinclair, 'and what you do need in a romance is a sexual spark.

'But there was no sexual spark between Joanna and Richard Warwick. There wasn't that sexual magic. Had there been, *The Breaking of Bumbo* could have worked. That spark simply wasn't there – but it was through no fault of Joanna's. It was nothing to do with Joanna's performance.'

With the help of a sparkling wardrobe, Joanna looked gorgeous throughout the film whether she was clad in a flimsy kaftan as in a party scene or dressed in the suede tasselled outfit and Davy Crockett-style fur hat she wore in her final scene where Susie is inciting a student protest outside the gates of Wellington Barracks.

Like many men who have encountered Joanna Lumley, Andrew Sinclair admits he couldn't help falling in love with her. 'On a film there's always a question of whether the star will fall for the direc-tor or whether the director will fall for the star,' he says. 'I thought she was wonderful. That marvellous walk and carriage and self-possession, and her beauty. Of course I fell in love with her.'

Most men will find it perfectly understandable that Andrew

Sinclair became so enamoured of Joanna. Quite apart from anything else, Joanna was the embodiment of the girl he had dreamed up for his best-selling book ten years before. At that point in her life Joanna was looking exceptionally beautiful but there was also a noticeable glow about her too. Her starring role in *The Breaking of Bumbo* had led to her being touted as 'The Face of the Seventies', she was driving around in a Silver Wraith Rolls-Royce and her son Jamie was by now up in London living with her at her flat in Addison Gardens. Life was looking good for Joanna Lumley and she radiated a new-found confidence. Her figure was in terrific shape, too, as the shot of Joanna stretched out on the bed in the movie's final love scene patently showed.

If Andrew Sinclair harboured any thoughts that his relationship with Joanna might become anything other than professional during the filming of *The Breaking of Bumbo*, then he was all set to find out at the end of a very pleasant evening the couple spent having a meal together in London.

Sinclair had taken Joanna out to dinner and they had then gone back to her flat in Addison Gardens. If any sort of romance was to develop, the scene was set and the players in place. 'But,' says Sinclair, his eyes twinkling with amusement at the memory, 'Joanna marched me up to a room where there was a small cot with a little infant sleeping in it and she said: "Andrew, meet Piglet! Piglet, meet Andrew!" In these Winnie the Pooh terms she told me beautifully that she was otherwise engaged.'

The infant was, of course, Joanna's son Jamie asleep in his cot, and Joanna's introduction to him, says Sinclair, was so subtle yet so clear a way of saying a romance was not on the agenda that he could not possibly take any offence. 'Nothing was said but it was all conveyed perfectly clearly in this Winnie the Pooh language,' he says, laughing. 'I loved it. I think this is the measure of Joanna. She has this coded language.'

When filming finally wrapped on *The Breaking of Bumbo* and the sets were being dismantled, Sinclair was hopeful of keeping for himself the delightful painting of Joanna which had hung on Susie's wall. But it was not to be. 'Bryan Forbes insisted on having it,' he says. 'And he's still got it.'

Looking back today at his film *The Breaking of Bumbo*, Andrew

Sinclair is philosophical. 'On set we shot it conventionally,' he says, 'and, in my opinion, the Army sequences are very good and the Swinging London sequences aren't. They are simply a bit old-fashioned now. But Joanna is very good in it. I loved working with Joanna, she was totally professional, and I thought for a first-time performance in a major role she was superb. I can only speak most highly of Joanna.'

As happens with every film, a marketing campaign was carefully prepared to accompany the release of *The Breaking of Bumbo*. Full-colour advertising posters were designed to show a Guards officer in red tunic lying prone on the ground with the outline of a scantily clad girl in black bra, lacy black knickers and black high heels, stepping over his back and his busby. The statutory advertising credits would ensure that Joanna's name was projected in large letters under that of Richard Warwick.

A special publicity brochure was also printed with various stills telling the story of the film. One was headlined 'Joanna Lumley is Revolting!' over a photograph of Joanna as Susie in a protest demonstration. 'She's the most seductive revolutionary you've ever seen,' trumpeted the brochure, adding the following unlikely but innocuous story about the female star: 'Joanna Lumley is very much a practical girl. That's why her reigning ambition is to make an enormous four-poster bed. With her own hands, to her own designs.

' "I've always had a thing about those gorgeous old four-posters," she admits, "and I've always longed to own and sleep in one at night. Because I'm mad about making things, I want to build my own. It will be very large, made of heavy dark old wood and have an ornate lion at each corner. The trouble is I'd probably adore it so much I'd want to lie in bed all day." '

As a teaser, this titillating little insight into Joanna Lumley added: 'Bed-postscript: Joanna spends a certain amount of time in bed in Bumbo during a passionate and daring love scene with Richard Warwick. Not, unfortunately for Joanna, a four-poster . . .'

The marketing brochure also noted that Richard Warwick's gruelling role as Bumbo had certain compensations. 'The compensations as far as Richard is concerned include several highly enjoyable love scenes with the gorgeous and delectable Joanna Lumley in the film. Richard's comment on his romantic sequences with Joanna? Roses, roses all the way!'

Despite the lack of screen fireworks between Joanna and Richard Warwick, hopes were still high for *The Breaking of Bumbo*. But just as Joanna was poised for her inauguration as a shining, sexy new star of British cinema, the launch of *The Breaking of Bumbo* on general release was suddenly aborted in the most unforeseen and mystifying fashion.

The received wisdom is that *The Breaking of Bumbo* encountered 'distribution difficulties' and thus was accorded the most limited of cinema screenings. In real terms, hardly anybody saw the film which was designed to launch Joanna to screen stardom simply because it never reached their local cinema.

Today it is difficult even to find *The Breaking of Bumbo* in some film reference books and what references there are tend to explain away its obscurity by blaming those 'distribution problems'. But Sinclair has a different explanation as to why his movie did not find its way into the cinemas.

'Forbes's occupancy of Elstree wasn't easy,' he says without malice but to try and set the record straight. 'When I came, you couldn't get to his table and when I left he sat alone with me. We were taken over. First we were ABC Pictures, then it was EMI, then it was EMI-MGM and this all happened on two days and the decision was taken that every single film should be scrapped and dumped as a tax loss. That's what happened to *The Breaking of Bumbo*. It wasn't a distribution problem as Joanna and others have thought.'

In the face of a studio take-over Sinclair was powerless to influence the fate of his film. 'It wasn't not shown on its merit,' he says. 'It was because of a studio coup. Only one of the ten films survived and that was *The Railway Children* because that had a child's market. Everything else was dumped including Bryan Forbes's own film *The Raging Moon*.'

Whatever the reason, the non-appearance of the film was a huge blow to Joanna's aspirations as an actress. She had worked so hard on the movie and turned in a highly creditable performance and now, quite literally, had nothing to show for it. Worse still, gossip about its failure to go on general release implied – wrongly, as it transpired – that *The Breaking of Bumbo* was not up to scratch, and the danger for Joanna was that she would be tarred with the same malicious brush. It was a bitter disappointment. Her hopes of at last establishing herself as an actress to be reckoned with had turned horribly sour through no fault of her own. 'The film was put aside for five years,' says Joanna sadly. 'Not many slight films can take the test of a year let alone five.'

After such high expectations, Joanna came down to earth with a bump. 'Success, so-called, is like a treacherous lover,' she said. 'It's any place it wants to put you at any time. When I got *The Breaking of Bumbo* I tried not to grin too much on the street. But I came out of the film with nothing to show but a very small cheque.'

Sinclair is the first to wish for Joanna's sake that it had been otherwise. He says: 'I went on to make *Under Milk Wood* with Elizabeth Taylor, Richard Burton and Peter O'Toole. So for me, *The Breaking of Bumbo* was a springboard into fortune. I was lucky.'

Unluckiest of all was Richard Warwick, and Joanna was there at his memorial service a month after his death to read 'When I Have Fears' by Noel Coward. They had remained lifelong friends.

Indeed some years after the ill-fated film Richard Warwick spoke frankly to one of the authors about his nude encounter with young Joanna. 'I am sure there are millions of men who think I am completely mad,' said Richard, 'but filming those nude scenes with Joanna was one of the most harrowing experiences of my life. I was desperately nervous about the whole idea and I tried to put it right at the back of my mind.

'I knew what it entailed and Andrew Sinclair kept encouraging me about how vitally important it was to the whole film. Bumbo had to look mesmerized by this fantastic vision of a woman, so that it was believable that he would do anything, betray anyone, just to please her. And the awful thing for me was that I could see perfectly well that Joanna was stunningly attractive. She was bright and vibrant and full of fun and when she took her clothes off she looked even more lovely. I could see that but it had no effect on me, I'm afraid. In that moment I would have given anything to have genuinely fancied her but the truth was I just didn't. I was awkward and embarrassed and hopelessly wooden in those scenes. I could not bear to watch them afterwards because I could see Jo trying so hard to display enough feeling and emotion for both of us.

'I tried to pretend. But there was no chemistry between us in that way. It was ghastly because as a person she is inspirational in so many ways. She is brave and strong and true to what she believes in. We became real friends and I always admired her so much. But I was a bit screwed up with myself at the time and when the cameras started rolling and Joanna went for it I just know I let her down. I'm sorry but I did.'

Joanna's acute disappointment over *The Breaking of Bumbo* was compounded by a similar fate befalling the other film she had made that year, *Tam Lin*. Infuriatingly *Tam Lin* also remained unreleased despite the fact that it starred one of the great legends of Hollywood, Ava Gardner, was produced by Alan Ladd and was directed by Roddy McDowall, a British child actor of the 1940s who had developed into a competent, if unpredictable, adult performer in a string of big movies.

Based on a Scottish ballad but re-set in England in the Swinging Sixties, *Tam Lin* featured Ava Gardner as a sinister, beautiful, middle-aged widow who has a diabolic influence on the bright young people she gathers around her. Ready to be lured into her coven are a number of very beautiful English actresses besides Joanna including Sinead Cusack, Stephanie Beacham, Madeleine Smith, and Jenny Hanley with whom Joanna had spent six cosseted weeks in Switzerland on the Bond film *On Her Majesty's Secret Service*. Ian McShane played the young man with whom the devilish widow falls in love.

It was a happy production so it was all the more galling when the film was stalled at the last hurdle. One of the major obstacles to *Tam Lin*'s release was that the plot involved hallucinatory drugs and that was not viewed with approval by the film censors of the time.

Coupled with the heartbreak over *The Breaking of Bumbo*, the non-appearance of *Tam Lin* was a double blow to Joanna's acting aspirations. Her breakthrough into films seemed fated to fail.

6

Mrs Jeremy Lloyd

When Joanna Lumley celebrated her twenty-fourth birthday on 1 May 1970, she can have had no inkling of the extraordinary chain of events that was to turn her life upside down that summer. Nor, for that matter, can Jeremy Lloyd.

While Joanna was blowing out the candles on her birthday cake, Jeremy Lloyd, the man she had not yet met but was to marry by the end of the month after a remarkable, whirlwind affair, was in Hollywood basking in the reputation of being not just a very funny English actor and writer of comedy sketches but a ladykiller of considerable standing.

Having carved a niche for himself as an actor in Britain on TV and in movies playing quintessential upper class twits or Guards officers, Jeremy had progressed to writing TV comedy sketches and to his surprise and unconcealed delight had been summoned to Hollywood to write scripts for and take small roles in Rowan and Martin's *Laugh-In*, a TV comedy show which had taken America by storm in 1968.

Hosted by Dan Rowan and Dick Martin, *Laugh-In* was one of those rare television programmes which was not only an overnight sensation but was highly innovative, crystallizing a kind of contemporary, fast-paced, unstructured comedy 'happening' which was exactly what an agitated America wanted in 1968.

Laugh-In had swept straight to the top of America's TV ratings that year and the show's producer George Slaughter, needing some 250 gags per *Laugh-In* show and eager to keep the programme fresh for a second season, had flown to Britain with the express purpose of searching for new comic talent. In London he heard of Jeremy's ability to write comedy sketches and invited him to join him for breakfast one morning at 8 a.m. sharp at the Dorchester Hotel.

Fellow guests breakfasting at the prestigious hotel in Park Lane were then treated to the sight of the six-foot-four-inch tall, frightfully English Jeremy Lloyd and the very upfront American, George Slaughter, trading rapid-fire jokes at a corner table. The silence which the decorum of a traditional breakfast at such an elite British hotel usually dictates was broken by the two men throwing back their heads in uproarious laughter.

Jeremy's *pièce de résistance* was yet to come. Springing up from the table, he took off his jacket, dropped on both knees then tugged his sweater down around his ankles and walked about on his haunches in a squatting position. 'Toulouse Lautrec!' he exclaimed, beaming hopefully at the startled Slaughter who let out a bellow of laughter which froze the forks of a dozen Dorchester diners in mid-air on the way to stiff upper lips. 'I'd love to be in the show,' enthused Jeremy, squat-walking under the table cloth and emerging with an asinine grin the other side. How could Slaughter turn him down?

Promptly whisked off to Hollywood, Jeremy arrived to a warm welcome not least from the statuesque, beautiful, sexy, six-feet tall and athletically inclined blonde actress Julie Newmar who generously made her apartment just off Sunset Strip in Los Angeles available for him, and much else besides.

Jeremy endeared himself to the rest of the *Laugh-In* gang from the moment he joined the team of fourteen other gag writers at the Tulaca Capri Hotel in Hollywood. At the first scriptwriters' meeting he was deliberately paired with another writer called Coslo Johnson who stood all of five feet tall in his stockinged feet so that, side by side, he and Jeremy would at least look funny. The hope was that if they looked funny together, reasoned Slaughter, they might come up with some funny lines together.

Jeremy immediately demonstrated he was on the *Laugh-In* wavelength by suggesting an outrageous sketch in which the giant-sized Harlem Globetrotters basketball team would be dressed up as foreign legionnaires and would then encounter a group of midgets dressed up in Arab costume. Jeremy's idea for the climax of this unequal confrontation was that the legionnaires would suddenly produce giant fly-swatters and swat the midgets.

Asked not only to write but perform in *Laugh-In* as well, Jeremy's burgeoning star status coupled with his very English accent, his innate sense of fun, his considerable self-deprecating charm and his debonair, flamboyant good looks, had an immediate impact on the many American girls he encountered. 'Aren't you that guy from the Beatles film?' was a much-quoted opening line from girls who wanted to get talking to him. Jeremy had indeed played a small, but conspicuous, role in the Fab Four's first film, *A Hard Day's Night*, in 1964, as an upper-crust, silly ass Englishman making a fool of himself by attempting to be groovy and bop on a dance floor with Ringo Starr in a disco scene. 'I was a remarkable nightclub dancer,' he says, 'and hurled myself into the air as if I was on a pogo stick.' It was an odd way for an upper-crust Englishman to dance but just being in a Beatles film brought fame by association. 'Gee, do you really know the Beatles?' Jeremy was repeatedly asked in America.

Jeremy's reputation for being such a hit with the ladies and for bringing so many attractive girls to the *Laugh-In* show prompted George Slaughter to make him an offer. 'Since you seem to be so good with the ladies, you might as well have the job of choosing the girls for *Laugh-In*'s dance segments,' said George. It was an invitation which Jeremy seized with relish and he lost no time in making it widely known that auditions would be held at his home the following Sunday morning.

By now he had moved out of Julie Newmar's apartment and was residing at the home of composer Leslie Bricusse and his wife Evie in a splendid mansion close to the plush Beverly Hills Hotel. What happened that Sunday morning became a legendary story in Hollywood circles because Bricusse arrived home for lunch to find no fewer than sixty-five liquid-limbed lovelies lined up in his garden, each one holding a portable tape recorder containing their own dance music with which they were preparing to cavort enthusiastically for the lanky TV hotshot from London holding the auditions.

In front of them, sitting regally under a striped sun-shade umbrella, wearing dark glasses and looking like the cat who had got the cream, was Jeremy Lloyd making notes and compiling a directory of names with telephone numbers of some of the sexiest girls in town.

Hollywood embraced Jeremy in every way, even his clothes. The Americans were mad about the way his trouser legs fell fully to the soles of his shoes while theirs all seemed to stop at half mast. 'That's why you have to wear long socks,' Jeremy jovially mocked them. With such warmth emanating from the Americans, Jeremy lived life to the full. In *Laugh-In* he worked with embryonic stars like Goldie Hawn, an instant hit with her giggling dumb blonde act, as well as the big names of showbusiness like Bob Hope, who queued up to make guest appearances. Even President Nixon had been persuaded to make a cameo appearance on the show to utter one of *Laugh-In*'s cult catchphrases 'Sock it to me.'

Jeremy was at the heart of America's top TV show and away from the set he enjoyed life thoroughly. On a holiday in Acapulco he had to pinch himself when one day he found himself dancing under the moonlight at a party with Merle Oberon. 'It was a fairly wild time,' he says. 'I lived some of the wildest adventures and there were lots of exotic cheroots going around at the time. They were called tea parties!'

Back in England, his future wife Joanna Lumley was at this time mulling over the offer of a film role in a comedy called *Two Girls*. 'The script was very funny,' she says, 'and I went along to see the director and he said: "We've got Jeremy Lloyd and Dickie Wattis in it", and I said: "Funny men. I'll do it." '

Jeremy was on a brief visit back to England halfway through his second year on *Laugh-In* when Joanna met him for the first time and in the most bizarre of circumstances. She introduced herself to the man who was to become her husband while he was doing his best to look fetching in fishnet stockings, high heels and a garish red dress.

Jeremy was being fitted at the film and theatre costumiers Berman's and Nathan's for his role as a homosexual in *Two Girls* when Joanna, also there for costume fittings for her role as a prostitute, cheerfully knocked on the door and said she'd like to say hello because they would be working together in the movie. She roared with laughter at Jeremy's get-up but told him he had jolly good legs. Such an unlikely beginning developed into a remarkable, whirlwind romance.

Joanna found Jeremy terrific company. He had a fund of funny stories, always engagingly told in a way which was to earn him in some quarters the title of 'the wittiest man in London'. Jeremy made Joanna laugh, he was polite, worldly, gentlemanly, attentive, very tall, good looking, charming. 'He could charm eagles off crags,' said Joanna who felt comfortable, even cosy, with him. She also considered him to be quite the most exciting man she had ever met. Jeremy thought Joanna enchanting, beautiful, intelligent and sexy. He remembered how he had seen her once before at a party some years back and how he had thought her very attractive then although they had not been introduced on that occasion.

Three days after the meeting at Berman's and Nathan's, Jeremy invited Joanna to dinner at a London restaurant on a Thursday evening and asked her to marry him. Sudden though this heady marriage proposal was, remarkably Joanna was not taken aback. On the contrary, she thought it was a terrific idea although she did not give her answer immediately. But on the Friday they excitedly drove down to her parents in Kent together so that Jeremy could formally ask her father for Joanna's hand in marriage over the weekend. Naturally it was a huge surprise for the Lumleys but if Joanna was happy, they said, then so were they. On the Saturday, Joanna accepted Jeremy's proposal and Jeremy promptly moved into Joanna's flat.

On the following Monday 18 May 1970, the England World Cup football squad improbably took the song 'Back Home' to the top of the pop charts en route to the Mexico tournament, Prime Minister Harold Wilson shook the world of politics by announcing he was calling a snap General Election for 18 June, and Joanna Lumley astounded her friends by announcing her engagement to Jeremy Lloyd after knowing him for just a matter of days.

Jeremy's sudden marriage proposal to Joanna did not, however, altogether come as any undue surprise to Jeremy's many friends. They had come to know that when Jeremy fell madly in love with a girl, his passion was total and all-consuming. Some four years earlier they had witnessed Jeremy being comprehensively swept off his feet in similar fashion by another young English actress, Charlotte Rampling.

Jeremy had fallen for the wild and ravishingly beautiful Charlotte the moment he had first encountered her at a trendy London party. He'd taken one look at the almond-eyed, coltish model and budding actress and become utterly and helplessly enamoured. His first glimpse of Charley, as she was then known to London's in-crowd before she made her name to great acclaim in movies like Visconti's *The Damned* and *The Night Porter*, had left Jeremy transfixed. She was coquettishly tossing her long mane of reddish-brown hair about while dancing with energetic abandon to the guitar riffs of 'You Really Got Me' which snarled from the speakers of pop's hottest new group to arrive on the London scene, the Kinks, who were playing raucously in the host's garden.

'You Really Got Me', delivered by the Kinks' rasping vocalist Ray Davies, resplendent in the group's trademark red hunting jacket, could hardly have been more fitting. Jeremy remembers he knew he simply had to speak to the stunning creature he saw prancing enthusiastically to the music like a mini-skirted marionette in front of him. He determined there and then that this was one girl he was going to become fully acquainted with.

When Charlotte later strode off into the kitchen to fetch herself a drink, Jeremy pursued her, struck up a conversation, and Army colonel's daughter Charlotte and Army colonel's son Jeremy clicked instantly. The sexually charged attraction was immediate and mutual. Jeremy offered Charlotte a lift home and he and Charlotte spent the remainder of that night hungrily entwined in each other's arms in Jeremy's car pausing between passionate kisses only to talk animatedly about life and love till the sun's rays filtered through the steamed-up windows heralding a new Swinging Sixties day. In no time at all Jeremy had moved into Charlotte's flat.

Jeremy, the man whom Joanna was now about to marry, had come very close to marrying Charlotte. Their marriage banns had actually been called twice and the wedding invitations were being prepared when Charlotte's stern father Colonel Godfrey Rampling broke the news to Jeremy on Charlotte's behalf that his daughter felt that she could not, after all, go through with the wedding.

Now, some five years on, here was Jeremy, head over heels about another beautiful, classy, young actress and about to be married for the second time. His first marriage to clergyman's daughter Dawn, a house model at top London store Liberty's, whom he had met while playing tennis, had collapsed under the strain of Jeremy's efforts to make his way in showbusiness. After ten years she had gone off with a man she had met sailing.

On 23 May 1970, Joanna duly married Jeremy at Chelsea Register Office in London. The bride looked gorgeous if a little nervous in a silk dress with a hemline several inches above the knee made by her former employer Jean Muir, a matching jacket and a broad-brimmed black hat. Not to be outdone, Jeremy wore a pair of smart tapered trousers, a long black velvet jacket, a frilly fronted open-neck shirt and a tightly tied neckerchief. Dangling foppishly from his neck on a chain was a monocle.

As they walked away down the King's Road as husband and wife after the brief ceremony, the newly joined Mr and Mrs Lloyd could have been just another couple in the colourful parade of peacock males and dolly birds who regularly paraded up and down Chelsea's most famous street on a Saturday afternoon.

Joanna said of the marriage: 'I must have been out of my tree and so must he. But we were working on the same film and on its completion he had to return to the States for another job. It was the urgency of his schedule which pushed us into marriage and had we waited longer things might have been different.'

For their honeymoon the couple decided to drive down from London to the south of France. They planned to extend the honeymoon in France through the summer, which would give Jeremy time to get down to some writing there.

Jeremy owned a wonderful collection of cars ranging from a Lotus Seven to a 1957 Rolls-Royce and he chose the latter for the journey because of its size and comfort. But before they set out Jeremy had a somewhat bizarre warning for Joanna about the typical French roads lined with trees on either side which they would inevitably encounter on their long journey.

He says: 'I told Joanna I suffered from a condition that can happen when you are passing a row of trees whereby it can have a sort of strobe effect on your brain and you pass out for a while. I told her I was therefore insuring the car for her to drive just in case I passed out so that she would be able to take over the wheel. Joanna was all for it and said: "I'm absolutely ready to do that." '

But neither of them bargained for it to happen quite so soon. 'We set off and I passed out just over Battersea Bridge,' Jeremy remembers with a huge laugh. 'So Joanna drove the Rolls all the way down to Dover, on to the boat and across most of France before I woke up and was able to continue the journey and arrive in some style. I think it was basically fatigue on my part – or the stress of packing!'

Joanna and Jeremy took Jamie with them, and they settled into a picturesque house at Saint Paul de Vence, tucked into the hills above Cannes. 'It was a beautiful town with a medieval belt of stone wall, looking down towards the sea,' Joanna recalls. 'It was a hot summer of fun, and fireflies which I hadn't seen since Malaya.'

The house belonged to Jack Davies, a great friend of Jeremy's whom he had got to know well during the making of the film *Those Magnificent Men In Their Flying Machines* for which Jack had written the screenplay. Jack was later to join them at the house with his son who revealed he was working on a new BBC comedy show called *It's Awfully Bad For Your Eyes, Darling* and suggested both Joanna and Jeremy should take roles in it.

This idyllic Côte d'Azur setting where the newlyweds were about to get acquainted was a former restaurant with a large barbecue in the garden which was put to frequent good use. Throughout the hot south of France summer various visitors took the winding, dusty roads up into the hills to Saint Paul to call on the honeymooning couple as word got around that the newly married Mr and Mrs Lloyd were in residence. Many a happy hour was spent lazing in the sunshine over a drink, laughing at Jeremy's endless fund of funny stories.

For Joanna and Jeremy, there was a lot of getting to know each other to be done, much personal history to unfold. By any standards Jeremy had lived an amazing life. His mother had been a dancing Tiller girl who had left his father, a colonel in the Army, when Jeremy was just eighteen months old. He had rarely seen his mother since.

Expelled from prep school before his thirteenth birthday, Jeremy was then packed off to live with his grandparents in a home for retired folk. Surrounded by people who were mostly fifty years or more older than himself, Jeremy spent a lonely childhood whiling away his time reading all the books in the retirement home's library.

Eventually bowing to family pressure, he tried to join the Army for National Service but cut such a sorry-looking figure at six feet four and weighing less than eight stone that the military sent him away. They were so concerned about his wellbeing that they even popped him into a taxi to take him home because it was raining.

Work had followed as a van loader, a plumber's mate and an industrial paint salesman during which he achieved the dubious distinction of negotiating a sale which brought about a change of paint to the railings in Regents Park – to grey. He also had a stint working as a management trainee at the London store Simpson's in Piccadilly which was later to inspire the creation of his hugely popular BBC comedy show *Are You Being Served?* He got the sack from Simpson's for selling ice cream and soft drinks in the gentlemen's fitting room.

But it was the rainy afternoons he spent hiding in cinemas when he was a paint salesman that first put him on the road to a showbusiness career. After watching one singularly unremarkable film, he decided he could do just as well. Earl St John, then head of Pinewood Studios, agreed with him because he bought Jeremy's resulting script, written in Jeremy's own fair hand in a school exercise book, for £1,000.

Jeremy followed this success with scripts for a wide range of TV programmes like the pop show *Six Five Special* and shows for performers like Harry Secombe, Billy Cotton and Dickie Henderson.

With the showbusiness life came a love of fancy cars and, by the time he met Joanna, Jeremy had owned at one stage or another a total of some fifty motorcars ranging from a 1928 Austin Seven to Bentleys to an obscure and exotic Italian sports Iso Grifo.

Jeremy had also briefly raced Lotus 6 cars at Goodwood. Legend had it in racing circles that once, while waiting on the starting grid, Jeremy had happened to glance in his racing mirror and was so struck by the elegance of his own marvellous image of half-tinted goggles, visor, helmet, the lot, that by the time he managed to tear his gaze away from his own reflection, everyone else had passed by him. It was a story Jeremy readily told against himself.

Jeremy's love of adventure had also extended to the skies after he became friends with a man who owned an old 1920 Spartan biplane. Their chief sport was to take off with Jeremy sitting in the front cockpit while his friend piloted the plane from the seat behind. Stored at Jeremy's feet were several bags of flour and the duo would fly daringly low over the Denham by-pass endeavouring to drop-bomb the flour bags on a car being driven beneath them at high speed by yet another friend.

Joanna also quickly learned that throughout much of his adult life Jeremy had consulted psychics, mediums and clairvoyants and claimed he had received many messages 'from people on the other side'. He had first become a keen devotee of spiritualism after meeting a woman who convinced him he was going to be a successful writer, appear on television and go to Hollywood.

Joanna was later to discover first-hand Jeremy's abiding interest in matters spiritual shortly after he had decided to volunteer to be hypnotized. Under hypnosis, Jeremy had been taken back in time and had been introduced to his spirit guide who turned out to be a plump oriental from Tibet. Excited by this spiritual encounter, the next time Jeremy got together with Joanna he asked her if she would like to see his spirit guide and she was inquisitive enough to say she would.

Together Joanna and Jeremy sat side by side on the sofa and under Jeremy's exhortation they both started to concentrate intensely. Joanna was tempted to giggle but suddenly, as she looked hard at Jeremy's face, she noticed his eyes had started to narrow and she was shocked to hear a quite terrifyingly gruff, guttural noise emerging from deep in his throat. Joanna was so taken aback she burst into tears. The experience, she confided chillingly to friends, was not an illusion.

Sitting together calling up Jeremy's spirit guide was one thing but an uninvited transfiguration of Jeremy was quite another, says Jeremy, 'It arrived in the form of a transfiguration uninvited when we were discussing something at Annabel's,' Jeremy remembers very vividly. 'Joanna had a fright fainting fit when it appeared.'

These strange phenomena continued after their marriage was

over and on a couple of occasions Jeremy had out-of-body experiences that took him into Joanna Lumley's home at night. 'I had one or two out-of-body experiences where I visited Joanna at her home and came back and was able to tell her exactly what had been going on,' he says. 'I was able to report accurately who was there and what they were talking about.'

On one of these occasions, Jeremy had retired to bed after a hot bath in his flat only a few miles from Joanna's and had only just put his head on the pillow when he heard what he could only describe as 'a vibrating noise' and suddenly he had an extraordinary sensation that he was being lifted out of his body.

He says he even clearly remembers putting his hands up to deflect the impact as he flew through the wall later to find himself standing in Joanna's bedroom. 'I was aware I had the same height but had the consistency of grey jelly but also my feet weren't on the floor but two inches below.'

Although the room was unoccupied, Jeremy swears he could hear Joanna talking to a friend in her sitting room and observed Joanna and her friend having a conversation. The time was two o'clock in the morning and Jeremy recognized the girl she was with as an actress with whom they had both worked.

Jeremy says he was desperate to speak but found he simply couldn't get the words out of his mouth and the effort in trying had expended any remaining energy he might have had and he found himself flying back through the wall into his own bedroom back into his own body where his head was still on the pillow.

It had all been so remarkably clear, he says, that he sat up and felt he had to telephone Joanna immediately and report the conversation he had heard. She said: 'Don't ever do that again,' says Jeremy.

But he says he did, however, one day have a curious call from Joanna to say that he had materialized in her living room holding up a newspaper and pointing to his obituary and that she was calling him to make sure he was all right.

It was not the first time Joanna had experienced strong feelings about something she cannot have known anything about. She once held in her hand a ring belonging to Evie Bricusse, wife of Jeremy's great composer friend Leslie who had been so generous to him in Hollywood, and she immediately had a strong image of a strange flower-bedecked room and Evie covered in diamonds. It transpired Evie had been painting in just such a room.

This, then, was the multi-faceted Jeremy Lloyd, the complex but immensely likeable man who had arrived so suddenly in Joanna's life and whom she was now getting to know and find out about during their extended honeymoon in the south of France. But almost at once there were differences to overcome, major differences that in the haste to wed had been overlooked or not considered at all.

Jeremy had fondly imagined that he would return to Los Angeles to continue with his highly successful writing and acting in *Laugh-In*. He was riding on the crest of a wave in television's hottest show and Joanna, he thought, would naturally come with him. He imagined they would live in California together while *Laugh-In* was riding high and all the signs were that it had a good few years of life in it yet.

But Joanna had other ideas. She had a young son to consider and she wanted him brought up in England. She certainly wouldn't dream of going to Los Angeles without Jamie and the idea of his being educated in America did not remotely appeal to her. She also reasoned that, since offers of work as an actress were not exactly plentiful in England, she also had no intention of going to Los Angeles to be seriously unemployed.

Joanna had also been influenced by seeing the film *Bob and Carol and Ted and Alice*. This was a movie starring Natalie Wood, Robert Culp, Elliott Gould and Dyan Cannon as two Californian couples who, after being influenced by a group therapy session advocating spontaneous behaviour, decide to admit their extra-marital affairs and end up narrowly avoiding a wife-swapping party. If that's the way California is, Joanna told her husband, then she didn't want to go. 'I could have stayed on,' says Jeremy, 'but I would have probably ended up as an old hippie if I'd stayed there.'

Within a matter of days the idea of relocating to Los Angeles became a major sticking point. Jeremy and Joanna argued and argued over it but she determinedly dug her heels in and won the day. She insisted she was not going over to America, mainly for her son Jamie's sake.

It was an impasse which ended when Jeremy reluctantly sent

word to *Laugh-In* that he would not be returning to the show. 'There's bound to be a woman behind this,' said one of the *Laugh-In* team knowingly when Jeremy's cable arrived at the show's production office and he was right. The entire *Laugh-In* team had come to like Jeremy enormously and they were genuinely sad he would not be rejoining them.

Looking back, Jeremy recognizes that resigning from his writer-performer's contract with *Laugh-In* was not the most brilliant of career moves. *Laugh-In* was a winner and, at that time, showed no signs of flagging. As it transpired, the programme was destined to run very successfully on television for a further two years. Jeremy felt he had a lot more to contribute to the show but from the moment he sent his cable of resignation, the writing was on the wall for his marriage to Joanna. There was now a tension between the two newlyweds, which was obvious to anyone who saw them together.

One heated argument resulted in Joanna jealously confining to the dustbin Jeremy's much treasured photo albums containing his collection of pictures of himself in Hollywood and in the various TV shows and films in which he had worked during his career. Joanna was not best pleased that the albums included pictures of many dazzling girls with whom Jeremy had worked. Jeremy was extremely upset that so many fond reminders of happy times past had been chucked away in such petty fashion.

Just four months after their wedding, Joanna and Jeremy decided to part. 'At the end of a wonderful summer Joanna and I both realized we had married in a hurry,' is how Jeremy puts it. 'That is to say, she realized she had married in a hurry.' With diplomatic gallantry he adds: 'I think that was her prerogative.'

By the end of that summer, England had failed in Mexico to hold on to the World Cup they had won in 1966, against all the opinion polls Harold Wilson had suffered a totally unexpected defeat by Tory Edward Heath in the General Election, and the marriage of Joanna Lumley and Jeremy Lloyd was over almost before it had begun.

The newlyweds, resigned to going their separate ways, returned from the south of France to London where the nightclubs were all pounding to the beat of a record which was to top the charts for six weeks. It was 'Band of Gold' by Freda Payne, a record with an unusual and daring lyric concerning the failure of a couple to consummate their marriage and the ultimate failure of the marriage itself. Ironically, non-consummation was the grounds on which Joanna and Jeremy were to have their marriage annulled the following year.

In the certainty of hindsight, Jeremy believes he married Joanna at a juncture in his life when he was feeling somewhat vulnerable. He was nearing forty and when he fell in love with Joanna he felt it might be his last chance of finding happiness or of settling down to a contented married life. Acutely conscious of the personal milestone he was approaching he was also, he concedes, becoming something of a hypochondriac.

Unbeknown to Joanna, not long before he had fallen in love with her, Jeremy had travelled over to Paris to collect phials of a supposedly youth-giving extract which had been manufactured in Switzerland and, although banned in England, was available to buy in Paris. The chief problem with the magic elixir was that it had to be kept at a very low temperature and, having returned with it to London, he delicately had to transport it around from fridge to fridge while taking on the role of an MI5 agent called Carruthers on a British stage tour of *The Avengers*.

To save money at one stopping-off point on the tour, Jeremy begged to share a room one night with two of his theatre co-stars, both female, both very glamorous. With Jeremy's charm, how could they refuse? One of the actresses was Kate O'Mara who later went on to find international fame in the glossy American soap opera *Dynasty* and many years later still was to play Joanna Lumley's sister Jackie in an episode of *Absolutely Fabulous*. The other was Sue Lloyd, an elegant former Dior model later to become a star of the ITV soap opera *Crossroads*.

It was a toss-up as to which of these two ravishing young beauties would take on the delicate task of injecting the Peter Pan potion into Jeremy's bare backside. When Jeremy dropped his trousers in front of them insisting his treatment must be continued, it fell somewhat appropriately to doctor's daughter Sue to administer the jab to Jeremy's buttocks while Kate looked on in astonishment before collapsing in a heap with the giggles.

Ironically, Sue Lloyd had won the stage role of Hannah Wild in *The Avengers* after Joanna had been turned down for it. 'I was a very hot contender for the leading lady,' says Joanna. 'Leslie Phillips was directing but he told me they could not afford to use a complete unknown like me. When they said they wanted Sue Lloyd, I was heartbroken.'

Just as Joanna's marriage to Jeremy was coming to a by now inevitable end, Jeremy's father suddenly died. He had been rushed off to hospital where doctors had given him just twenty-four hours to live. Loyally Joanna accompanied Jeremy to give him comfort and support as he sped off to see his father one last time and she was solidly there for him doing her best to console his grief while he wept inconsolably on her shoulder all the way home.

Although their marriage was irrevocably over, Joanna was never going to stop liking Jeremy. They had got on so well before they had married and she was determined that, although their brief conjugal fling had come to an end, there should be no reason why they could not go on being friends. 'I don't think either of us meant to get married,' she explained as news of the abrupt separation began to break in showbiz circles. 'We got carried away with the idea. But the parting doesn't mean we are not friends. In fact we adore each other. My family know about it. All they say is that I should be happy. It was really a matter of adapting to each other. Some people are better at conforming than others. I don't know what went wrong. There were no rows nor hurling of lamps.'

'Marry in haste, repent at leisure' goes the adage and, in the months which followed her separation from Jeremy, Joanna had time to ponder why it was that she had married so very quickly after meeting Jeremy. It was crazy, she admitted, but explained her decision by saying that there were times in life when people did crazy things. Throughout her life Joanna has frequently said that she relishes life-changing upheavals, sudden changes of direction, and her career bears this out as much as her personal life. Marrying Jeremy Lloyd was certainly a huge step but she countered the doubters at the time by saying that she felt ready for marriage and she would like more children.

Although this was the Swinging Sixties, there was a social pressure upon a 21-year-old single mother of a two-year-old boy to get married, partly to have a father around for her son. That wasn't Joanna's idea, but it was the general idea and it tilted her thinking towards marrying Jeremy Lloyd. Many people readily told her that marriage would be good for both her and for Jamie.

But not everyone was convinced. Some of Joanna's friends, mindful of her overwhelming enthusiasm for the match at the time, had been reluctant to voice their doubts about the wisdom of such a hurried marriage. They had secretly feared that a two-week courtship was not nearly enough time for Joanna and Jeremy to discover whether they really were suited. Now the marriage was over they were, however, far too loyal and far too concerned for her feelings to turn round and say: 'I told you so.' Rather, they regarded it as extremely brave of her to admit so quickly it had all been a mistake and to get out of the marriage so swiftly before further hurt was caused.

Having been Mrs Lloyd for such a short period of time, Joanna was dismayed to discover that ending the marriage was much more complicated than she imagined. It had seemed so easy to get married and she thought that it would be just as simple to terminate the union. 'I thought one could just have the marriage rubbed out,' she said naively. 'I went down to the register office one day and discovered that as the marriage is entered on the files you cannot do that. We've discussed every possibility. Annulment would be a nice way out.'

In December of 1970, just six months after they had wed, divorce proceedings began and on 11 February 1971 Jeremy was granted a *decree nisi* in the London Divorce Court on the grounds of Joanna's incapacity to consummate the marriage. That very night they were, however, putting on brave faces in each other's company in London at the première at the Odeon, Kensington of their film *Two Girls* which had now depressingly for them become a risqué *Games That Lovers Play*.

Joanna was all too aware that the end of the marriage and the sudden death of Jeremy's father had hit Jeremy extremely hard. He was utterly miserable and kept questioning himself as to why it hadn't worked out especially as before they had wed a medium had told him that the marriage would be a success. In retrospect, however, he believes the medium was not wrong because it was probably their long-term relationship she was foreseeing and that has more than stood the test of time. But in early 1971 all the gloom he had felt when Charlotte Rampling had called off their wedding some years before returned to engulf him. This time he had married and it had been a failure.

By severing his link with *Laugh-In*, Jeremy was also almost broke when he separated from Joanna and, without a home to call his own, he went off despondently to live with friends. Such was his desperation at one point that his great friend and comedy co-writer David Croft remembers that Jeremy took to ironing his mattress at night just to have a warm bed to sleep in. Friends had never seen Jeremy so low. For such a famously funny man it was pitiful to see.

Almost inevitably it all took its toll on Jeremy and soon afterwards he suffered a full-scale nervous breakdown. He frequently broke down in floods of tears and became so deeply depressed and sorely plunged in gloom that he even very seriously considered committing suicide.

Instead he somehow found the money and the resolve to take himself off to the Caribbean for a holiday to try to forget all about Joanna Lumley and what might have been. There he bumped into the British film director Bryan Forbes who managed to convince him that life was worth living after all, even without Joanna, and that with his talent to amuse he had much to offer the world.

'That was the turning point,' says Jeremy who flew back to London and moved into one room of a friend's house in Kensington, little more than one mile away from Joanna's flat, and set about rebuilding his life. He started to write again and bolstered his self-esteem by penning little notes to himself which he stuck up on the mirror telling himself he must cheer up.

As fate would have it, Joanna and Jeremy piquantly soon found themselves not only acting opposite each other, but playing girl-friend and boyfriend in a new TV situation-comedy pilot for the BBC's Comedy Playhouse written by Jilly Cooper. For most just-separated couples it might have been an experience too distressing even to contemplate. For two impecunious actors hungry for work it was something they could not afford to turn down. 'We didn't really mind,' says Jeremy. 'After all, it was work for us both.'

Joanna and Jeremy had both signed to appear in *It's Awfully Bad For Your Eyes, Darling*, a play about the lives and loves of four girls sharing a flat and now, two months after their divorce, they were required to play lovey-dovey for the television cameras.

Writer Jilly Cooper remembers Joanna very fondly at the centre of rather an unhappy experience: 'I first met her at a time of great conflict. Joanna was starring as one of the four debs. The screaming matches on the set were pyrotechnic. An Australian director had tried to take the whole thing down market. All those involved, including the actors, kept changing the scripts and threatened to take their names off the series when these changes were not accepted. Heavy reproof descended constantly from on high because of the blueness of the jokes. People stalked out, everyone fought. Except Joanna. She was not only wonderfully beautiful in the part, even looking stunning in a bath cap with no hair showing, but also utterly professional. She knew her lines, was always on time and always brought something extra and original to the character she was playing. More important she was sweet to everyone, a still centre, who listened to all of us, but never backbiting or taking sides, and put in a wonderful performance, which I like to think put her several rungs up the ladder to stardom.'

Joanna said: 'Some people hated the show, probably because nice girls aren't supposed to discuss men so uninhibitedly. But if you think men get a bit near the mark about sex when they're together, you've never heard girls when they're alone.'

It's Awfully Bad For Your Eyes, Darling made for intriguing viewing when it was screened that April and the BBC deemed the show to have been enough of a success and to contain enough potential for it to be extended into a series. With both of them needing the money, Joanna and Jeremy gratefully agreed to recreate their roles for six more shows.

Aiming to capture the mood of the times, *It's Awfully Bad For Your Eyes, Darling* was essentially a comedy about four very different young girls sharing a flat but encountering such common problems as lack of money, interfering parents, and a dearth of suitable boyfriends.

In a largely unknown cast, Jane Carr played the sensible, plump girl Gillian Page-Wood, nicknamed 'Pudding', Jennifer Croxton played the posh one, Virginia Walker, Elizabeth Knight was the scatty one, Clover Mason, and Joanna took the role of the sexy one, the aristocratically named Samantha Ryder-Ross. Jeremy Lloyd played Samantha's boyfriend Bobby Dutton who lived in the flat as her lover but who had to be hidden away when any of the parents were on the scene since they were bound to disapprove.

Jeremy, whose writing success with *Laugh-In* had not gone unnoticed at the BBC, also managed to secure for himself the job of doing some scriptwriting on *It's Awfully Bad For Your Eyes, Darling* in addition to playing Bobby. It was an opportunity which Jeremy found simply too good to miss.

With a mischievous sense of fun Jeremy contrived to write into the shows various minutiae to gently needle Joanna. Cleverly he fashioned certain subservient characteristics for sexy Samantha which he knew would stick in Joanna's craw.

Jeremy had Joanna as Samantha willingly ironing Bobby's shirts for him and adoringly toiling over a stove for him. 'As I could get my hands on the script I was able to get her to cook Bobby's eggs for him in the morning and other things like that which I would never have dared to do in my normal life,' laughs Jeremy. Samantha even found herself agreeing with everything Bobby said.

There was little Joanna could do about it while Jeremy viewed the fruits of his script editing with an impish twinkle in his eye and an expression which veered from triumph to that of a naughty choirboy who has just slipped a frog into the collection plate. 'As we were divorcing at the time it was a very funny situation but Joanna took it very well,' he says chivalrously.

Since Joanna as Samantha was supposed to be the sexpot of the quartet, she was also frequently required to wander around the fictional flat in her underwear or in other various states of undress and, annoyingly for Joanna, for many viewers that appeared to be the highlight of a series which never really found its feet nor a committed audience.

In the years since, Joanna and Jeremy have, however, managed to remain good friends. Jeremy went on to further success as the creator of shows like *'Allo, 'Allo*, and *Captain Beaky* and *Are You*

Being Served?, in which Joanna appeared three times. 'As an actress she probably wouldn't have done,' he says, 'but as a friend for fun she very kindly did.' Jeremy also gallantly dedicated his book *The Further Adventures of Captain Dangerfield* to her. Joanna, in turn, wrote the foreword to Jeremy's book about *Are You Being Served?*

'We should have just had a raging affair which is different from being in love,' Joanna concludes of her marriage to Jeremy. 'But because he was such a sweetheart we emerged unscathed. It taught me to be more circumspect about really important things. The worst thing is to be unhappily married. Being happily married is marvellous. The next best thing is being happily unmarried.' After the briefest of marriages to Jeremy, Joanna was to remain unmarried, mostly happily, for another sixteen years.

These days the sudden images Jeremy Lloyd has of Joanna Lumley are perhaps more easily explained. Her distinctive voice still comes through to him as voice-overs on TV commercials while he is dozing in front of his fire.

Jeremy remains a staunch friend. 'At the end of the day it's a great shame if you marry someone who isn't going to be one of your best friends,' he says. 'I don't think marriage should ever interfere with friendship – or divorce.

'I'm a great admirer of Joanna's. I always thought she had that star quality. I've picked out one or two people I thought were going to be great and they were and she is one of them. It's very hard to take your eyes off her when she's on the stage or on screen. Some people were surprised when she was terribly funny in *Absolutely Fabulous* but I always knew how funny she was. She has a great sense of humour.'

7

Seventies Struggle

The transformation of Joanna Lumley from in-demand model to credible actress was never going to be smooth. But Joanna can not have imagined it would be quite such a long, painful and often humiliating process, nor that, on occasions, it would be downright demeaning. In essence, Joanna found herself having to spend some eight years apologizing for being a model before she was taken seriously.

Blown up before the credits in *Some Girls Do* and then a blur in a Bond film, Joanna's first two excursions into the world of movies gave her no opportunity whatsoever to parade any of the acting potential she had displayed so promisingly at school. Depressingly for Joanna, her first stab at television was as much a chastening experience as her first film and at the end of it she was left with much the same feelings of inadequacy and disappointment.

While in Switzerland filming *On Her Majesty's Secret Service*, Joanna had been introduced to Diana Rigg's then boyfriend Philip Saville who was a respected TV director and he had suggested Joanna for a small part in a TV play called *Mark Two Wife*. 'It was the title part,' said Joanna, 'but he told me I would just come in at the very end of this very long, gruelling play and say just one line and that was then the end of the play.

'All kinds of very good actors were in this play, like Faith Brook and Philip Madoc, all tearing their hair out, sobbing, ripping clothes, weeping, high tension. I didn't go to rehearsals as I only had one line at the end. So I only arrived on the day of the shooting, I had no idea who anybody was, I'd never been in a TV studio before and, although I'd done a bit of filming, I found TV was so different.

'I came in rather overweight in a terrible lurex crocheted mini-dress. I was ghastly in it and I hated it. It was a part of my life I wanted to snip out. I had one line but one has to start somewhere.'

Despite such a humiliating start there was no doubting Joanna's eagerness to watch and learn her craft, however, and many an evening she was to be found at the theatre in London absorbed in stage performances by acting luminaries of the day including Laurence Olivier, Vanessa Redgrave and Jill Bennett and dreaming of the day when she too would be treading the boards in the West End in some highly prestigious production.

But it seemed that every which way Joanna turned, her natural beauty and modelling background proved an enormous handicap. When it came to casting, Joanna Lumley was labelled as a very pretty model who had got where she was on her natural physical beauty, and through the first half of the 1970s Joanna had to endure playing a succession of roles where she was employed almost entirely for her looks and thus was never given a real chance to prove herself.

She also hated the pressure on her and other young actresses to take their clothes off for their art. Many years later it still rankled with Joanna that she had been made to feel in her early days that she wasn't a proper actress unless she stripped off. 'We all hated it,' she railed, 'but we knew we would lose the job if we didn't take off our pathetic little tops or shorts. No one was spared. It was humil-iating.'

The nadir for Joanna was the film *Games That Lovers Play*, the movie in which she had first met Jeremy Lloyd and which had started out as a comedy shot under the title of *Two Girls*. 'Somehow along the line it got changed from a funny 1920s–30s comedy into what was then shown as a rude sort of skin-flick,' Joanna fumed. 'But it didn't stand up as a skin-flick. It was nonsense as a rude film. I thought it was going to be a bright little comedy but it turned into a dreary, foul, desperate, unfunny, dismal film. It was totally unerotic.'

On the very first day Joanna started shooting she had to clamber out of bed stark naked while an equally naked actor had to get out the other side. She said: 'I knew then I should never have agreed to do it but everybody kept coming up to me and saying: "Come on darlin'. It's nothing. We've all got bodies, haven't we?" But they hadn't all got my body.'

Joanna only agreed to the nudity because she wanted to be professional about it. But she was sickened by it and resolved that never again would she allow herself to be exploited so blatantly in this way.

If *Games That Lovers Play* was a depressingly low point, there were, however, other encouraging signs for Joanna both in films and in TV. In the horror film *The Satanic Rites of Dracula*, starring Peter Cushing as Professor Van Helsing, Joanna had an important role playing Cushing's vulnerable granddaughter in a tale involving the investigation of a sinister black magic circle of government ministers, the uncovering of a deadly experiment with a plague virus, a cellarful of chained nubile vampires, and Christopher Lee as Dracula who came within a fang's breadth of adding Joanna to his victims.

And on TV, even in some of her more menial roles, it was apparent to those around her that Joanna was destined to go places. Tony Adams, who played dashing Dr Neville Bywaters in *General Hospital*, remembers Joanna joining the 1970s ITV medical serial for a handful of episodes.

'She was natural and warm and friendly and very down to earth,' recalls Tony. 'Joanna was playing a flirty patient and as she was lying in bed I had to examine her. I think it was one of the most pleasant scenes I've ever encountered. I can't remember what illness she was suffering from but I can remember the nightdress she was wearing and I can distinctly remember her cleavage. I can also remember she always used to refer to me as "the old tart". That was quite outrageous as I was a heart-throb then. Even if I am a coronary now.

'She always used to say, "Come on you old tart, let's get this scene in the can." There was a lot of giggling and horseplay between us as I tried to make my examination last as long as possible. She really was a very, very nice woman. Working with Joanna was a lovely experience. Acting alongside her was rather like smelling a very expensive scent. You can smell talent. She had everything it takes to make a star. She lit up my life working with her. She made you feel good. She has that effect on people. It was only a small part for her in *General Hospital* but it was obvious to all of us that one day she would be a leading lady in her own right.'

But even in 1975, by the time she was nearing thirty and had proved by her appearances on the BBC's word game *Call My Bluff* that she did have a brain and could actually talk, Joanna was still so desperately trying to change everyone's perception of her that she was to be found on stage at Greenwich in a play starring Rachel Roberts called *The End of Me Old Cigar*. She had taken a small role in the play in the knowledge that the author was the much vaunted John Osborne and Greenwich Theatre had snob value. 'I thought a deep play would change public opinion of me,' she explained. 'No chance.'

Unfortunately, on this particular occasion, Joanna's plea to be taken seriously was not helped by *The End of Me Old Cigar*'s subject matter or the outfit she had to wear for much of the play. The plot involved a country house brothel for the rich and influential run by a Lady Regine, played by Rachel Roberts, whose purpose was to destroy the power structure in Britain by means of accumulated compromising films and tapes. Joanna spent much of the play with very little to say and dressed in black leather shorts, boots, and stockings and suspenders.

Keith Barron who was also in the cast recalls: 'Joanna was lovely. It was one of her earlier jobs and even though it was a very, very large cast she stood out. She just had something special about her. She was desperate to be taken more seriously and not to be simply decorative. But she ended up in leather shorts I'm afraid. It was that sort of play.

'Then years later Jack Tinker roped me into a production about Terence Rattigan at Brighton. It was a con job really because it was readings from Rattigan dressed up as a real play. We had a wonderful week with Robin Bailey and Joanna and I both agreed it was not quite right to charge people for readings. It was called *In Praise of Rattigan* and I said you can't charge people eight quid to come in and watch a few lunatics walking about with a big black book. And Joanna was about my only ally in that because she felt exactly the same. She is very unstuffy and very talented. She is quite rare because she is very, very stylish.'

But Joanna had known all along right from when she set out to become an actress that she could not afford to be picky in her choice of roles. She had Jamie to feed, clothe and eventually to educate so she was initially grateful simply to be offered an acting role at all even if it did mean having to play the glamorous girl-friend or decorative secretary in TV situation comedies like *Steptoe and Son*, *On The Buses*, and *Up The Workers!* At least it helped pay the bills. She bit the bullet and took the parts but the tag of 'pretty girl' still annoyed her.

'At one time I was very confused and angry about it,' she says. 'It was when I had long fair hair, so I had it all chopped off and dyed what was left brown and went around looking terrible in fear-ful old clothes so that I didn't look pretty. It didn't make a ha'porth of difference. The BBC, for instance, had me pigeon-holed as light, not serious, and that stuck.'

It was a vicious circle. The more 'dishy dolly bird' roles she played, the more she was typecasting herself and the further she was distancing herself from consideration for roles of any substance. Such was Joanna's frustration that in April 1971 she took a small part in rep to make her professional stage debut in *Not Now, Darling* for £20 a week at the Marlowe Theatre, Canterbury, in the hope that she might then be taken seriously as an actress. 'I hoped people might think I was real and stop thinking of me as a starlet,' she said. 'I tried really hard to prove myself. I went to out-of-town theatres to say just one line. But it didn't make any difference.'

How sweet was the moment for Joanna nearly twenty years later when she opened Kent University's drama building. Even sweeter was when in 1994 she received an honorary Doctorate of Letters from Kent University at Canterbury 'for her contribution to the entertainment industry and her active charitable work'.

Back in 1971 when a chance arose to play a glum, mousy labora-tory assistant in a Vincent Price horror film, *The Abominable Dr Phibes*, Joanna saw it as another opportunity to help lose her image. But to her chagrin her scenes ended up on the cutting-room floor.

Salt was later rubbed into the wounds when friends like Susan

Hampshire and Gayle Hunnicutt managed to break out of the 'pretty girl' mould to become accepted as straight actresses. Jacqueline Bissett, another British beauty who had started out as a model, even managed to decamp to Hollywood and build a flourishing film career.

In September 1971 Brian Rix was ready to celebrate twenty-one years as the West End of London's king of farce in a new show at the Garrick Theatre by Michael Pertwee, called *Don't Just Lie There, Say Something!*, and Joanna went up for a role as one of a bevy of beautiful girls involved in the improbable exploits of junior cabinet ministers. 'They had parts for the tall girl, the bosomy girl, the short girl and the secretary,' Joanna remembers, 'and when they asked me which part I wanted to read for, I said the bosomy girl.'

It was neither vanity nor an inflated pride in her bust measurements, however, which prompted Joanna to volunteer for the role. It was lack of self-confidence. She chose to audition for the role of the busty girl because it was the smallest. She never imagined as such a relative newcomer that she would be considered for anything else.

'But they called me back,' she says. 'They asked me to come back and bring a bikini and I said: "I haven't got a bikini but I'll get down to bra and pants and I've got some socks with me to make my bust look bigger." They started falling about with laughter.'

The role of Miss Parkyn, secretary to a Minister of State played by Alfred Marks, was hers and there was enough interest in *Don't Just Lie There, Say Something!* for the play to be later adapted into a film with Joanna reprising her role as Miss Parkyn. As a film it neither found favour with the critics nor set the box office tills jingling. The promotional front of house stills included one of a bare-shouldered Joanna sitting up in bed sandwiched between Brian Rix and Leslie Phillips.

On the stage, *Don't Just Lie There, Say Something!* was a typical Rix farce with a plot in which two eminently respectable politicians who are piloting a Morality Bill through the House of Commons are caught in private lechery.

Theatre critic Felix Barker noted in his lukewarm review in the *London Evening News* that at one point as many as three beautiful girls in bra and pants were hiding under beds, in wardrobes and broom cupboards. 'As the Minister, Mr Marks huffs and puffs,' he added. 'As his secretary, Joanna Lumley looks gorgeously, if anti-septically, beautiful stripped down to her white briefs.'

Shakespeare it was not, but, typically, Joanna made the most of it as the play toured Birmingham and the provinces before coming into the West End. She says: 'I was lucky enough to work with Alfred Marks and he was very generous to me on stage. We were able to build up an incredibly funny scene together and the sound of people falling off their chairs with laughter was magic. I've always loved comedy for that reason. When it works, it has to be the best thing ever.'

Despite the uplifting company Joanna had one of the most difficult times of her life towards the end of the run as all the many pressures in her life appeared to weigh ever more heavily on her elegant shoulders. She would find herself on stage hallu-cinating that a machine gun was about to wipe out the cast and she was forced to struggle to stop herself from throwing herself on her friend Alfred Marks to protect him from this vile attack. Her grip on reality was becoming loosened yet she fought hard to hang on.

When Joanna left the farce at the Garrick she experienced a kind of nervous collapse or breakdown. All the anxieties of previous years came back to haunt her in the worst form of depression she had ever experienced. It built up steadily over days and then weeks until this vibrant and resourceful young woman, who had bounced back from so many setbacks before, would find herself sobbing on her bedroom floor.

She was worried about many things. Her beloved cousin Maybe was fading away badly and close to death in St Stephens. A nanny had departed dramatically back to her home in Scotland. Joanna was recovering from an operation which had already taken her out of the show and she was suddenly facing real financial problems for her and son Jamie. It all seemed to add up to a weight that was impossible to bear and something had to give.

It was perhaps the lowest time in Joanna's life and to this day it gives her pause for thought as to just how fragile the balance of the mind can be. Years later when she talked to Dr Anthony Clare for Radio 4's *In The Psychiatrist's Chair* Joanna described the experience as like going into a black hole and said: 'Stage fright, if it comes to get you, which it has in my life once or twice, is the worst thing because it lives with you until it goes and there is nothing you can do about that. That kind of panic we call stage fright because we're actors but I suspect that it might be a kind of panic that visits all sort of people at different times in their lives, a kind of nervous breakdown they call it but it's probably just a real insecurity attack.'

Joanna found help in her loving family. Fortunately her parents and her sister Ælene and family had already booked the annexe of a small hotel in Zeneggen in Switzerland for a holiday. As soon as Joanna's condition became known to them the party was enlarged and Joanna and Jamie headed for the Alps with the best possible company. It was a simple family time that restored Joanna. And happily Maybe made a full recovery and was able to share another of Joanna's adventurous trips to the Far East many years later.

Quite apart from her breakdown, Joanna found that the first half of the 1970s proved to be extremely difficult years. After Jamie's birth Joanna had, in 1968, moved out of the Earls Court flat she had shared with Ælene into a new rented flat on the top floor of a Victorian house at 86 Addison Road in Kensington, round the corner from showbiz friends like Anoushka Hempel, Patrick Mower and John Cleese.

In the summer Joanna learned how to unpick the lock the land-lord had placed on the gate leading to the roof so she could climb up and sunbathe, but the flat also had the advantage of being close to Holland Park which, for Jamie, served as a huge rambling garden where he and his mother could walk, play with a ball, and take bread to feed the ducks.

Joanna was broke when she moved in but the flat was to be home for her and Jamie for the next eighteen years and gradually she turned it into a stylish but cosy abode for the two of them with beautiful pieces of furniture picked up from junk shops for practically nothing. Houseplants eventually abounded throughout her flat and in Joanna's bedroom at the foot of her carved bed she kept either a bay tree or a daisy tree. 'They're so nice to look at first thing in the morning,' she decided.

The days when she was able to enhance the flat with ornate brass oil lamps, antique vases, glass and cane coffee tables, plant stands, exotic shells and a stylish magnolia-coloured sofa were, however, a long time coming.

But a role that really registered with millions of television viewers arrived to brighten up Joanna's life in July 1973 when she joined *Coronation Street* as beautiful and sophisticated Elaine Perkins, the headmaster's daughter who had a lesson or two in life for Ken Barlow, played by Bill Roache.

It was already a dramatic month in the soap when Bet Lynch (Julie Goodyear) was mugged on the way home from The Rovers and taken to hospital, and Elsie Tanner (Pat Phoenix), in London to visit Dennis in Pentonville prison for hustling double glazing to pensioners, gets knocked down by a taxi in Oxford Street and lies in hospital unidentified, suffering from concussion.

But elegant Elaine arrived like a breath of fresh southern air. Teacher Ken was clearly very taken with his boss's spirited young daughter and she had quite an effect on him. Stylish Elaine soon had Ken switching from his usual collar and tie appearance for more adventurous open-necked shirts and the first cravats ever seen in Weatherfield. They looked made for each other, but when he proposed marriage she broke his heart when she turned him down.

Joanna recalled the experience with great fondness to one of the authors: 'I think I was very strange for *Coronation Street*. I was a girl who changed her accent. I wasn't allowed in The Rovers Return because I would not have got on with them. I got lovely letters from the fans. People spoke to me for ages afterwards saying, "You should have married Ken."

'We never kissed, we just exchanged a lot of sincere looks. Then I brought the faithful viewing fans' wrath upon my head because I broke Ken's heart. He delicately proposed "Marry me" and I declined rather gracelessly, saying, "No! You're a bore." So I wasn't forgiven for being a horrid thing.' Years afterwards, after she had become Mrs Barlow for real, she noted the curious coincidence of the names and said: 'I'm pleased really that I didn't become Mrs Ken Barlow. Mrs Stephen Barlow is much nicer.'

Bill Roache still remembers Joanna as one of his more alluring screen loves. He said: 'She was very good to work with. I like to think the Street helped her on her way to things like *The Avengers*. It was definitely Ken's loss. Poor old Ken, ever the loser.'

But offscreen Joanna really enjoyed herself: 'The regular *Coronation Street* cast were charming, lovely, sweet people. They couldn't have been nicer to me.

'I always had to drink sherry every scene to demonstrate that I was a cut above everyone else. The sad thing was that the writers admitted they didn't know how to write for such a character and so I became terribly wooden and said things like: "Oh Ken, I want to travel, the world will be mine", while sitting on the sofa with yet another glass of sherry in my hand, which I found very difficult to act convincingly.

'I did it for a month and although it was fun I also found it terribly frightening and nerve-wracking. It's difficult when you are a late-comer, as it were, and with an established cast you feel you never fit in. I've always thought it harder to play the small parts than leads. I'd far rather play Hamlet than someone who says "A sail, a sail".'

Joanna almost found herself in more drama after she left the studios as she chose a somewhat insalubrious place to stay in Manchester. 'I took a service flat in Manchester because I don't like hotels very much, particularly where they have rules about having to eat by eight in the morning. It was rather odd and I subsequently discovered it was a brothel! People would go there and rent rooms. Shortly after I got there, they realized I was in *Coronation Street* and they rushed around improving everything and gave me a nice sofa and things. But *Coronation Street* did not instantly help me. For six months afterwards I didn't do a thing.'

The one essential accessory for all beautiful blondes in show-business was the same in the 1970s as it is today, an outrageous rock star on the arm. Joanna Lumley was never too impressed by precisely who was parading their latest hit on *Top of the Pops* but the rasping voice of Rod Stewart, whose international anthem 'Maggie May' topped the charts on both sides of the Atlantic in 1971, certainly made an impression. Their first encounter was at a football awards dinner when Joanna had been recruited to hand a Player of the Year prize to taciturn Scot Kenny Dalglish, while football-loving Rod had been brought in to hand over the award for most entertaining team of the year to, would you believe, Queens Park Rangers.

The chemistry between the two was instant. The cut glass vowels of the Major's daughter and the strangulated cockney accent of the Scottish Londoner were instantly mixed in a flirty conversation that was leading in one direction only. But usually confident Rod was intimidated somewhat by the intelligence and authority behind the pretty face and failed dismally to make his usual move. He left the evening completely smitten by Joanna and deeply disappointed that he had not even managed to gain her telephone number. But there are advantages in being the hottest rock star in town. Rod decided to enlist the services of energetic pop journalist John Blake, then working on the now defunct *London Evening News*, to try to track down Joanna.

Blake, now an affluent publisher, recalled: 'Rod rang up out of the blue and asked, "Can you do me a favour? I really want to get Joanna Lumley's phone number." He had chatted her up and really fallen for her and now he wanted to get discreetly in touch. I agreed, on the understanding that if they really hit it off, I would get the exclusive story of the new relationship. About two months later Rod phoned again and said, "Do you still want to do the story about me and Joanna" which had not then been in the papers. I was delighted and went round to this lovely house in Holland Park. We had a few beers, played football in the garden, and did the story. Rod was so grateful for my help he even let me borrow his yellow Lamborghini Miura for the afternoon. He knew I was car mad. Joanna was lovely and it was obvious they were crazy about each other.'

Rod's public relations adviser Sally Croft was also involved in the early arrangements and she firmly warned the hard-living singer that he was to be on his best behaviour for their first date. Sally forcefully told her employer: 'Joanna is educated, Rod. She is not like one of your usual type of girls. So you are not to try to leap into bed with her on the first date, are you?' Rod meekly agreed but Sally later learned they had gone back to Rod's house on that first date and, when Sally asked if the singer had behaved himself, Joanna swooned, 'Oh yes. He's wonderful, really wonderful.' Perhaps wisely Sally decided not to inquire any further.

Joanna and Rod fell for each other in a big way. After their first night out the notoriously thrifty rock star was quoted as reacting enthusiastically: 'It was the cheapest night out I've had for some time. The meal was £8.90. I thought to myself, "There's a nice girl,"' while Joanna said: 'I love him to death.' The romance lasted some two months. She took him to the Greenwich Theatre. He took her on his yacht for a Mediterranean cruise.

They might have been intellectually and socially miles apart but Rod adored Joanna's sense of humour as well as her obvious sex appeal and Joanna loved Rod's earthy charm. Rod became very fond of Joanna's young son Jamie and he admired the actress's fierce independence in bringing the boy up alone and refusing to name the father.

For her part Joanna was entranced by Rod's beautiful Georgian house near Windsor, which had been bought from Lord Bethell. She gasped visibly at the rambling rose gardens and the tennis courts, and was enraptured by the huge staircase sweeping up to a spacious bedroom lined from top to bottom with cupboards stacked with clothes. Rod shrugged at her reaction, saying: 'I liked it better when I slept on a mattress and hung all me clothes around the walls.' Joanna really warmed to the millionaire rock star's nostalgia for the days struggling to make it in the music business, criss-crossing the country in ancient vans to lacklustre gigs in unknown clubs.

She was perhaps a little less impressed by sleeping with Rod in an enormous bed with a giant flag hanging over them. Sally Croft noted: 'It didn't last very long. I think Rod found Jo too clinging in the end. When he was losing interest in her he made me and Cyril the chauffeur come out to dinner with him and Jo. Jo had a hairdo like the one she had for Purdey in *The New Avengers* and she asked him if he liked it. "It's awful," replied Rod. "I don't like it at all." So we had this row over dinner. It was very tense. To cap it all, Rod ordered drinks just for the men and I snorted, "We drink too, you know." He was being so rude. I knew that there was another girl on his mind – obviously she was waiting for him somewhere else. Cyril got as pissed as hell and going home he nearly had us all killed going the wrong way up a one-way street in the Rolls. But then Rod found someone else and that was the end of that.'

Afterwards Sally recalls having Joanna on the phone at two o'clock in the morning saying, 'Darling, what has happened to Rod? He said he would collect me at eleven o'clock and I'm still waiting. Could you phone him for me, darling? Please, phone him.' Sally would phone Rod the next day to be greeted by: 'Oh God, I got caught up with some tart somewhere.' Knowing Rod, she would then phone Joanna and advise her not to take it all too seriously. But the romance inevitably floundered. Sally said: 'Rod was a rat to her, he was always arranging to meet and then never turning up. I liked Jo but she was out of Rod's class. In the end I advised her to get rid of Rod. And she agreed to dump him. She suddenly said, "Yes, nobody treats me like that," and she dumped him.'

Afterwards Rod had genuine regrets about the end of the fling with Joanna. He said, 'She was a smashing bird and I was very fond of her. She was dead classy and I was dead common and we got on like a house on fire.' For her part, Joanna displayed all her class when she soon afterwards commented on Rod's subsequent relationship with Britt Ekland: 'I am very fond of both of them and I wish them all the luck in the world. Rod's very charming, feckless, very conservative, very correct really apart from having those applied bad manners that all these rock stars seem to have to wreck hotel rooms and things like that. But I think he grew out of that a long time ago like his public image of drinking. The image is of always having a bottle in his hands, when he doesn't really drink to excess at all. I never saw him drinking more than the odd pint of bitter. He is very agreeable, engaging, friendly and warm-hearted. Awful things have been written and said about Rod but the truth is that underneath the image, he is very like me really. A true romantic. All hearts and flowers. It didn't last, but he was one of the most exciting men I had ever met. We just weren't meant for each other.'

Joanna almost always remains friends with her lovers and she certainly still has a soft spot in her heart for Rod although, as she told one of the authors: 'He did not take up that much space in my life any more than I did in his life. It was blown up by the press into quite a giant thing but it was really a very short-term encounter. I did like him a lot. It was a fascinating world to drift into. Everyone comes alive at night time frequenting recording studios and clubs, then like owls they go to sleep during the daytime. It was weird. I watched how Rod dealt with the fame. It was quite interesting. I could see that if he behaved quite normally then he was left alone but if he arrived in dark glasses and jumped out of a big car then people started to flock round him. You can almost turn it on by having security men saying, "Stand aside please," when no one is taking any notice. Jolly interesting.'

By 1979 she was able to say: 'I'm no longer on the party circuit when it was zowie and wowie and sobbing into your pillow next morning. I don't regret any of my affairs. There are lots of proposals of marriage but some of them approach you like they are asking for a match or a drink.'

When times were hard Joanna surreptitiously returned to modelling just to get some money coming in. But there were bleak periods when she was earning nothing at all and one year she earned just £60. It was not until she starred in the sci-fi TV series *Sapphire and Steel* in 1979, fully ten years after she had set out to be an actress, that she managed to get out of the red financially. It was a further three years, 1982, before she allowed herself the luxury of a washing machine.

'Once I went ten months without a single job,' she says, 'without any work at all, not even a single phone call. It was a nightmare. You begin to have awful self-doubts. I think many people in that situation drop out. They weigh up their life and think is it worth it with my mortgage or whatever. Other people hang on but many people who do hang on don't get there. It's a gamble. You have to be ready with your expertise. It's like one of those old fairground machines where you have to put a penny in and that terrible grabber comes down to get a gob stopper and you might get a toy as well. It's a gamble.

'But the times I sat thinking "what on earth can I do" with tears racing down my face. Months and months out of work begging people to do a £10-a-week lunchtime play and getting no replies, writing off to all the reps and getting no replies. And when I'd all but lost my nerve, thinking, "I'm going under for good this time." I did get to the stage where supper for me would be bread because eating eggs would have meant that there were no eggs for the day after.'

Necessity decreed that she lived simply and it helped that by now Joanna had become a vegetarian. Always a great lover of animals, Joanna was sitting down one day to the usual steak and grapefruit diet prescribed for models in those days when she suddenly knew she did not want to eat meat any more. 'I was halfway through a rare steak and I thought: "I don't want to eat this," ' she says. 'The steak was slightly bloody and warm and it suddenly struck me it was flesh, not meat, I was eating. It had been joined on to an animal, it wasn't just something in a packet. So I put down my fork and that was the end of it.' Joanna had owned a racoon coat and had modelled furs when it was fashionable but now she swore never again.

But although she lived as simply as she could and often voraciously read books for entertainment rather than go out, she admits: 'There were long nights when I sat there crying working out possible ways I could make money. I always thought I'd be able to get out of it some way, by cunning or by hard graft, and that I'd swim because I don't believe in sinking. If I'd thought I was going to dive into an endless spiral of poverty then I would have sold everything I'd got and I would have lived in a very different way.' As it was, Joanna was so impecunious one year that she sold her beloved Tiffany lamp worth at least £90 for £35 to help make ends meet.

During the good times when she had been signed up for *The Breaking of Bumbo* and *Tam Lin*, Joanna had splashed out on a beautiful 1949 Silver Wraith Rolls-Royce. She bought it for £550 with the help of an aunt who generously contributed £350 towards the purchase. But the insurance, running costs and repairs were a drain on her finances and when Jeremy Lloyd, whose knowledge of motorcars could scarcely be bettered, told her she simply could not afford to keep it, she realized he was right and in December 1970 she placed an advertisement for it to be sold. Her asking price was £975.

To her surprise Robert Bradshaw, the then Premier of the Caribbean Island group of St Kitts-Nevis, was one of the first to show an interest. He was in London for talks on the future of Anguilla and Joanna took him and an official for a drive in it. But he was disappointed to find Joanna had had the car painted cream and said he liked conservative colours on a Rolls. Eventually Joanna sold it to a dealer for £700.

'One regret I have in my life was having to sell that Rolls,' Joanna says, however. 'She didn't have a glossy, rich look about her but a beautiful rather faded look. She was a lovely car and everyone admired it. But I was so skint I had to sell it. When I sold it for £700 I knew it was worth more, but what can you do?'

Ridding herself of the Rolls probably helped Joanna towards her ambition to lose her 'glamorous' tag. But it was *The New Avengers* and a call from a Sunday newspaper asking her to sit a Common Entrance exam that really helped to alter the public's perception of Joanna Lumley. *The New Avengers* made her a star at last and an exam result that almost equalled historian A.J.P. Taylor's showed everyone she was bright as well as beautiful.

'I was a pretty girl till I was thirty,' she says. 'People didn't expect anything. It wasn't until I sat an exam and got higher marks than A.J.P. Taylor that anyone accepted I had a brain.'

8

New Avengers

Joanna Lumley was a fifteen-year-old schoolgirl, Elvis Presley was top of the pop charts with 'Wooden Heart', the Pill was about to go on sale in Britain for the first time and *West Side Story* and *The Guns of Navarone* were the big films of the year when a comedy suspense series called *The Avengers* was launched on ITV in 1961.

Conceived as a highbrow poke at James Bond-style movies, *The Avengers* introduced viewers to a mysterious, elite squad of British crime-busters led by aristocratic actor Patrick Macnee as the impeccably dressed, elegant, bowler-hatted John Steed, accompanied by Honor Blackman as his redoubtable, leather-clad, macho partner, judo expert Cathy Gale.

Right from the outset this secret agent spoof captured the imagination of millions of TV viewers with its tongue-in-cheek style, its fantasy violence, its zany villains and its macabre plots solved by amusing and ambiguous leading characters whose hair never even got ruffled. Despite, or perhaps because of, changes of key female personnel, *The Avengers* managed to maintain its fresh appeal and its momentum for eight highly profitable years and became one of the most successful British TV series ever.

Then, in 1969, after five series, 83 episodes, 19 gallons of champagne, 192 karate chops and 30 bowler hats, *The Avengers* finally came to an end when Tara King, the third of Steed's right-hand girls, played by Linda Thorson, was seen by millions of fans of the series accidentally pressing the lift-off button on a rocket. Tara and Steed thereupon soared into space, theoretically never to be seen again.

But in 1975 the drinks company Laurent Perrier approached Patrick Macnee and Linda Thorson with a request to recreate their Avengers roles for a TV champagne commercial. The two stars conferred and agreed to team up once more providing the advertisement did not tarnish or cheapen the image of *The Avengers* which was still being screened on TV in various countries around the world and continuing to prove a money-spinner.

The commercial was duly made at Elstree Studios in the summer of 1975 largely focusing on Linda Thorson with Macnee included as a reminder of *The Avengers*. Macnee was at that time appearing in a play in Chichester and he arrived at Elstree studios anxious that the filming should go as smoothly as possible so that he could return to the Sussex coast in good time for curtain up. But Rudolph Roffi, the French producer making the commercial, soon had Macnee fretting and glancing anxiously at his watch. Roffi wanted Macnee to speak his lines in French but the Old Etonian was finding it none too easy.

When finally everyone was satisfied and filming was in the can, Macnee turned to go, far from pleased that he would now be driving against the clock on the 100-mile journey ahead of him to the Sussex coast. He had grabbed his coat and was dashing out of the door when Roffi idly asked him: 'Would you like to do *The Avengers* again?'

'I certainly can't do it in French,' snapped Macnee acidly and never gave it another thought as he headed off to Chichester. But Roffi was already so enthusiastic about the commercial he had just filmed that he believed there was real potential for reviving the series. Plot-wise it was certainly feasible since Steed and Tara had merely been shot into space in the last episode of *The Avengers* and had not been irrevocably killed off in TV terms. Roffi saw the door was therefore open for their return. All he had to do was simply bring them both back to Earth.

But would Macnee and Linda Thorson want to star in a revival? Were the viewing public ready for it? And would an ITV company be prepared to make it? These were questions he needed to put to Avengers writer-producer Brian Clemens.

Clemens was not immediately hopeful. He advised Roffi that a series would cost around £2 million and at that price no British TV company would consider it. Clemens expected that to be the end of the matter but a fortnight later he was contacted by an excited Roffi triumphantly saying : 'I've got the money. When do we start?'

Clemens then quickly set about forming a company with Albert Fennell who, like Clemens, had also been closely involved in the creation, writing and producing of *The Avengers*. Laurie Johnson who had been the music arranger on *The Avengers* was also brought in and together they formed The Avengers (Film and TV) Enterprises Ltd, to make *The New Avengers* in association with Roffi's IDTV Paris.

Clemens recognized full well that the return of Patrick Macnee was imperative if the revival was to be a success, not just in Britain but, crucially, in America where he naturally had his sights set on a lucrative network sale. Originally *The Avengers* had been able to offer Hollywood something that it could never procure – England – and they didn't come much more English than John Steed of 3 Stable Mews, London.

Macnee's creation of cool, upper-class dandy Steed, who stepped out on assignment in a dapper three-piece suit, bowler hat and umbrella, had gone down especially well with the Americans first time round and Macnee would be a trump card when it came to selling *The New Avengers* to American TV stations. Clemens succinctly said of Macnee: 'Avengers girls can come and go. But if Patrick Macnee fell down a manhole tomorrow, it would be the end of *The Avengers* for good.'

Macnee was appearing in the play *Absurd Person Singular* with Judy Carne, Shirley Macrae and Betsy von Furstenberg at the Schubert Theater in Chicago when he received the telephone call from Clemens asking him to dust off his bowler hat once more. At first he was so astonished at Clemens's proposition that he was convinced he must be pulling his leg. When the penny finally dropped, Macnee said it had come as such a shock to him that he must have time to think it over. He also insisted that Clemens send him out a script as soon as possible.

A script never did drop through Macnee's letterbox but he agreed to sign up for another ride as Steed regardless. Returning to film a *New Avengers* series in the sanity of England most certainly appealed to Macnee after what had become a trying American run of *Absurd Person Singular*. One performance of the play had ended in chaos and uproar when co-stars Judy Carne and Betsy von Furstenberg came to blows in the first act. Betsy had spilled a glass of wine on to Judy's costume and the two women started trading insults which became more and more heated. The audience thought the spat was all part of the show until they observed the two stars starting to fight, eventually rolling around on the stage clawing and kicking each other. In the middle of this unscheduled affray, Shirley Macrae, who was a committed Christian Scientist, did her best to restore order by walking to the footlights, kneeling down on the stage and inviting the audience to join her in prayer. The curtain was then hastily lowered and the bewildered audience was offered a refund. It would never happen in England, thought Macnee, as he gratefully grasped the opportunity to head back to London to recreate his role of Steed.

Macnee was by now fifty-three years old and the plan was to give old-stager Steed a slightly reduced role with not one but two assistants, one male and one female, to provide the action-packed heroics. This time round, Steed would suavely mastermind everything while largely leaving the fisticuffs to his daring duo. Steed's distinctive traits would, of course, remain sacrosanct. 'Steed is the one vital element from the old *Avengers* to be regarded as untouchable' was the directive to the production team from Brian Clemens and Albert Fennell. Steed would still twirl his tightly rolled umbrella, still stir his coffee anti-clockwise as habitually as ever and still continue to regard villains as opponents who were involved in something that 'simply isn't cricket.' But he would leave it to his sidekicks to give them their come-uppance in the field of combat and deliver the physical *coup de grâce*.

Gareth Hunt, a thirty-two-year-old dark-haired, firm-jawed, heavily handsome actor was picked to play Steed's heir apparent and right-hand man Mike Gambit. Hunt had impressive credentials of drama school, Bristol Old Vic and the National Theatre and had already garnered a female fan following from his appearances in another very British TV drama series, the gaslight saga *Upstairs Downstairs*.

Choosing *The New Avengers* girl proved to be more difficult, especially as just about every young actress, starlet and model in the country, Joanna Lumley included, coveted the role and the chance to follow in the footsteps of Honor Blackman, who had played Cathy Gale, Diana Rigg who had succeeded her as Emma Peel, and Linda Thorson who, as Tara King, had replaced Diana when she left the show following a row about wages.

Joanna had, in fact, been something of a latecomer to *The Avengers*, since the Lumley family didn't own a television set when the first two series were broadcast in black and white. But now she was as aware as any young actress that a revival of the show presented a major opportunity for her.

Joanna had first come to hear about *The New Avengers* from Leita Don, the *Coronation Street* press officer at Granada TV who had remained on friendly terms after Joanna's stint in the soap. 'She suddenly rang me up,' Joanna remembers, 'and said: "They're looking for a new Avengers girl. Have you tried for it?" I'd heard nothing about it so I immediately phoned up my agent who told me they were looking for someone like Faye Dunaway. So I said: "Oh, all right", and quietly forgot about it.

'For a month I did nothing about it. Then I kept on seeing pictures in the papers of girls with names like Rita Bosom bicycling in shorts or running in the park saying they were hoping to be the next Avengers girl. There seemed to be no point in my going up for it.'

Jeremy Lloyd, who had remained on friendly terms with Joanna since their divorce five years before, was also reading in the newspapers of all the unlikely girls who claimed to be candidates for the plum role and he was one of several friends who now urged Joanna to try for it. But he also did more than that. 'I phoned Joanna,' Jeremy remembers, 'and said: "This is appalling. Why haven't they chosen you? You're ideal for the part." So I got on to the agent Dennis Selinger and he said he could get Joanna in to see *The New Avengers*' producers and he did.'

Joanna remembers: 'A lot of people told me I must have a go. So after a lot of wrangling I decided to do so but I was superstitious enough not to tell anyone. One sure way to lose a job, I'd found, was to tell someone you were up for a film or a role. The other sure way to lose a job was to get on very well with everybody. Spend three hours with the director of a film and he'll tell you "wonderful, marvellous" and they love you to death and the part is just right for you and you don't get it.'

Totally unbeknown to her, however, Joanna had a head start in the competition to be *The New Avengers* girl. The name Joanna Lumley had sprung instantly to mind the moment Brian Clemens had decided to get the project off the ground. More than that, the longer he thought about it, the more Clemens resolutely believed Joanna was perfect for the role.

Clemens had first met Joanna during the making of a horror film called *The Abominable Dr Phibes*. His great friend Bob Feast was directing the movie and Clemens often visited the set of the film in which Joanna was playing a tiny role as a laboratory assistant. During breaks in filming Clemens briefly got to know Joanna socially and was immediately impressed by her. He thought Joanna possessed striking good looks but he also liked her style, her femininity, her enthusiasm, her personality and her general demeanour. It did not escape Clemens's notice, either, that Joanna was able to more than hold her own as a raconteur with Vincent Price without blushing. That took some doing since Price was known in the film industry as one of the great story-tellers, not to mention a champion recounter without equal of dirty jokes.

Clemens would eventually have suggested to Joanna that she try for the part so he was therefore delighted when she added her name to the list of hopefuls and put herself forward for consideration. Joanna was nevertheless none too optimistic about her chances as she drove down to Pinewood where the auditions were being held and took her place alongside the other actresses waiting for their eight minutes in which to prove themselves worthy successors to Honor Blackman, Diana Rigg and Linda Thorson.

When it was her turn to be summoned, Joanna made an immediate impression. 'She looked great in a fur hat,' noted Clemens. But as her audition progressed, Joanna began to fear that her lack of experience in major TV roles and her reputation as a model were probably weighing heavily against her. 'So, finally,' she remembers, 'I did something that I didn't normally do. I told Albert Fennell and Brian Clemens that they really must screen test me. I said I wanted to test for the role and that I wasn't prepared just to join a list of possibles.'

The list had, in fact, been whittled down by this time from some 300 actresses to just a dozen and by laying down her conditions in such a spirited manner Joanna was in effect daring the producers to reject her without finding out what she looked like on screen. It was a brave but wise move because the casting director, Mary Selway, did indeed have grave doubts about Joanna. Mary was concerned that any real success Joanna had achieved was not as an actress. She had been trained as a model but not in acting. 'Mary Selway was against Joanna Lumley,' Clemens recalls. 'She didn't think Joanna could act. She thought she was just a model who was playing at it.'

Mary Selway's misgivings were not unjustified. Still fresh in everyone's memory was the mauling Jean Shrimpton had taken from the critics when she had tried to branch out into acting. Easily the best known of the 1960s models and undeniably beautiful, Jean's photogenic charisma had failed dismally to transfer from the photographic studio to the big screen in the film *Privilege*, when she was required to act opposite Manfred Mann pop singer Paul Jones, and the reviews had been scathing in the extreme. The thinking in movie and TV circles still pervaded that models did not make great actresses and *Avengers* history had shown that Honor Blackman, Diana Rigg and Linda Thorson had all been thoroughbred, trained actresses, not converted clothes horses.

Joanna was all too well aware of these misgivings about her modelling background. 'Yes, they were terribly worried about the fact that I had been a model,' she recalls. 'I had to bludgeon them even to look at me. They thought because I was a model I wouldn't be able to learn my lines. But I said to them: "You must test me, and if I can't do it, then I can't." I think they could see in my face how much I wanted the role.' Clemens and Fennell admired this spirited approach from Joanna and agreed first to giving her a reading test – 'perhaps they thought I couldn't read' remembered Joanna scornfully – and two subsequent physical tests.

For her first test Joanna was paired with Gareth Hunt who was to play Steed's henchman Gambit. Together they had to act a scene specially written by Clemens to contain some action and a modicum of humour. After coming through it comfortably, Joanna and Hunt paused to sit for a moment on an ornate table on the set and promptly broke it. Joanna's heart sank.

For the second test Joanna was teamed with a stunt man, Vic Armstrong, to see if she was up to the physical demands of the part. Interestingly, some footage from this audition was later considered good enough to be used in the title credits of American versions of *The New Avengers* episodes. It showed Joanna with brown, shoulder-length hair, standing behind a door as a man rushed into the room.

'Quite honestly, I didn't think I had a hope of getting the role,' says Joanna. 'Straight afterwards I had to fly off to Italy to do a modelling job for a catalogue. I was in Amalfi when I got a call asking me to come back to London and do yet another test. By now it was down to three actresses, me and two others, but apparently Brian Clemens was very keen for me to do it, which was nice.'

Among the contenders was formidable competition – Diana Quick, a slinky, dark-haired beauty with an acting CV which was streets ahead of Joanna's up to that point. For Albert Fennell and Brian Clemens there would have been no fears about Diana Quick's acting credentials. Like Joanna she was from Kent, daughter of a doctor and almost exactly the same age as Joanna, but her pedigree as an actress was impeccable. Diana was already performing with the National Youth Theatre while still at school and, after becoming the first woman president of the Oxford University Dramatics Society, she had gone straight into London's Royal Court Theatre, the Bristol Old Vic and Royal Exchange, Manchester.

The other actress in the running was both beautiful and talented but her handicap was her laugh. Clemens is too gallant to name her but he says: 'She was super in almost every other way except she had an awful laugh, the kind of laugh you'd hate to be stuck with on a desert island.'

Joanna arrived for her final screen test in a whirl. She had flown out to Italy for the Grattan catalogue modelling assignment, then rushed to catch a plane back to England again with hardly a pause for breath. 'I was so tired for this new test,' she says, 'that I didn't have the energy to be nervous. In fact I didn't have any nerves at all.'

Afterwards Joanna went straight back to the airport and sank wearily into another hastily arranged seat on a flight taking her back to Naples so she could complete her modelling assignment. As the plane roared along the runway, nosed through the clouds and banked towards the English channel, Joanna was able to close her eyes and reflect on a gruelling eighteen hours, hoping it had all been worthwhile.

Back at Pinewood, Clemens, Fennell and Johnson were running through the screen tests of their three possible leading ladies one last time and they all agreed that Joanna clearly stood out. 'It was no contest,' says Clemens. 'Albert and Laurie had to agree that Joanna was the best.'

'She was outstanding,' admits Johnson, 'head and shoulders above the others. There had been some big names going for it including some well-known stage actresses. Joanna had had limited experience but what counts is a magic that someone either has or hasn't got. It's when you see someone on screen, see them at work, that's when you can judge them. Joanna just had what it takes. You did need a very special personality to fill that strange no man's land we frequented with *The Avengers*. You needed style and wit and elegance and Joanna Lumley had it immediately.'

The triumvirate of Clemens, Fennell and Johnson were all in accordance but when they revealed their choice of Joanna Lumley to Mary Selway she was dumbfounded. Clemens says: 'I remember Mary Selway saying: "Oh my god, we can't have spent all these weeks and conducted all these interviews with 300 girls just to end up with Joanna Lumley."

'Mary is now one of the most important casting directors in the country if not the world. I haven't seen Mary since Joanna became Patsy in *Absolutely Fabulous* but I'd love to see her and remind her of that now!

'Joanna was always my first choice and to some extent I went through the motions of interviewing the 300 other girls in order to persuade the others Joanna was right for the role. I said to Albert Fennell and Laurie Johnson before we even began that I would like it to be Joanna Lumley but that if anyone else came through I would, of course, back down.

'During the auditions, any actresses whom I thought were good

I wheeled in to Albert and then we tested them because you never know whether the camera likes them or not. But I always had faith in Joanna right from the start. From the first time I'd met her socially on *The Abominable Dr Phibes* I thought that she was glamorous and sexy and she had that wonderful asset of being a clothes horse. She always looked good. Put a black sack on her and she looked good. But I also loved her personality and I thought that if we could ever get that personality on to the screen then Joanna would be a star.'

Despite Mary Selway's reservations, the triumvirate were not about to change their minds. Laurie Johnson says simply: 'We owned the company so we had the vote on it.'

By the time the aircraft bearing Joanna back to Italy had landed, she was so exhausted she barely knew which day it was or which country she was in. Wearily she waited at the baggage collection point to pick up her cases only to find that they were nowhere to be seen on the carousel. After such a hectic two days, she discovered to her annoyance that her bags had mistakenly been flown to Budapest.

Joanna was fit to drop when her taxi pulled up outside her hotel. Collecting her key from the counter she made her way to her room promising herself a much-needed sleep. 'I'd got the call in Amalfi on a Tuesday night, flown back to do the screen test on the Wednesday almost collapsing with exhaustion, and then got the plane back to Italy again on the Thursday morning,' Joanna remembers. 'All the travelling had taken eighteen hours. When at last I crawled back to my hotel room, the phone rang. It was my agent phoning from London to say: "Are you sitting down? You've got it!" It's funny, I really wasn't terribly excited. I was so tired I could barely take it in.'

Word of Joanna's success quickly spread among the other models and the accompanying entourage of photographers, stylists and make-up girls on the fashion shoot. The moment called for champagne and Joanna's fatigue was briefly forgotten as everyone gathered round her at the hotel bar and raised their glasses to toast her success. Joanna's chief feeling was one of relief. For the first time she could look forward to a solid period of work as an actress on television. Regular work also meant regular pay. Impecunious for so long, Joanna and Jamie could now look to the future with some confidence. She learned she would be paid £600 per episode for the first series of thirteen episodes with an increase to £800 an episode for a second series if the first was a success.

In her moment of triumph Joanna did not forget the part Jeremy Lloyd had played in helping to pave the way for her to be tested for the role. 'She phoned me up and said: "I'm jolly grateful, I've got the part." I said: "You deserve it." She was eminently suitable for it.' Lloyd remembers that Joanna followed up her phone call of thanks with a letter to him expressing her gratitude.

For Joanna, the weeks that followed were filled with endless meetings as the outline of the woman she was to play in *The New Avengers* began to emerge. Brian Clemens had originally intended to call Joanna's character Charlie but there happened to be a perfume of the same name on the market at the time and it seemed incongruous to give it priceless free publicity. Joanna was given the chance to help come up with another name and obliged with Purdey, partly derived from the name of a top model called Sue Purdie.

All agreed Purdey was perfect, that the name had a nice ring to it. The first syllable had an unmistakably kittenish quality of purring about it and would therefore be a worthy successor to Emma Peel which had been devised as a pun on M Appeal, short for man appeal. But the name Purdey had another pertinent connotation. It was also the name of the most revered and expensive shotgun in the world. To those in the know, a Purdey gun was a superb, hand-crafted piece of weaponry. Lastly, Purdey would also appeal to the Americans who, it was felt, would interpret it as 'purty', their slang version of the word pretty.

Purdey, it was decided, was to be a former ballerina who also ran like an Olympic athlete. She was the daughter of a spy who had been shot and she then went on to have a bishop as a stepfather. She was tough yet vulnerable and with a sharp sense of humour. She would be dressed in feminine frills and soft flowing fabrics and drive a yellow MGB drophead sports car to reflect her sporty nature. Occasionally she would be seen on a motorbike.

Home for Purdey was to be a sensuously decorated art nouveau basement bedsit in London with a predominantly lilac look to it.

There was a piano and, on one wall, a full-length mirror with a barre in front of it. This was to enable Purdey to practise her ballet exercises – and allow male viewers the occasional pleasing glimpse of Joanna in figure-hugging leotards.

A curtain of hanging beads would serve as an inviting door to Purdey's bedroom where she slept in a big brass double bed. *New Avengers* viewers were to conjecture that Purdey was not a virgin but, since she seemed to share her bedroom with just a large teddy bear, she was in no way to be considered promiscuous. There was to be the odd occasion when Mike Gambit would arrive at Purdey's flat while she was still asleep and he would linger to gaze longingly at Purdey in bed. But, although he would never actually join her under the covers, their flirtatious relationship was based on a promise that one day Purdey would allow him to do so.

'*The New Avengers* are very close as a team,' Joanna explained, 'but they don't have any love affairs between them. They all have love affairs outside them. Whenever confronted, we are all coy as if we don't ever go to bed with anybody. But it's implied that we do.'

Clemens essentially saw Purdey's character as an extension of Joanna's own. 'Upper-crust, liberated, with a sense of humour, quite tough but with a touch of vulnerability,' he said. Joanna, for her part, made up her mind to keep as much of herself as possible in Purdey and simply flesh out the character which had been outlined to her. She also resolved to play up the British elegance, comedy and lightness which had so marked the original Avengers, and the typically British humour which had sold Patrick Macnee and Diana Rigg so convincingly to the Americans.

Pre-publicity described Purdey as 'a girl for the Eighties. A girl who mixes ultra-femininity with a fighting style that is as effective as it is unique. A girl who can shoot the pips out of an apple at 20 paces. A stockings-and-suspenders girl giving lots of glimpses of thigh, a man's woman, a male chauvinist pig's dream. *The Avengers* girls will have grown full circle with Joanna. So much so that she won't have to burn her bra – she can put it back on.'

Clemens says: 'I wanted to get away from the Diana Rigg and Linda Thorson catsuits and leathers and I thought that women were so emancipated that they could put their bras back on and return to femininity. The stockings and suspenders were my idea but Jo didn't completely go along with it and we had problems of actually doing the fights and action scenes without getting ladders in her stockings.'

One of the authors was present on 8 March 1976 at London's Dorchester hotel as a television staff reporter for the *Daily Mail* when Joanna was openly presented to the press for the first time as *The New Avengers* girl. Naturally there was tremendous interest in the revival of such a popular television series and the press launch attracted huge numbers of showbiz writers and photographers to the Dorchester.

In the run-up to the press launch there had been much discussion in the press as to what kind of clothes *The New Avengers* girl was likely to wear and which designers she would favour, and much excitement among the tabloids over the pre-publicity promise that stockings and suspenders would be the order of the day for whichever lucky actress clinched the role.

In their dummy pages Fleet Street picture editors had therefore prominently pencilled in just such a picture of Joanna for the following day's papers and there were groans of dismay from the ranks of photographers assembled at the Dorchester Hotel when Joanna arrived and announced that they would not be able to photograph her showing stocking tops as she was in fact wearing tights.

News photographers are never the most tactful bunch, never the most sensitive to other people's feelings. Dispatched by their bosses to the Dorchester anticipating the opportunity to photograph a pretty starlet showing a glimpse of thigh at a carefully orchestrated press launch, this group's disappointment at being thwarted quickly turned to annoyance and resentment. 'Come on, love, where's the sexy underwear?' one demanded of Joanna completely ignoring the fact that she looked stunning in an exceptionally floaty, feminine dress. 'We were told you'd be in stockings and suspenders and that's the picture we want. If we don't get it, we're off.' With that, the cameraman turned his back on Joanna and went into a huddle with his Fleet Street colleagues amid murmurings of 'unprofessional' and much worse aimed in Joanna's direction.

Gamely Joanna kept smiling and took the absurdity of it all in her stride while the journalists, who mostly view photographers with contempt anyway, looked suitably embarrassed for her, distanced themselves from the 'monkeys' as they like to call cameramen, and studied the press release they had been handed.

'A girl in a thousand' was how it trumpeted Joanna, a PR man's spin conveniently more than tripling the number of actresses Joanna had been chosen from. 'A thousand faces, three months of expectations, scores upon scores of auditions, the resultant screen tests and the role of John Steed's lady was cast.

'With a birth sign of Taurus, Joanna rubs the height chalk-mark at 5' 8", other vital statistics are 34-24-35. She remarks: "I longed to be short, 5' 1" with brown shiny hair. So it was a great disappointment I shot up to five-eight."' How great the disappointment might have been for Brian Clemens and Albert Fennell if their Purdey really had rubbed the chalk-mark at only five feet one.

While the photographers began surrounding the hapless public relations man, berating him for 'allowing Joanna to have the nerve to turn up in tights', the budding star proved to be a good interviewee for the journalists. Not only was she warm and courteous but she came over as genuinely grateful, humble even, at having been chosen to play Purdey and at pains to point out she was not taking over from Diana Rigg.

'Apparently Diana got all these people coming up to her saying: "Poor love, too old for the part, are you?"' said Joanna. 'People are so awful. Can you imagine saying that to Diana? I'm not taking over from her, not playing the same part.

'I had come to have a very jaundiced view of England and I was even thinking of trying my luck in America as I hadn't done anything I could call memorable for a very long time. Now I can take the dish away from under the leaking pipe in my loo and call in the plumber. I'll also be able to get the sash cords on my windows repaired. Up till now I've had to jam cans of hairspray under the windows to keep them open.' The poverty-to-stardom story was a nice line for the showbiz reporters. What was needed now was an eye-catching photograph to go with it.

Keeping a watchful eye over proceedings, Brian Clemens and Albert Fennell were naturally anxious about the mood of the photographers and the imminent threat of a boycott of their star.

At an appropriate moment Fennell took Joanna aside to warn

her that the cameramen were now seriously threatening to depart unless they got their stockings and suspenders photograph. Joanna told him she was unable to oblige, she simply didn't have stockings on.

In desperation a member of the PR team was dispatched to find suitable underwear for Joanna and returned triumphant unexpectedly soon. Joanna was unobtrusively beckoned from the room to the Ladies at the Dorchester where a woman was being persuaded to be gallant enough to take off her own stockings and suspender belt to loan to Joanna.

Once she was suitably attired, Joanna sallied forth to meet the grumbling hordes of photographers once more. She was amused to see their faces visibly brighten at the news she would now be photographed just as they had requested. With a Steed-style bowler hat perched jauntily on her head and a Steed-style rolled umbrella clasped in one hand, Joanna posed in front of a Rolls-Royce with one leg up on the bumper to reveal a suspendered stocking with a revolver tucked into the top.

The clamouring photographers were given more expanse of exposed thigh than they bargained for since the stockings had been borrowed from a woman of much smaller stature than Joanna and were really much too short for her long legs. The photographers could hardly believe their luck and they fired off photo after photo, jockeying and elbowing each other out of the way in a flashbulb frenzy while Joanna shrewdly added the quotes to match their pictures. 'Purdey is a stockings and suspenders girl,' said Joanna most helpfully. 'I knew that was the kind of girl they were looking for when I went for the audition. I know that men are hung up on stockings and there will be a glimpse of them in the series.' She added obligingly with a broad smile: 'I always wear stockings. They are so much prettier than tights.'

Of course the readers of the newspapers the following day were not party to the extraordinary lingerie-swapping shenanigans which had occurred in the Ladies of the prestigious Dorchester Hotel and which had engineered such extensive coverage for a rising new star called Joanna Lumley. All they saw were simply tantalizing pictures of Joanna plus accompanying stories and the headlines screaming: 'I'm a stockings and suspenders girl.'

Joanna had played the publicity game to perfection but, even at a moment in her life when she appeared to have the world at her feet, she confided she was still not entirely sure whether she should not be doing something more worthy. She was full of self-doubt. 'Acting is fun,' she said, 'but it's not being a brain surgeon, it's not being on a trawler in appalling seas bringing in food and it's not being a starving person in Peru.

'I'm not sure it's in my blood. I'm not sure that I'm a trouper. I haven't done years and years of rep work. I'd like to give acting up – I'd hate it to give me up. It's like love affairs – you don't want to be the one left there at the end of the day. Always try and get the boot in first, though it's not very attractive.

'I love stars but I don't think I'll ever be one. I think stars should go about in mink coats and grumble and be late on the set and have pink Cadillacs and rip off their clothes in public. I would never do that but I love people who do. It must be terrible to climb down so I'm determined never to climb up. Going downhill is awful, those awful corners in the newspapers saying: "Where are they now?"

'But it will be quite nice if people recognize me in Greece. Last time I was there they thought I was Julie Christie. They wouldn't believe I wasn't. In the end I signed my name Julie Christie just to make them happy.'

Shortly before filming was due to start on *The New Avengers*, Joanna took it upon herself to have her shoulder-length hair cropped short which came as a severe shock to the producers. 'It's fine if you have long, healthy, shiny hair like Diana Rigg,' Joanna explained, 'but look at mine – it's really quite tatty. As I'm going to be leaping about the place and working outside a lot, it's bound to get frizzy, so I thought I'd have it shortened. I pointed out that a secret agent would have a hairstyle she could look after herself. She couldn't afford the time to go to a hairdresser.'

It was hard to argue against Joanna's reasoned feminine logic although she was later to discover that it took a great deal more care than she had imagined and that she needed to have it cut often. But Clemens nevertheless viewed her newly shorn crop with dismay. 'I wasn't very happy about it,' he says. 'In fact I didn't think it was good news at all and we were all a bit cross about it. Joanna had nice long hair and America then, and even now, prefers its blondes with long hair. I think it would have made Joanna more of a star in America if she had kept it long. Long hair has a softening effect and Joanna, though she's not hard, could be horsey if you weren't careful. Once she'd had it cut, we had the problem that we couldn't glue it back on again. The next best thing we could do was to exploit it.'

When the famous Purdey cut went to the head of thousands of young girls, Clemens was delighted. 'We said it was the best idea we'd ever had!' he laughs.

For *The New Avengers* to live up to, and hopefully eclipse, the action-packed reputation of its forerunner, it was made abundantly clear to both Joanna and Gareth Hunt that they could expect their roles to be physically demanding.

The show's resident director, Ray Austin, had been a stunt and fight arranger before taking to directing and he was determined that his two young stars should be extremely fit for the on-screen gymnastics he had planned for them. He also knew just the person to put his new charges through their paces – Women's European Heavyweight Judo Champion, Cyd Child.

Cyd had been involved in the training of the British judo team and Austin had worked with her on fight arrangements in *The Avengers*. He duly called her up to join the new team as one of the fight arrangers and made available to her the Bandroom at Pinewood. It was normally reserved for orchestras to rehearse in and record their film scores but it was offered to Cyd to turn into a gymnasium so Joanna and Gareth Hunt could receive their training on the lot.

The prospect of submitting to some regular fitness training held no qualms for Joanna. She prided herself on being an athletic young woman. 'For my own personal comfort I like to be able to touch the ground,' she said, 'and I like to be able to put my foot on a table or put my head on my knee because I don't like the idea of seizing up.

'I thought the training was going to be quite fun and that it would be nice to be able to bend over and touch my toes. But I was in for a shock. The training was quite unbelievable. Oh those training sessions! That rubber-smelling gymnasium in Pinewood at the top of K block! That great, lugubrious gym with rubber mats and barbells! It was relentless.

'Cyd Child was a terribly nice girl who started us off but it was none of that try-to-work-up-to-it-gently-at-first business. They said gently at first as they rammed your head into the ground and put a foot behind your neck. We trained for two hours a day for three weeks.

'We did an exercise called the Shuttle Run where you either died or became a very strong person with a very slow heartbeat. It was sprinting up and down – ten minutes sprinting with one minute to catch your breath. By the fourth or fifth I was crying and saying: "I simply can't go on, this is the end." But no, I was told: "Off you go again." It was sprinting, sprinting and more sprinting. I'm sure most people in this world would welcome a bit of enforced physical training every week and you can groan and moan and hate it and spit but in the end you'll feel better. At the end of my training I felt fit and I found I could sprint long distances.'

Cyd Child was impressed with the effort both Joanna and Gareth Hunt put in. She says: 'I'd asked Ray Austin how fit he wanted me to get them and he'd said: "Give it the full works." So together we just went for it, as much as Joanna and Gareth could take. I trained them early in the morning and then Gareth would go off and do weight training and Joanna would have a session with a ballet instructor.

'It was mainly Shuttle Runs and lots of stretching exercises. The Shuttle Run meant running up to a wall and back again in a minute. If you did it really quickly you'd get to rest until the next minute ticked round and then you'd be off again. As the minutes tick by it takes you longer and you get less rest. I think it was all a bit of a shock to them at first but they didn't hate me too much and I got them very fit. I knew Joanna was a smoker and if she hadn't smoked she might have been a bit fitter still but you couldn't say it handicapped her.

'There was one scene she subsequently filmed which required Joanna as Purdey running hard and, because of her training, the camera crew couldn't keep up with her.' Joanna was running so fast, in fact, that resident director Ray Austin had to reconstruct the action shots to make sure the film crew captured them in one take. 'I wasn't there to watch the scene but Joanna later told me how chuffed she felt about that,' remembers Cyd. 'She was quite cocky about it.'

Much of the whole process of filming was new to Joanna. For the first time in a television production she was given her own chair in which to rest between takes on set and her own dressing room with her name on the door which she immediately tried to make more homely with pictures of Jamie and boyfriend Michael Kitchen.

Without wishing to appear the least bit ungrateful for the star treatment she was being accorded and the invaluable opportunity *The New Avengers* was giving her to learn about acting in front of the camera, Joanna could not help but ponder on the irony of it all. She was enjoying herself hugely filming the show while her flat-mate Jane Carr, boyfriend Michael Kitchen, and other actor friends like Stuart Wilson and Jonathan Pryce were all with prestigious national theatre companies often rehearsing difficult speeches in scruffy warehouses, battling away at tricky scenes and having to cope with the tantrums of fellow actors and temperamental directors. 'Why can't I be put through the mill like that?' Joanna queried to herself. 'Why don't I have some of those pressures. All I do is learn a line like "I say Steed, where do you think the Russians will land?" and deliver it.' To Joanna's way of thinking, although she was working hard over long hours and doing her professional best, she considered she was having great fun. She was enjoying herself so much, she confided, that it hardly felt like work compared with the intensity her nearest and dearest were undergoing for their art. 'I was getting the best table at a restaurant, the whole bezazz but no scripts through the door,' she said.

As the weeks went by, Joanna's confidence visibly soared, buoyed by the rapid strides she was making in her various forms of physical training. Brian Clemens was especially pleased. 'If we'd found Joanna Lumley when she was about nine she'd have won a couple of Olympic gold medals by now,' he enthusiastically told the crew.

Cyd Child had also devised a special fighting style for Purdey based on an old French martial art called Panache. The aim was to make Purdey's fighting style elegant, ballet-like but lethal. As an ex-dancer, Purdey's strength was supposed to lie in her thighs and her feet and consequently this was the way she would fight. 'We threw in the occasional kung fu or karate-type kick,' said Cyd. 'Purdey rarely used her hands but once every five episodes or so she'd lash out with her right fist.'

Joanna's action scenes were plotted and choreographed with meticulous care and precision. She rehearsed them in slow motion and for close-up high-kicking scenes, her leg was supported by a tripod to get the correct height. 'The new girl will be shot so as to capitalize on her grace and sexuality,' was the brief to the production team.

Joanna threw herself into it all with gusto. 'Apart from getting fit, I enjoyed doing the dance fighting,' she said, 'and I developed a strong right hook which could floor a man. I really loved doing all that action stuff. I loved the hokum, all that standing behind doors looking anxious, the kind of thing *The X-Files* does so well now. What always worried me was that people might think I was really an expert and pick on me for a fight. But I never hit anyone. I always worked with stunt men and pulled my punches.'

Gareth Hunt was not so fortunate. Filming a karate sequence up and down a staircase late one night for an episode called 'The Last of the Cybernauts. . . ?', Hunt mistimed a punch and laid out stunt man Rocky Taylor who proceeded to tumble backwards down two flights of stairs, still wearing his Cybernaut helmet. Hunt's tough guy image from *The New Avengers* almost inevitably attracted unwelcome attention from a tiny minority of men who considered themselves macho enough to want to find out just how tough he really was. It earned him a few scars when he got involved in a fight in a Hackney pub.

Everyone was impressed by how clear-headed Joanna was and full of energy at 7.30 in the morning after getting up at 6 a.m. Macnee, who was enchanted with Joanna and described her appearance as that of a Dresden shepherdess, confided: 'She just radiates – whether with fire and brimstone early in the morning when confronted with yet another inadequacy or, conversely, with compassion and understanding of other people's problems at all times of night and day.'

Macnee gelled with both Joanna and Gareth Hunt and it was as well for the production team that he did. Initially Macnee was appalled when he finally got to see the first scripts. He found that his role as Steed had been considerably reduced this time round.

'I'd all but been put out to grass,' he fumed while Rudolf Roffi kept assuring him that all would be well. But Macnee later confessed that if he had not enjoyed working with his co-stars so much and had not been tied by contractual obligations, he would have walked out.

Such was the pace of filming that at one point five different episodes were in production at the same time. As with most films and TV shows, scenes were shot out of sequence and Joanna decided the best way to cope was to concentrate hard on her own scenes and not worry too much about what else was going on.

Saturdays were spent shopping for Joanna's wardrobe. Sunday was her one day off but frequently it saw the most heightened activity of her week. Sundays meant doing the washing by hand – because she didn't allow herself the luxury of a washing machine – the ironing and other domestic chores, as well as catching up with letters. Occasionally she would drive down to Rolvenden for a simple Sunday lunch of cheese on toast or a bowl of soup at home with her parents.

During filming the demands on Joanna during the week often left her strung out by the end of each day. On one occasion she was so exhausted driving away from the studios after filming that fatigue caused her to lose her way home. From then on she was accorded the star status she deserved of a car and a driver to ferry her to and from the studios.

Fatigue was not the only worry. 'I also picked up a lot of bruises from chucking myself over walls and barriers,' she says. 'One day we screamed up in a car and they said: "Right, leap over the gate!" It was wire. I just ran at it and somehow got over. It was only when I was over and I'd sprinted off then stopped that I realized I'd got cuts, bruises and lacerations.

'Unless it's something that's very, very skilled, I realized it's just a mental block that stops you doing it. But a lot of it is personal courage. I'm amazed at some of the things I've done. I had to vault walls, stride up bars set wide apart and walk out on a wire with only a parallel wire above me to hold on to.

'Patrick Macnee told me I was mad to do some of the things I did.

One dewy morning I arrived at Aldershot with these exhausted seventeen-year-old boys all training to be parachutists on this assault course. I had to climb on to a very high platform and swing off on a huge great rope. In the distance was a net to catch me. "Go on, you can do it," they said. "I can't, I can't," I pleaded. The whole of me was shaking. Suddenly my hands went all wet with fear as I realized I could just plummet on to my face. I swung off and I did my knee in and immediately got a great big black bruise.

'In another scene where a helicopter was dive-bombing a man, I had to run in under the helicopter's blades. I know those blades are not going to hit you but they do go at a pace and the downdraft flattens you and I rushed through, rugger-tackled the man and hit my chin so badly a great lump came up. I looked like Desperate Dan.' Years later an X-ray was to reveal that Joanna had chipped and cracked two vertebrae while performing her Purdey stunts. Nowadays, to ease the discomfort she practises the Alexander technique and, when sitting, sits with her back ramrod straight.

At the time, Joanna accepted her lot cheerfully enough. She even wrote the producers comically sarcastic little notes of gratitude for some of the hardships she suffered in the name of Purdey such as: 'Thank you for allowing me to grovel in drains.' Laurie Johnson says: 'I'm sure at times Joanna's enthusiasm must have flagged but she said she was lucky to learn her art in front of a movie camera for two and a half years. She appreciated it and it shows in her work. She knows how to use a camera.'

It wasn't just Joanna who anxiously had her heart in her mouth the day the plotline in an episode called 'Target!' called for her to walk perilously along the gable of a four-storey house. 'If you really must do this stunt yourself,' said Ray Austin nervously, 'then hang on with your hands and crawl.' But Joanna proceeded to tread surefooted and swiftly without a pause across the roof. 'It wouldn't have been Avengers-style woman to have crawled,' she explained with satisfaction when she was safely back on terra firma. It wasn't till much later when he viewed the sequence on film that Brian Clemens realized it really was Joanna up on the roof. 'It was all very well,' he said, 'but if she'd fallen and broken her leg we'd have lost the series and if our insurance people had got tough they'd have put the premium up.'

Gamely though she tackled most of the physical action required of Purdey, there were times when sheer fatigue took its toll and tested Joanna's will and endurance to the limit. Joanna's spirit was almost always willing but on occasions the flesh was momentarily weak. 'I once wept openly in front of everybody about something I didn't want to do,' she recalls. 'I was very tired and shattered at the time and they said if you don't want to do it, then don't do it.'

It was at moments like these that Joanna longed for a double to stand in for her. In general, *The New Avengers* production team wanted Joanna to accomplish as much as she could of her own accord and they were reluctant to use doubles. 'Joanna was very good at the action stuff,' Cyd stresses, 'and she was quite agile and very keen to do as much as she could. But obviously there were limitations and there was always the insurance aspect.'

When one or two doubles were tried but found to be wanting or unsatisfactory for one reason or another, Joanna began to press for Cyd Child to double for her. Cyd had successfully doubled for Diana Rigg and then Linda Thorson during the making of *The Avengers* and Joanna saw no reason why she shouldn't double for her too. 'But they didn't want that,' says Cyd. 'For some reason they decided that it wouldn't do. Joanna was very keen but they wouldn't listen. They said originally that it wouldn't work because I wasn't thin enough. They said I wouldn't look like Joanna who was very thin at that time. So I went on a diet and lost quite a lot of weight and Joanna kept saying: "Cyd can do it," but still they said no, it wouldn't look like Joanna.

'So finally Joanna said to me, "I've had enough of this. Will you go to my hairdresser and we'll have a wig cut on you to look like me?" This we did, quietly without telling anyone, and then Joanna arranged for me to meet her at the studio and to hide away in her dressing room. She'd borrowed an outfit from wardrobe and had copies made from it and then, when she and I were ready, we both walked out on to the set together looking exactly the same wearing exactly the same. Everyone was taken aback. Joanna then insisted upon a screen test and we took it in turns to run past the camera and they seemed happy enough. After that they let me double for Joanna.'

In the weeks leading up to the launch of *The New Avengers* on

ITV there was feverish speculation as to how Joanna would be dressed as Purdey. Catherine Buckley, who owned a little shop in Westbourne Grove in West London, had been chosen as the designer for the series and the first sketches of her clothes to emerge indicated that Purdey's wardrobe would be delightfully feminine, frilled and flowing, a sharp departure from the aggressive leather of previous *Avengers* girls.

The sketches included a yellow batik-patterned silk dress and a skirt in pleated chiffon that gathered at the waist and tied at each shoulder. 'Delightful to wear on a summer evening for dinner,' Joanna commented. There was also a velvet, pin-stripe suit with black trilby worn with white shirt striped with mauve and lavender. 'It made me feel very elegant,' said Joanna. For Purdey to relax in at home there was an orange, black, green, red and yellow flower-print silk kimono with buttons on one side but otherwise loose. The sleeves were long with side splits. Clearly designed for action was a black cotton jump suit with lion Avenger motif and the name Purdey trimmed in white. It was to be worn with a white polo-necked jumper underneath, motor-cycle gloves and long boots.

All the hype persistently hailed Joanna's Purdey as a stockings and suspenders heroine as per the image she had been encouraged to project at the Dorchester launch. The *TV Times*, then very much the mouthpiece magazine for ITV, excitedly featured a sketch among Catherine Buckley's clothes of Joanna as they expected her to look in navy blue Janet Reger underwear consisting of a lace bra, a front-lacing satin corset, a satin suspender belt and a lacy garter.

'They announced even before I joined the series that I was going to be a very feminine secret agent with frilly underclothes, stockings and suspenders and high heels,' said Joanna. 'But I just wish some directors had to wear stockings, suspenders, high heels and a dress just for one day. I had to chase crooks, climb walls and kick people in the face in them. It was hell.'

Joanna argued repeatedly that if Purdey really was supposed to be the most effective sleuth in the world or a vital component in a secret crime-busting organization then she would have to wear very efficient, probably sporty clothes. 'I kept begging for plimsolls and a track suit but not likely,' she says. 'It's not practical for a secret agent to spend her life with her bum hanging out of her pants and her cleavage tumbling over a gate. I'm all for an occasional flash of thigh but how can Purdey justify constantly twitching in her undies?'

Despite director Ray Austin saying that Purdey was 'the complete sexual animal', her character generally emerged as deliciously feminine rather than blatantly sexy and, despite all the excited speculation, stocking tops and suspender belts were destined to become conspicuous only by their absence when the series finally hit the screen. There was a glimpse of Purdey's white stocking in 'Target!' when she shinned up a drainpipe, and a titillating close-up of her black stocking tops in another episode, 'To Catch A Rat'. But far more eye-catching was the wardrobe designed for Purdey by Catherine Buckley.

The first episode, 'The Eagle's Nest', set the trend. It featured Joanna emerging from a frogman's outfit wearing a fetching red, green and blue Lurex dress and a velvet top with Lurex pieces dangling from large buttons at the shoulder. Ingeniously the wrap-around skirt contained drawstrings to hitch up the hem to reveal Joanna's legs and allow freer movement for Purdey's ballet-like fighting style. Thus Joanna was able to pirouette out of the dress, emerging in a leotard and red boots, kicking villains into oblivion.

Joanna rarely looked anything less than dazzlingly pretty in Catherine Buckley's creations. Only once in the first series was Purdey presented as a sex object. An episode called 'Faces' fleetingly transformed Joanna from a uniformed Salvation Army officer paying a visit to a hotel for homeless men into a Lolita figure. One moment she was soberly attired and then later she emerged dressed as a gum-chewing sexpot complete with a permed wig, a string of pearls, a cockney accent, broadly layered eye shadow, freshly applied glistening lipstick and a sexy sway of the hips in the walk. 'That was her Patsy of *Absolutely Fabulous*,' reflects Brian Clemens.

Inevitably there was massive interest in *The New Avengers* as ITV prepared to launch the series in the autumn of 1976 at the end of one of the hottest summers on record. The omens were mostly favourable and at a press screening Kingsley Amis was to be found enthusiastically lashing out with his feet each time Purdey executed a kick.

The word was that Joanna was every bit as good and as sparky on screen as the producers had hoped when they had chosen her. Once he had first seen her work, Laurie Johnson had always felt Joanna was destined to be a success in the role. But he positively knew for sure she was going to be a sensation the moment he viewed two completed episodes. The two programmes had yet to be broadcast and did not even have a transmission date but Johnson had himself seen enough in them to take Joanna aside to tell her what to expect once the series was launched. 'I told her that I hoped she was prepared for becoming the biggest thing to hit British TV screens,' he says. To this day Johnson remembers Joanna's reaction. 'She just looked at me and laughed,' he says. 'But I genuinely felt that. And I was right.'

'The Eagle's Nest' was filmed in Scotland with Peter Cushing as a popular and important guest star and featured a story about a group of Nazis who were secretly living on an isolated Scottish island masquerading as Trappist monks. It encapsulated many of the elements of escapist fun which had made the original Avengers so popular – a bizarre plot, clever dialogue, plenty of action and a fast-paced new title sequence accompanied by a punchy new arrangement of the theme music. Joanna was all cheekbones and charm as she, Patrick Macnee and Gareth Hunt prevented the ruthless band of cloaked Nazis from bringing Adolf Hitler back to life. Not too many marks for credibility, but Joanna did look stunning in her frogman's outfit, which she proceeded to swap for a green leotard in order to polish off a brigade of stormtroopers in a high-kicking fight sequence.

It met with the approval of the critics. 'Avenging is better than ever before,' said Shaun Usher reviewing 'The Eagle's Nest' in the *Daily Mail*. 'Pay no heed to that title,' he continued, '*The New Avengers* are, thank goodness, the old Avengers, in fact the very old ones in the Sixties heyday before the show declined in a noticeably wan and shabby final season.'

The *Daily Mirror* also enthused, summing up the new show with a typically tabloid vote of confidence: 'It's Wham! Bam! Pow! stuff!' Clive James in the *Observer* was more taken with Joanna's physical attributes: 'An amazing pair of legs which go all the way up to the mouth which in turn goes all the way across to each ear,' he commented. But not everyone was totally enamoured. Joan Bakewell likened Joanna as Purdey to 'a hockey captain attending a royal garden party'.

The impact of the series on the British public was significantly lessened by the political flaws of the ITV system in place at the time. Instead of the big five ITV companies making a collective decision that *The New Avengers* should be screened fully networked on the same night of the week at the same time, several ITV companies were permitted to opt for different scheduling. Some channels screened the series on Sunday evenings, others on Tuesdays, others on Fridays. 'It was total madness,' says Clemens. 'With a proper network show we could have emptied the streets on our opening night.'

The split scheduling meant that the show frequently missed out on priceless previews in the daily newspapers. Television editors were reluctant to write about a programme which many of their readers might not be able to tune into that night in their particular region. Nevertheless *The New Avengers*, staying largely faithful to the original concept of outrageous plots and dry British wit, quickly established itself with the British viewing public and pulled in big enough audiences to rank as one of the top TV series of 1976.

That was no mean feat in a vintage television year which saw Derek Jacobi winning awards as the ridiculed runt with a speech impediment in the BBC's bloodthirsty historical mini-series; *I, Claudius*, and 20 million viewers tuning in every week to see incest and sexual infidelity make a middle-class Surrey family miserable in ITV's *A Bouquet of Barbed Wire*. The TV year also included the monster hit from America *Rich Man, Poor Man*, the rags-to-riches drama of a maid turned caterer to the rich in the BBC's *The Duchess of Duke Street*, Sir Lew Grade's innovative *The Muppet Show* with its lovable cast of madly designed technicolour glove puppet creatures, Burt Lancaster starring in Sir Lew's spectacular *Moses The Lawgiver*, the Ronnie Barker–David Jason sit-com for the BBC *Open All Hours*, and the preposterous police pals of Los Angeles in the American import *Starsky and Hutch*. All things considered, *The New Avengers* did remarkably well to attract its huge following in the face of such varied competition.

Naturally the series was cleverly balanced to attract fans of the original *Avengers* as well as newcomers. An episode called 'The Last of the Cybernauts. . . ?' saw the return of monsters from a previous Avengers incarnation while new dangers surfaced in the shape of cardboard targets at a shooting range, which ingeniously fought back with deadly curare-tipped darts, in 'Target!' and the emergence of giant rats in London's underground system in 'Gnaws'.

For many, the fascination was the eccentricity and charm Joanna Lumley brought to the role of Purdey. Although *The Avengers* had a long history of liberated women, Joanna had always held very definite views on how she intended to portray Purdey. 'I decided right away that Purdey was a complete professional,' she said. 'She didn't care about being pretty or trying to attract men, because that seemed to happen all the time anyway. I thought she'd be a very cool head, very bossy and organized – and unapproachable.'

One thing was clear. Joanna did not see Purdey as overtly sexual. She wanted her to be a thoroughly normal woman whom, if people liked her, they would automatically find attractive or sexy. Joanna's view was that if people didn't like Purdey as she was, then that was just too bad. Joanna resented being sold as sexy. 'I'm certainly not a sex symbol so anyone who expects to find something kinky will be disappointed,' she declared.

But one scene in particular irritated Joanna intensely and led to heated arguments. It was a scene in which Steed calls Purdey up in the middle of the night and tells her to come over straight away. The scene read: 'Purdey leaps out of bed and throws off her pyjamas.'

Joanna considered this was ridiculous and was not afraid to say so. 'It's a comic strip for children,' she protested. 'That's all it is and children don't want to see Purdey without her clothes on. We argued and argued and, sure enough, finally I had to throw my clothes off. But they agreed only to show the back view. They said there would be no photographs, no sensationalism. Nevertheless someone took a photo and it appeared in the newspapers saying Purdey will be seen in bed . . . new sexy angle . . . all bullshit. Really it made me so angry, particularly after all the arguments we'd had in the first place.

'If you happen to be five feet eight inches tall and you were once a model you always get stuck with the "sexy" roles which are the most boring parts in the world. Actresses always want to play the nice drunken woman or the bitch. But you always get landed with the false eyelashes and the lip gloss.'

What vexed Joanna more than the actual casting off of her pyjamas was that the sexy image began to rub off on to her rather than on to Purdey. 'I began to be asked for comments on sex and the men in my life, all that sort of thing,' said Joanna ruefully.

Joanna's insistence she would not be seen as just a pretty face and a sexy body was a determined stand and she conveyed her feelings to those around her on *The New Avengers* production.

'The only one of *The Avengers* girls I never saw naked was Joanna Lumley,' Patrick Macnee confided some years later, 'which says everything about her. In those days she was like Fort Belvedere. She came wrapped in concrete. I just felt very fortunate that I was too old for her. She treated me like an old uncle and we got on famously but she was a real ice maiden when it came to sex.

'Jo was by far the most beautiful of *The Avengers* girls but she was really anti-sex, she was very jolly hockey sticks and head girl. Because she was so pretty she didn't like the idea of anyone thinking she was sexy. She was as prickly as a porcupine about it. She used to go out with the type of men who would make her feel less attractive or wanted for her looks. She gave herself quite a hard time.'

As the years went by and Joanna and Macnee stayed friends, he noticed a transformation in her. 'She changed completely, she's got a wonderful husband and she's much happier,' he said. 'I don't feel she minds people thinking she is sexy now. She's got over having to assert herself and feeling the need to be taken seriously. I think people go off that sort of person. Ironically when Jo softened, people started to take notice of her and listened.'

But during the spring recess of 1977, it was very different. Rudolf Roffi, the Frenchman initially responsible for *The New Avengers*, took it upon himself to complain that Purdey wasn't sexy enough. 'Purdey is short of lip gloss and cleavage and her wardrobe is dull and drab,' Roffi ventured to declare. He wanted Purdey to add a touch of ooh la la in outfits by top French designers like Yves Saint Laurent. 'The stories could be sexier, more violent also, but still remain sophisticated,' said Roffi adding that the ratings would soar if Joanna Lumley looked a little more like the girl cops in *Charlie's Angels*.

This was a reference to the heavenly trio of American actresses Farrah Fawcett, Kate Jackson and Jaclyn Smith who had burst on to TV screens with the unlikely claim of being police-trained detectives in a series which relied hugely on what the Americans called 'jiggle appeal'. The formula of bimbos with big hair and bronzed, bikini-clad bodies battling crime for a mystery boss had swept *Charlie's Angels* to the top of the ratings with a bewildering array of plots involving health spas, nightclubs or beaches where they could appear out of uniform and out of almost everything.

If Roffi's remarks were aimed to stir up some controversy for publicity purposes, then he was not disappointed. Just how sexy Purdey should be was an argument which became hotly debated in the press with Joanna stoutly defending her corner against the Angels: 'We don't want to see bottoms and breasts, do we? I think the public have had quite enough of that on TV and everywhere else. Aren't people bored with actresses who lick their lips trying to be sexy?'

The suggestion that *The New Avengers* should follow the example of *Charlie's Angels* particularly rankled with Joanna. 'I don't mind anyone saying other women are prettier,' she said. 'I'm the first to agree that Charlie's ladies are lovely. My son James keeps telling me they are gorgeous. They are – all that sitting around in the Californian sunshine in open cars with dark brown suntans that make their teeth look twice as white. If you're golden all over you don't need a diamond bracelet – you can look marvellous in an elastic band. But I'd like to see an Angel, pale as a lily, crawling round a backlot in Pinewood in March.'

Joanna was also anxious to avoid antagonizing women. 'With Purdey, I didn't want women getting bitchy about me in the same way that they are about Farrah Fawcett. You know, because she's so lovely, and so sexy and wears push 'em up bras and runs around in shorts all the time.

'Do you wonder I've tried to make Purdey into something more than just wobbling boobs? I don't resent the comparison but I do think it would be madness to model *The Avengers* on the Angels.

If we copy the Americans, instead of doing our own very British thing, then we've had it.'

Purdey's role was, however, made slightly sexier in the second series and there was more of an adult tinge about the programmes. In an episode called 'Obsession' Purdey actually fell for an old flame played by Martin Shaw. Her wardrobe changed in the second series, too. Half of it was French as Rudolf Roffi had requested, and the other half Joanna picked out from Quorum.

Joanna may have laughed at Laurie Johnson's pre-launch prediction that she was to become the hottest female star on British TV but she did not have to wait long to gauge the impact she was making on the millions of viewers tuning in each week. Thames TV was deluged with shoals of fan letters for Joanna who, to this day, modestly puts that huge postbag down to the fact that Purdey was a much less aggressive character than the previous Avengers girls. 'People saw me as less of a threat and therefore the letters were kinder,' she says.

Once *The New Avengers* had hit the screen, Joanna discovered her first flickers of recognition from passers-by and they rapidly progressed to stares, nudges and requests for autographs as the show gathered momentum and her face became increasingly familiar to the public.

What took Joanna and everyone else connected with *The New Avengers* totally by surprise was the way Purdey's distinctive, smooth, mushroom haircut suddenly went to the heads of millions of young girls. Up and down the country hairdressing salons were crammed with clients rushing to get the Purdey look which was essentially a fringe on top, back and sides. This Henry V crop was, of course, the style which Joanna's bosses had initially been so horrified to observe atop the head of their star actress. Now they were not slow to take the credit for having invented it and to exploit it.

Joanna was later to discover just how much she had done for the hairdressing fraternity whilst she was holidaying in the Seychelles. She was approached by a British hairstylist who wanted to thank her for the luxury holiday he was currently enjoying with his wife and two children. 'I'm only here thanks to the Purdey cut,' he gratefully explained. 'Thanks to you, business has never been better.'

While hair salons claimed their own cut of the profits from the show, shops and stores across the country were busy stocking up on *The New Avengers* merchandise. On shop walls and windows Joanna's face stared down from a giant-size poster featuring *The New Avengers* trio of stars. The poster was rapidly snapped up by fans of the series and almost immediately sold out.

On the toy counter, young girl fans of the series could find the official Purdey doll. Ten inches tall, the Purdey doll was packaged in a plastic bubble on a cardboard display board which featured a drawing of Joanna on the cover. The doll was dressed in a purple leotard similar to the one Joanna wore in the first *New Avengers* episode, 'The Eagle's Nest', as well as shoes and a patterned shirt. Other Purdey outfits were advertised on the back of the packaging with the manufacturer's proclamation that 'Purdey leads such an exciting life she needs an outfit for every occasion.'

Young boys were not forgotten either in the marketing of Joanna and *The New Avengers*. For them there was a choice of a Dinky toy or a plastic assembly kit of Purdey's TR7, registration number OGW 562R, the yellow motor car she drove in the second series. Jigsaws, a set of rub-on transfers and a *New Avengers* board game, complete with a bowler hat and an umbrella spinner, all helped to keep the show to the fore.

There was much rejoicing when the series was sold to America for a coast-to-coast screening on the giant CBS network just as the second series was going into production, although it transpired that CBS was never to give it the prime-time slot of its predecessor. Instead it went out on Friday evenings at 11.30 p.m. from September 1978 to March 1979.

For the second season Joanna's fee was significantly increased. 'For an actress to get this role of Purdey is like winning the pools,' Brian Clemens had announced at Joanna's press launch at the Dorchester Hotel. 'She will become quite wealthy from the series.' Now he was able to increase her fee from £600 to £800 per episode and Joanna began squirrelling what she could away to pay for a public school education for Jamie.

After the first six episodes had been shot, the production team moved to France to shoot a further three but then money problems began to beset the show. By the time everyone assembled to start work on the second series it was obvious that the production was in trouble. Promised French funding had failed to materialise and Brian Clemens and Albert Fennell personally paid Joanna's salary and the salary of the other artistes for six episodes. Even though the francs had dried up, they were determined to keep the show going from their own pockets and succeeded until Canada came to the rescue – but with one condition. 'Canada would only put in the money if we shot it in Canada,' recalls Clemens, 'and there's nothing so anti-*Avengers* as Canada. They've got no sense of humour anyway and I always think Canada looks as though the bomb's been dropped on it. It looks very empty on screen.'

But the producers had no choice but to agree and Albert Fennell drew the short straw and went off to Canada with Joanna and the rest of the cast and crew while Clemens remained behind in England working on their new major project, a hard-hitting drama series called *The Professionals*.

In Canada Joanna found the purse strings were being pulled ever tighter on the production. Corners were cut and compromises made but production staggered on and in the midst of growing discomfort Joanna was called upon to perform one of her most demanding scenes yet. On a bitterly cold day she had to subject herself to a severe drenching while going through a car wash.

The storyline involved a vital hand print left on the roof of a car. The hand print is destined to be erased for ever by the powerful water jets of a car wash until Purdey springs into action and gallantly flings herself on to the car to protect the priceless clue.

Chris Jackson, one of the Canadian production team, remembers it well. 'You couldn't help admiring Joanna for going through with it on such a freezing cold day,' he says. 'First she was smothered in a bucket of soapy washing powder so her hair and clothes would all foam up when the water hit her and then she had to go through it all again for the cameras a second time. It looked pretty spectacular but you had to feel so sorry for Joanna when the rest of us were all standing around in coats to keep us from the cold. At the end of it all she emerged drenched, shivering, covered in foam and half choking on the soap suds. She was hosed down by the water jets then stripped down to her underclothes before being whisked off for a hot bath.'

The thirteen episodes for the second series were finally in the can but it was the end for *The New Avengers*. For all its faults and limitations caused by financial problems, the second season still managed to attract a strong following, but the Canadian episodes were generally agreed to have been well below par. 'All three of us would love to have done another thirteen episodes,' Joanna reflected, 'but under very different circumstances. We wanted script control.'

Towards the end Joanna, Gareth Hunt and Patrick Macnee had been disturbed that much of the spoofy humour had been written out and Joanna and Hunt were particularly aware that, as Steed abhorred weapons, it was left to them to blast the villains endlessly. 'I was awfully angry that we tried to kind of sneak into the *Starsky and Hutch* area,' she said. '*The Avengers* had to be British and umbrellas and rain and OK behaviour and I thought we'd rather gone off the feeling that Diana and Patrick achieved, with very tight scripts and very bizarre sort of things.'

Naturally there have been periodic rumours that *The New Avengers* would be resurrected and as the 1970s drew to a close the American network CBS was said to be considering additional shooting for its Late Movie package but that never materialized.

The New Avengers was shown in more than 100 countries and in its heyday generated massive interest in Joanna Lumley particularly on the Continent. In Holland, for example, she was greeted like royalty, and the motorcades and the extraordinary red carpet treatment she received in South Africa she remembers to this day. Albert Fennell died more than a decade ago but Joanna remains great friends with Brian Clemens and Laurie Johnson, the two men who put their faith in her and launched her to stardom.

'What I've always loved about Joanna,' says Johnson, 'is that she takes her work seriously but she doesn't take herself seriously. *The New Avengers* was a launching pad for her. But the talent was always there and she did a wonderful job. Joanna's a one-off. She has a remarkably strong personality and she has an exceptional ability to play caricature which is a very difficult thing to do. She and Gareth Hunt had a great rapport and we would have liked to have seen the two of them go on to do a series together but at the time *The New Avengers* finished we were very wrapped up in *The Professionals* so it never happened.'

More than twenty years on, *The New Avengers* continues to be screened on TV stations around the world and the videos have also proved popular. Joanna still remembers the show with pride and with great affection and gratitude on several levels. 'Because Honor Blackman, Diana Rigg and Linda Thorson had such immense impact, it had become rather like a James Bond role,' Joanna reflected. 'I'd have been dumb not to do it. Sure, you get type-cast, but what a nice way to be type-cast. It was a rare show, wonderfully British, the kind of Britain with an elegant kind of nonchalance that had gone.'

Purdey came to Joanna's rescue at a time when she had almost given up hope of breaking through as an actress and when her financial situation was little short of seriously precarious. She was able to use the money from the show to send Jamie to a preparatory school and then on to top public school Harrow. For two and a half years *The New Avengers* also gave Joanna the priceless opportunity to learn her art in front of a movie camera, and the audience who watched her high-kicking her way to stardom all those years ago have grown up with her and have stayed loyal to her. 'Playing Purdey helped me more than I can say,' Joanna concludes. 'Before that series I was a nothing and a nobody. I appeared more in the gossip columns than anywhere else.'

9

Into the Eighties

'All irregularities will be handled by the forces controlling each dimension. Transuranic heavy elements may not be used where there is life. Medium atomic weights are available: Gold, Lead, Copper, Jet, Diamond, Radium, Sapphire, Silver and Steel. Sapphire and Steel have been assigned.'

These words, eerily spoken above the opening titles to *Sapphire and Steel*, began another chapter in Joanna Lumley's career. Hot on the heels of *The New Avengers*, Joanna was approached in 1979 to star in a science-fiction thriller being made by ATV, the company then holding the Midlands ITV franchise.

Joanna's character, Sapphire, and Steel, played by David McCallum, were two elements sent to earth by a universal power to try to contain a negative force, responsible for all disturbances in the natural order. Steel was the macho, hard-nosed technocrat, a strong being who could block tremendous forces with his body and exert vast power. Sapphire was enigmatic and sensitive, with extra-sensory powers able to switch into other people's thoughts – indicated by her eyes glowing bright sapphire blue. Steel wore a grey flannel suit, while Sapphire was always dressed in blue.

The stories included a search for parents who had vanished while visiting a child's bedroom, a railway station inhabited by ghosts of servicemen, an attack by the spirits of dead animals and a battle against a faceless man who had appeared in every photograph ever taken.

Sapphire and Steel was mysterious, even to those involved in its creation. It offered viewers few neat conclusions or easy explanations to the many weird goings-on. The spooky atmosphere was heightened by claustrophobic lighting and moody music. In a way, the bizarre and dangerous forces faced by Sapphire and Steel, and their complete seriousness in tackling them, was a precursor to series such as today's *The X-Files*.

The series was the brainchild of Peter J. Hammond, a writer who cut his teeth as script editor of *Z-Cars*. *Sapphire and Steel* followed his success on a number of children's shows for Thames Television, notably *Ace of Wands*, in which magical opponents fought against each other in an ordinary English setting.

P.J., as he is known, explained: 'The very first episode of *Sapphire and Steel* was a one-off pilot for a children's series and the then boss of Thames decided it wouldn't run. Then ATV picked it up and realized when it went into production that this could be an adult programme. They told me I could then up it to suit an evening slot. That was very good news. I've always written creepy stuff, I like psychological drama rather than violence, leaving the audience guessing all the time.'

David Reid, head of drama, passed the script to his friend, producer/director Shaun O'Riordan, who had been busy directing ATV boss Lew Grade's *Thriller* series.

Said Shaun: 'David and I trained together and he knew that I was very interested in science generally. He said, "Look I don't know what to make of this, the only person I can think might be interested in it is you. What do you think?"

'I took it away and read three episodes and I was knocked out by them, I thought they were absolutely brilliant. P.J. Hammond was a writer of some note. He had this burning injustice he had to write about and he wrote very vividly, from the balls. It was haunting stuff.

'I went back to David and said: "It's wonderful, but you're going to have to cast it up. It's not worth making *Sapphire and Steel* unless you get star casting." He said he would try and asked me who I was thinking of. So I gave him a list of people, pretty fancy names, and one of them was David McCallum.

'I said: "You've got to put a woman with him who's magic," and then Joanna's name came up. There was no doubt in my mind. I sent scripts to both of them and they both said yes.'

P.J. Hammond was delighted to hear the news. 'Shaun rang me and said: "Guess who we've got?" It was a wonderful surprise to have McCallum and Lumley. They were perfect. I couldn't think of anyone that would be as good. They worked closely together to make the characters gel. That was valuable and it was very unselfish on both their parts.'

Joanna was intrigued by this 'rather different kind of mystery series' and delighted to be off on another major series again, particularly alongside an established star such as David McCallum who, she noted charitably, had hardly changed since he broke so many female hearts as charismatic Illya Kuryakin in *The Man from U.N.C.L.E.*

The first episode went out on ITV on 10 July 1979. In all thirty-four episodes were made, the last of which was transmitted on 31 August 1982. Actors and actresses who guest-starred in the series included Patience Collier, Jeffry Wickham, Christopher Fairbank and Alyson Spiro, now Sarah Sugden in *Emmerdale*. At its height, *Sapphire and Steel* attracted about 22 per cent of the viewing audience, although ratings were affected by a strike at ATV which closed down the ITV regions completely.

P.J. Hammond, who wrote all but one of the adventures, recalled: 'At the moment this sort of programme is fashionable but at the time it was quite a novelty. I think it hooked people. The first six went out and did well. The first two of the next story followed and then there was a strike and it was off air for about three weeks. There was a problem picking it up again and the strike didn't do us a lot of good.'

Producer–director Shaun O'Riordan trained as an actor and began his career in comedies such as *The Larkins* before moving into directing. Over the years they worked together, he developed a deep respect and fondness for Joanna – but was frequently surprised by her.

'One had a feeling of Joanna being a good person. She's very sweet and kind and attentive. She makes most people feel wonderful – that's her gift. She was also very humorous and wry, and her education was apparent. She would come out with Latin tags and quotes the whole time. One felt she'd been to a boy's public school by her general presentation. She should have been a countess or a duchess.

'But Joanna was also a naughty person. She was very wilful. After the first series, where she had blonde hair, she came back with this spiky haircut all reddish and brown. She just turned up to the first rehearsal and my jaw dropped. I said, "Joanna, what the hell's this?" She replied, "Oh, Sapphire can do all things, can't she?" She frightened the life out of me that time. In the end, I think she had to wear a blonde wig.'

Although she took her portrayal of Sapphire very seriously, Joanna's sense of fun shone through behind the scenes. Shaun explained, 'Joanna was very generous, although it was always tinged with naughtiness and you couldn't trust her an inch. After the episode when we tried to make her weep, she gave me a small silver fox about an inch and a half long with "You silver-tongued fox" written underneath it. I think she meant that I fancied myself as a silver-tongued fox but I couldn't persuade her to do anything that she didn't want to do!'

P.J. Hammond, too, was to benefit from Joanna's generous nature: 'At the end of the first series we weren't sure we were going to get a second. Joanna had these wonderful cut glass goblets made with the name Sapphire carved into them and gave them to us. I still have mine today.'

Shaun O'Riordan admits that he didn't foresee the full extent of Joanna's comic talent which was later revealed in *Absolutely Fabulous*. 'Joanna came to me to do *Sapphire and Steel* after she'd been in *The New Avengers*. She was talking one day towards the end of one of the series, saying she wanted to get out of playing straight parts. I said that to make the transition from *The Avengers* and then Sapphire and waltz on to the London stage as a normal human girl might throw the audience. I thought she should make a soft landing into the world of the theatre and play a policewoman in uniform or something normal like that to begin with and then slowly become the sex kitten or whatever.

'I think I offended her and she was very insulted by me saying that. I was proved wrong of course. Because the first thing I seem to remember she did after she left *Sapphire and Steel* was play the ghost in Noel Coward's *Blithe Spirit*, who has to be the sexiest, naughtiest, most feminine creature of recent theatre.

'I didn't see the comedy in her. I saw it in Joanna the girl, but I didn't see it in Joanna the actress. Patsy is the most outrageous piece of comic send-up character that you've ever seen. Trying to sort out Sapphire from that junkie is wonderful. I think she's done incredibly well and she's got incredible talent.'

As ever, Joanna guarded her private life jealously. Although her son Jamie visited the set of *Sapphire and Steel*, she still refused to reveal who his father was.

'She had this amazing secret,' said Shaun O'Riordan. 'She appears to be a very straight up-and-down girl but then again she isn't. She leads a very odd private life which nobody ever knows anything about. We did ask her who her son's father was but she just said: "Nobody you know." It was very deftly put aside. But how did she pay for him to be educated at such a fine school as Harrow? One never knew.'

Despite her protection of Jamie, Joanna was not stand-offish. She enjoyed the company of the largely male production team on *Sapphire and Steel* and chose to spend lunchtimes in the Elstree studio canteen with the cast and crew, rather than alone in her dressing room.

The conversations would cover a variety of topics but one day in particular stayed in Shaun O'Riordan's memory.

'We were sitting at the table and it was a nice, sunny day. We were chatting and laughing and, apart from Joanna, we were all men. Joanna suddenly said, "Do you know what I'd really like? I'd like to have a baby by each of my friends. That would be nice."

'It was said without any lasciviousness or sexual connotation, but she so enjoyed being amongst these people she thought it would be very nice to have a child by each of us. It was the happiness of the moment, a sort of spontaneous way of keeping each of the friends going and keeping them alive. Always her remarks were clean and innocent which was her amazing quality. It wasn't a sexual offer to a group of men, it was very sweet.'

The chemistry between Joanna and David McCallum worked from the start and the pair of them became friends. Shaun O'Riordan said: 'I could never work out if they were having an affair or not because they used to have breakfast together occasionally. I used to try and get information but I never found out.

'But Joanna used to smoke Gauloises and David was the most fastidious man. He wouldn't eat salt with his food, he limited the amount of fat and looked after his body. He took care of himself, so smoking was an absolute anathema to him.'

In fact David McCallum and Shaun O'Riordan became great friends, something Joanna found difficult occasionally.

'Joanna regarded McCallum and me as a kind of male Mafia. She thought we were bullies, determined to run the show as we thought it should be run and ganging up on her. But we were just trying to get it right. I can remember sitting on the floor of my office with McCallum, a pair of scissors and a blue pen cutting up pages of the script, rearranging them and trying to get a sort of end to the first series.'

Shaun, who has retired from programme-making and now teaches at RADA, added: 'Of all the actors I've worked with, McCallum was the one who remained a friend. My first wife loved him dearly and even now, every time he comes to England he comes and stays.'

Special effects were a feature of *Sapphire and Steel* from the start. But with a studio-based production and computer wizardry still in its infancy, achieving the 'tricks', as P.J. Hammond called them, meant long hours in the studio, with the crew frequently giving up their break times to try to get an effect to work.

Sapphire's trademark glowing blue eyes were achieved by an electronic colour separation effect known as chromakey. From a close-up of Joanna, the vision mixer used an invisible mask to select her eyes and then keyed on a colour to make them shine blue. During the various series, the exact shade used was taken from dresses worn by Joanna and a make-up artist.

Originally, though, the sign that Sapphire's psychic powers were at work was to be a vein which would start throbbing in her head.

Shaun O'Riordan explained, 'The make-up girl created this throbbing vein with a rubber patch, but it looked grotesque, it was horrendous – the ugliest, nastiest thing, like a huge growth on her head. That was a disaster because Sapphire had to be elegant and beautiful. We talked endlessly about it and I think

P.J. wanted her eyes to change colour, it all fitted in with her being Sapphire.'

P.J. Hammond added: 'It was very expensive to do the tricks and at the beginning it was all more or less done with a knife and fork. Once we started to put the show out the audience expected tricks and you virtually had to have a trick on every page. Because of the time scale it would be in production while I was still writing episodes and they used to ring me and say what kind of effects they could do, then I'd fit it in. We were surprising ourselves because you could never tell what was going to happen.'

The pressure of the production's fast turnaround and the technical difficulties led Shaun O'Riordan to bring in a second director to share the workload with him. David Foster had a strong background as a cameraman and technician and had worked with Joanna early in her career in *Emergency Ward 10*.

David Foster explained, 'I'd been doing various experiments with special effects on one or two other things and this one was really a challenge because we were doing special effects which hadn't been used before in television.

'It was one of those things where the less you explained, the more mysterious it gets. So I couldn't say we ever knew exactly where *Sapphire and Steel* came from or where they were going. That was where P.J. Hammond was so good. He could suggest these things and they all worked. None of us completely understood what he was talking about, in fact half the time he said he didn't know where it had come from! But it just fell together.

'It was a very happy team. We all found ourselves on the same wavelength. When we got in the studio the crew was very keen, very good at suggesting ways of getting things right and making sure they worked.

'The funny thing was that the last series was delayed. By the time it went out we could have done a lot of the effects easily in about three minutes in the editing suite. It took at least two or three hours in the studio.'

Like many of her colleagues, David Foster was very impressed with Joanna's professionalism: 'Jo was marvellous to work with. There were no temperaments. She just got on with it. She didn't mind what she had to do to get the thing right. I think she is completely professional and completely straight. She and David McCallum believed in the script and unless you do that nothing works. None of us felt we were doing a send-up, we were making the script work. They joined in and that was why it worked so well.

'*Sapphire and Steel* had some gentle humour. Quite often Sapphire would be ahead of Steel and he would be left running after her. In theory, his character thought he was in charge but quite often found he wasn't.

'Jo had one very painful scene where this creeping darkness had taken her over. As we move in on her she's reacting to stress, then she opens her eyes and they're completely black. This meant wearing contact lenses that covered her entire eyeball which were very painful. She had to put in these huge contact lenses and she couldn't see at all.

'On another occasion we debated quite a lot among the production team as to whether we should see her as she'd been dealt with by this particular creeping force. She and I thought we should keep it as in the minds of the viewers, but Shaun decided that we should see her face. This meant having her covered in a mixture of spaghetti and raw minced meat. She didn't mind at all.'

Joanna's skill in a scene set in a derelict railway station is one which David particularly remembers: 'She had to come into the room and see a fresh rose on the far side. The script called on her to walk over to the rose and as she walked towards it her clothes changed into a 1917 costume. To do that we had to shoot it twice and she had to do the same walk in different clothes. I asked her if she'd like some marks, but she said, "No I think we can do it." So we did the first walk, then she went away and changed, then did the second walk.

'When we came to do the edit when we had to make the clothes change, I assumed there would be somewhere in the middle where the walk matched. In fact it matched all the way across, she'd matched herself completely. The editor, while we were playing with it, did the clothes change about six times. We didn't need that, but that was the sort of actress she was.

'Also, she had a mind for getting on top of the script. We were doing a lot of things out of order because of set changes and I apologized for her having to react to something before it had happened. She said, "Oh that's no bother; when I was doing *The Avengers* we did scenes from six episodes in one day once."

'She was very good at somehow suggesting the forces she was fighting when in fact there was nothing there to actually play against. We had one scene with a man with no face in a very strange house. The crunch between the two of them came when this character was changing shape at the bottom of the staircase, trying to overcome her, and she was just staring at him and willing him not to win.

'She knew what was happening and knew what she was going to see but there was nothing there at the time. At the end of it she was looking absolutely limp as if she'd run twenty-five miles.'

David Foster added: 'She had a different hairstyle for every series. It was a softer one than Purdey and longer. At that time she wanted to do something different. She wasn't bothered with being Purdey but she didn't want to be just Purdey.

'We were all very pleased when she got *Ab Fab*. In that one she didn't mind looking a slag. I think that sums up her attitude to the business. "Whatever it needs, I'll do it." So often people just want a smudge of dirt. On *Absolutely Fabulous*, I remember the scene where they had the explosion in the kitchen and she came up covered in soot. That really is her to a tee.

'The cameras love her. She was a very pleasant and quite attractive young lady when you worked with her on the floor but the camera just went for her. You'd go into editing and she just shone. She still does, she comes across as a complete person in the same way that a lot of people can't.

'The only time she got cross was with her various causes, the green causes. When it came to working she was very much in control and calm. She was a joy to work with. When she won her BAFTA I wrote and said I was glad she'd been recognized. It must have been about fifteen years later but she wrote back and said how much she'd enjoyed *Sapphire and Steel*.'

In fact, Joanna's concerns for the environment and living creatures were to inspire P. J. Hammond in writing the series. He said, 'I've always been vegetarian and Joanna was very ecologically minded and cared about animals. That inspired me in the second series when I wrote one episode about animals getting their revenge. She really believed in that one.'

Of course there were times when the stress of the job got the better of Joanna. Glen Cardno, film editor on the series who went on to produce *A Kind of Living*, *Apollo* and *The Day I Nearly Died*, recalled, 'There's one image of Joanna which makes me laugh. Shaun invited me to pop along to rehearsals one day. I didn't want to spoil the atmosphere, so I just sat on the windowsill, but I was right in Joanna's eye-line.

'They were doing a scene where Joanna has to break down and cry because there is a rift in time. She started to break down. I don't know whether it was because I as a strange entity was sitting in her eye-line just in the background or what, but she went: "Oh, for ****'s sake, I can't do this. I don't understand it Shaun, I really don't ****ing understand it."

'Shaun just asked, "How would you play it, Joanna?" which I loved him for. She pulled herself back in again and started to do it from right inside very quietly and I tiptoed out. But for me to see her swear and get cross was not at all what you expect.'

Glen added, 'After that she became quite friendly. I can remember sitting on the roof of ATV House on a cold morning wearing these multi-coloured gloves which were very in and Joanna came over wearing identical ones. She said, "Where did you get your gloves?" I said, "Oh, John Lewis I think, where did you get yours?" She said, "The Mill in Scotland, you know, that's where they make them." It just cracked me up.

'*Sapphire and Steel* gives you a really intimate view of Joanna because the camera goes right up close and you realize how sexy she is. You see the caring side of the character, as opposed to just the physically sexy one like in *The New Avengers*.

'Joanna is incredibly bright, she's not an idiot or a bimbo, she's actually a very intelligent woman. She plays the game awfully well. She's come up the hard way and anyone who's done that tends not to lose the knack of talking to people.

'I don't think it's manners with Joanna, it's just breeding. She's the sort of woman who enjoys people and is comfortable with them. A lot of good-looking women I suspect get a bit twitchy with a lot of men around them, because they don't know who's going to hit on them. She's totally in charge. You wouldn't dream of hitting on her. I wouldn't want those blue eyes turning on me. I'd just fall through a hole in the floor!'

Sapphire and Steel met their end when executive changes at ATV brought in a new programming policy. The company then lost its franchise to Central and the final series was transmitted months after the demise of ATV. Ironically, the final scenes saw the duo, along with another element, Silver, played by David Collings, trapped by their enemies in the infinite void of space.

Home videos of *Sapphire and Steel* were released in the early 1990s, a decade after its run ended, sparking fresh interest. Most recently, the series lives on through the Internet, with several sites set up in tribute, providing fans with information on the making and transmission of each episode, 'fan fiction' taking the characters into new adventures and photographs, some even featuring Sapphire's eyes glowing blue.

P.J. Hammond, who has since worked on *The Bill*, *Wycliffe*, *Dr Finlay*, *Perfect Scoundrels* and the Ruth Rendell adaptations said, 'It's one thing I've done that doesn't go away. It's zany and culty. I've got a whole cabinet full of fan letters. People who have grown up and are still fans and new people, kids and teenagers who've seen it. They send these questionnaires and pictures, asking me what Sapphire did next and about the other characters that were never used, like Brass and Copper. So it lives with them.

'It is something that I'm very fond of. There is a possibility it may be repeated on Channel 4 and I think it would go down a bomb. There are also talks of reviving it and doing it again.'

Ever since she had set her heart on becoming an actress, Joanna Lumley had looked forward to playing Shakespeare, and so she was delighted when the Old Harrovian Players offered her the role of Rosalind in a one-off performance of *As You Like It*. A complete contrast to *Sapphire and Steel*, it was to leave Joanna with a most unwanted legacy – stage fright, a fear which she was not to conquer for almost ten years.

To be fair, for much of those ten years Joanna was busy working in major television series and films and was therefore often unavailable for theatre work, but the stage fright which kept her off the boards for so long can be traced back to her contracting viral meningitis while rehearsing for *As You Like It*. The onset of the disease came in the run up to the performance which, however, Joanna bravely managed to struggle through before succumbing to her illness and taking to her sickbed.

Explaining just how badly it affected her Joanna said, 'Viral meningitis is a horrible brain disease which rather robs you of the powers of memory and so I had a fear that not only would I forget my lines and dry but I wouldn't even remember what play I was in! Which could be a distressing evening in the theatre for the audience. So I was off the stage for ten years. Then suddenly a play came up and I said, "Yes, I'd love it." But I just became afraid.

'Despite all of this, I eventually agreed to do the play even though I was going through this dreadful period of stage fright and I had a massive lack of self-confidence. It was just because I had been off the stage for so long. It's the most ghastly feeling, I can tell you: when you know that you have to go on and do the entire play and your heart is hammering. Eventually I did appear again in front of a speaking, breathing public. I didn't lose my nerve. And now I think it's the greatest fun. I love it.'

Confidence eventually restored, throughout the 1980s Joanna set herself a target to appear regularly in stage plays and her comeback in an eleven-week tour of *Private Lives* in 1981 remains memorable for the extraordinary manner in which comedy unpredictably turned into black farce.

For the first half of the tour Noel Coward's comedy of bad manners went smoothly, with Joanna playing Amanda Prynne, the glamorous role Coward wrote for Gertrude Lawrence, and James Villiers playing Elyot Chase, the clever part he wrote for himself. James Villiers was best-known for playing languid, witty and sometimes arrogant fops. His lordly manner was not all pose since he claimed he was descended from George Villiers, Duke of Buckingham. However, real drama was in store when the production moved on to the Alhambra Theatre in Bradford, Yorkshire, seven weeks into the tour.

As a slice of theatre, *Private Lives* offered a night of escapism for an almost full house who had paid good money at a time when industrial Yorkshire was gripped by the recession. Joanna was an obvious draw, and as the audience took their seats there were many who were there to see the actress from *The New Avengers* in person, live, and on stage.

The first act had Joanna, resplendently dressed in 1930s period costume, and Villiers sipping cocktails and trading typical Coward *bons mots* on the terrace of a French seaside hotel. The laughter from the audience indicated to both that all was going well, and as the first act drew to a close Joanna and Villiers confidently delivered their final lines and made their stage exit together.

As they reached the wings Villiers suddenly clutched his leg, his face contorting with pain. 'Bloody hell! You kicked me,' he said, grimacing and casting a look of thunder at a bewildered Joanna. She could not believe what her co-star was saying. She was absolutely certain her shoe had made no contact whatsoever with her co-star's leg. 'James was hopping about saying I had kicked him on the calf,' she said. 'I helped him back to the dressing room and offered to massage his calf but James was seething and wouldn't let me touch him.'

In the circumstances Joanna decided it would be best if she went off to her own dressing room for her quick costume change and then returned to try and help Villiers. By then, she hoped, his mood might have changed and she prayed that no real harm had been done to his leg.

Villiers was in slightly better humour by the time Joanna rejoined him although he was still insisting the toe cap of her shoe had done the damage. Joanna remained astonished at the accusation, totally convinced she had not even touched him. But there was no time to argue the point. Worryingly for everyone but most of all for Villiers, after much massaging of his calf he hauled himself painfully to his feet and announced to Joanna, 'Darling, I can't walk.'

Gamely, and in the true traditions of showbusiness, Villiers decided the show must go on and he half hopped, half limped his way back on to the stage for the second act. But, incapacitated as he was, Villiers was unable to perform much of what the script required. He was unable to dance, unable to get up and open and shut doors and confined himself to speaking his lines while sitting on the sofa. When he did drag himself to his feet and limped to a table to pour a brandy, the audience started to realize something was very wrong.

Act Three required much movement from Villiers and by now it was evident to everyone that he had badly hurt himself. Poor Joanna was left to give him as much on stage support as she could. She knew she was in no way responsible for Villiers's injury but as he was so insistent she was to blame she couldn't help feeling some sort of guilt.

Somehow the show tottered on to the finale, and when the curtain came down Joanna accompanied James Villiers to the casualty department of Leeds Infirmary. There, to their incredulity, they were informed he would have to wait for two hours before he could be attended to 'because people are coming in with broken bottles sticking out of their heads'. Despite being in such pain Villiers decided he was not prepared to wait that long and that he would be better off going home and seeking specialist advice in the morning.

The following day Villiers was diagnosed as having a ruptured calf muscle. While she naturally had great sympathy for him, Joanna was relieved when the doctor cited that a symptom of such damage was often an impression by the victim of being kicked in the calf. Joanna's relief that she was, after all, blameless and that Villiers would recover with complete rest was tempered by the fact that if the *Private Lives* tour was to continue, a new co-star was required to play Elyot Chase opposite her.

Next night, a Saturday, the company manager bravely stepped into the breach but once the show was over there was much soul-searching about what now would be for the best. At the Theatre Royal in Newcastle, the next leg of the tour, posters had already gone up announcing the imminent arrival of *Private Lives*. Joanna gallantly chose to go back to London to help settle James Villiers into his home before going on to her own flat where she would wait to be informed whether the tour was still on.

That Saturday night Simon Cadell, an actor then becoming hugely popular playing dithering holiday camp entertainments manager Jeffrey Fairbrother in the BBC's TV sit-com *Hi-de-Hi*, was dining with friends in West London when he got a telephone call asking him if he would answer the emergency by taking over the role of Elyot for the rest of the tour. He had played Elyot in a previous *Private Lives* production at Birmingham. Ever the trouper, Cadell agreed but as soon as he put the phone down he decided he must be out of his mind. He had even agreed to join the tour for the opening night in Newcastle on the Monday.

Cadell got up early on Sunday morning to give himself as much time as possible to refamiliarize himself with the role of Elyot and it was arranged that he should meet Joanna at King's Cross station on the Monday morning for the 10 a.m. train to Newcastle. As luck would have it the train was packed and the two stars of *Private Lives* finished up in the buffet car running through the play together. 'The most frightening part of it was getting to the theatre and knowing it was for real,' said Joanna.

But the drama was not quite over. The message to Birmingham Rep to send on Simon Cadell's Elyot clothes to Newcastle had somehow not got through quickly enough and his costumes were therefore not expected to arrive in time for curtain up. There was only one thing for it, Cadell would have to go on stage in his thoroughly modern suit, tie and sneakers.

In light of the frenzied activity of the weekend, the play's director James Roose-Evans went on stage on the opening night to tell the Newcastle audience of the extraordinary events that had befallen the production and to ask for their understanding. His explanation was so eloquently delivered with such wit and charm that he had the audience eating out of his hand and they were warming to the play before they had even heard the first note of Coward's opening overture.

Simon Cadell's entrance was greeted with a roar of applause and Joanna remembers, 'We went through the play on a rare bubble of love and support from the audience.' Cadell slipped so effortlessly into the role that by the Wednesday Joanna found herself having the 'nerve and blind insensitivity' to nag Cadell about not shutting a door behind him.

The following year saw Joanna playing Gertrude Lawrence in fringe theatre at the King's Head, Islington, in *Noel and Gertie*, a stylish musical devised by Sheridan Morley which explored Noel Coward's friendship with Gertrude based on their memoirs. Joanna donned a brown wig to play Gertie and looked strikingly beautiful in a silver and white chiffon, *diamanté*-studded gown with a plunging backline. Designer David Shilling made the gown especially for Joanna with sixteen godets of sheer chiffon in the skirt and a deep, dipping backline dramatically veiled with a cowl of silk.

While a show like *Noel and Gertie* was light and enjoyable for Joanna, she also worked hard to dispel any lingering illusions or doubts that might have remained that she was serious about her acting. Roles in *The Curse of the Pink Panther* and *Trail of the Pink Panther*, two of the weakest of the movies in the Peter Sellers series of comedies about the bumbling French detective Clouseau, cannot have helped her cause. But the fees she earned from those roles and others in TV projects like the American mini-series *Mistral's Daughter* and a part as a high class prostitute in the film *Shirley Valentine* did, however, allow her to accept the much smaller wages offered by the theatre.

Joanna took on *Hedda Gabler* in Dundee for her own satisfaction, and it elicited the following review from the *Daily Mail*'s theatre critic Jack Tinker: 'Dundee can boast as fine and true a performance of Ibsen's notoriously knotted heroine Hedda Gabler as I ever expect to alight on anywhere. I can only add that I have seldom seen a clearer, more comprehensible account of that woman's moral cowardice than in Miss Lumley's splendid and haughty restraint.'

Joanna was thrilled to receive a call early in 1984 to appear alongside Rod Steiger, one of her Hollywood heroes, who was to star with Anthony Perkins in Yorkshire Television's ambitious three-part mini-series *The Glory Boys*, based on the thriller by Gerald Seymour set in the murky world of international espionage and terrorism. But before she took up the role she was given one of her more demanding and appealing instructions. She must look plain, frumpy and unattractive at all times as homely Helen, secretary to British security chief Philip Jones, who was to be played by Alfred Burke, once famous as Frank Marker in *Public Eye*.

It was anything but the usual glamour role, which delighted Joanna who was heartily sick of being expected to do little more than pout and look decorative. As she started work on the role Joanna said, 'She is just dull little Helen. Her hair is dirty because she does not have much time to wash it. She goes about all the time looking a muck. This is not a glamorous role and one has to play it as such.' Writer Seymour enthused, 'Anyone who works in a large office would know of the Helens of this world as played by Joanna. They are real people, unsung people, and they are brewing tea outside the boss's office every day.'

But the part was made more interesting because Helen was locked in a torrid affair with sinister Jimmy, the ageing but still ruthlessly efficient British secret agent with a drink problem. Jimmy had the tedious task of preventing Rod Steiger's character, Professor David Sokarev, a top Israeli nuclear physicist, from being bumped off by the two deadly assassins who were on his trail. The deeply unlikely story revolved around a mysterious new alliance between the IRA and fanatical Palestinian freedom fighters. Seymour said of Joanna's character, 'Helen is a good, tough girl who keeps Jimmy on the rails. Life is littered with men like him who are kept on the rails by good, tough ladies.' For Tony Perkins he could not have spoken a truer word.

Perkins, who spent much of his life trying to forget his astonishing early success playing clean-cut college-kid killer Norman Bates, who wielded the knife in the memorable shower scene in Alfred Hitchcock's *Psycho*, was interviewed on location at Manchester Airport by one of the authors. 'I've had more enjoyable jobs,' said the anxious actor surveying the rain and his frequently changing shooting schedule, 'but what has made this job worth flying over for is a lady called Joanna Lumley. I guess you know her pretty well but to me she's been a revelation. I've never met anyone who surprised me so much.

'I had seen a picture of her, sent by the producer, and I was expecting a real tight-ass. How wrong can you be? We hit it off right away. I especially warmed to her because she didn't once mention knives and showers and all that crap. She was just warm and natural and very funny. We joked about the differences between our languages, what a crazy business acting is as I prepared to pretend to go out and shoot some guy I'd never met, and about our friends and families.

'I've got a reputation for being nervous and a shade screwed up and I guess I can become a little tense. But working with Joanna was just about the most relaxing thing I've done in a long time. Our love scenes were a hell of a long way from being over passionate but I was still dreading them. Joanna's sense of fun made me forget all that and stop taking myself so seriously. That smile can melt your heart without even trying and I was downright astonished to find she's just the sort of dame I could really go for in a big way. She certainly knows how to turn a guy on when it comes to playing at lovers. I had to pinch myself to remember we were still acting when she felt like she was really coming on to me. She's a real classy lady and she taught me that maybe there's a whole lot more to the English upper classes than I thought. Best thing about her was that she treated everyone the same. She'd just as soon yarn to one of the gophers as to me or Steiger. Funny thing was she really wanted to work with Steiger but her scenes were all with me.'

10
Marriage and Revelations

Joanna Lumley was feeling distinctly unwell as the car in which she was a front seat passenger wound its way over the Pennines in a snowstorm, its windscreen wipers defiantly flicking fast falling flakes of snow to left and right.

It wasn't the weather that had Joanna feeling below par. She was suffering from an unpleasant bout of food poisoning and she was looking forward to reaching the railway station and the chance to settle herself into a corner seat in a warm carriage for a train journey taking her back south.

It was then that the driver chose his moment to cheer her up considerably. He asked Joanna to marry him. 'I said yes,' Joanna joyfully recalled to one of the authors, 'after a subtle thirty-second pause!' Then Joanna boarded the train, sat down and thought to herself, 'Gosh, I'm going to get married to Stephen Barlow.'

As well as experiencing a feeling of great excitement, Joanna's innermost emotion was one of relief. It was as if a personal photo negative which she had been expecting to develop over the past nineteen years was now at last coming sharply into focus.

The picture was finally complete some six months later on 23 October 1986, at a register office in Fort William in the Scottish highlands. Joanna, now forty, elegantly attired in a pink floral dress with matching pink tights and red shoes, exchanged her wedding vows with the gifted, bearded operatic conductor Stephen Barlow, eight years her junior, standing proudly by her side.

In accordance with the couple's wishes for privacy, registrar Mrs

Janet Gallon had loyally kept Joanna's wedding to Stephen a closely guarded secret. Only sixteen close family members and friends and a handful of housewives and a group of inquisitive shop girls saw them emerge into the pale autumn sunlight as man and wife. It was three hours before the newspapers had caught up with the newlyweds, by which time they were enjoying a celebratory drink at Inverlochy Castle.

The marriage was, and remains, a union which Joanna believes was somehow always meant to be. The very mention of the name Stephen Barlow, she remembers, made her heart inexplicably thump when she heard it for the first time when she was twenty-one. Why it did so she could not understand at the time because she was then twenty-one and the name Stephen Barlow belonged to a mere boy of thirteen she had not even met.

Joanna had first heard of Stephen while visiting the Armitages, family friends who lived at Godmersham near Canterbury in Kent. On one of Joanna's visits it was announced that the Armitages' son St Clair was bringing a school friend home with him for Sunday lunch, a boy called Stephen Barlow.

'For some reason he never turned up,' Joanna recalls. 'I can remember feeling terribly disappointed that I wasn't going to meet this boy. But even then that struck me as odd. I was eight years older than this child and I had never met him. But the name Stephen Barlow burned into me or it came from me as if it was a memory for the future if you can imagine something as strange as that.'

More than a decade later Joanna was delighted to accept an invitation to St Clair's wedding in Devon and she took the train to Dawlish where she was met at the end of her journey by members of the Armitage family who took her on to the church. As she stepped through the porch into the church in her turquoise coat, Joanna saw a man with a white face and very black hair at the organ and just at that moment he turned round and looked straight at her. 'It was as though someone had pushed me sharply in the chest with a great bang,' she says. 'I felt like I'd had some kind of electric shock. It wasn't a matter of falling instantly in love, it was the impact of a colossal shock, completely memorable.'

It was not, however, the most propitious moment for Joanna

Lumley to meet Stephen Barlow because he was frantically and irately rummaging through sheaves of sheet music, with an angry scowl spreading darkly across his face. Joanna was nevertheless introduced to Stephen and she quickly ascertained why he bore such a look of thunder. He had been conducting *The Rake's Progress* the previous night in Norwich and he was due to go on to work in Southampton the next day so he had arrived in a highly tired and emotional state and had forgotten to bring the music for the wedding which was 'Zadok the Priest' and 'The Arrival of the Queen of Sheba'. Now he was feverishly looking through the church's own collection of music to see if he could find copies and he was grateful when Joanna offered to help.

The wedding ceremony passed off successfully and the reception was followed by a party which stretched long into the night. But just as Stephen was realizing that he really ought to go to bed because he had a concert the following night, the bridegroom's sister brought word that Joanna would like to talk to him and together they briefly chatted about music before going their separate ways.

Their paths did not cross again until a mutual friend invited them both to a first night party for a play starring Joanna's former flatmate, actress Jane Carr. Stephen remembers Joanna turning up in a flashy black Renault 5 and wondering whether he would be able to cope with all the theatricality of the occasion.

They went out to dinner afterwards and Stephen spent the night in Joanna's former au pair's room. In the morning he was off and away which, since Joanna was still very much involved with Michael Kitchen, did not at the time concern her one iota. And yet when she later heard news from the Armitage family that Stephen had married a singer she found herself shocking both herself and them with the petulant comment, 'How stupid, how ridiculous.'

Communication between Joanna and Stephen continued only by Christmas cards until one day in 1984 he found himself rehearsing with the Chelsea Opera Group in Addison Road, Holland Park, and it struck him that it was the street where Joanna lived. He left a note saying, 'How's life?'

'We bumped apart again like ships,' says Joanna, 'and then the great net drew us closer together and for the first time we ran across each other and although we only talked and Stephen would drop in for tea, finally we got to know each other and it became apparent, we both agreed, that it was exactly as if each of us had found our other half.'

When Stephen asked Joanna to be his wife she admits that she liked the idea of marriage, but her main concern was that she might find it very difficult to live with someone. 'After all,' she said, 'apart from my first marriage, and that hardly counts, I'd lived on my own all my adult life. I thought I'd be very set in my ways and that I'd find living with someone very oppressive. But it proved to be the easiest thing in the world.'

Joanna was also determined that this time her marriage was going to work. She recognized she simply didn't have the emotional stamina for it to go wrong. 'When I met Stephen I wasn't looking for anyone,' she said. 'I wasn't fussed about getting involved, all of which probably helped. I'd loosened up rather than trying too hard to make it work which is hopeless. It's very odd with Stephen because I think he's the only man in the world I could have married and he's the only man who wanted to marry me.

'It took me a long time to find Mr Right because in my profession there are so many good-looking and talented people, it's terribly hard to choose the one you want to stay with for ever. With Stephen it was not only a case of eyes meeting across a crowded room but something deeper as well. An inner voice told me he was the one and when that happens you've got to go with it because your heart is open and you feel marvellous. The first thing that struck me about him was his enormous enthusiasm for life. He's full of attack and passion and intensely good-humoured.'

When Joanna and Stephen initially decided to get married they found Joanna's Holland Park flat too cramped for the two of them and they took a series of temporary homes while Stephen waited for his divorce to come through. After their marriage Joanna and Stephen went back to their Kentish roots and bought a rambling seven-bedroom eighteenth-century parsonage at Goodnestone, near Ramsgate, with a delightful garden and steeped in history. M.R. James was born there when his father was perpetual curate of the parish.

The house was in the middle of an estate where Joanna delighted in finding that pheasants would strut confidently to her door waiting for her to feed them with peanuts and bird seed she had bought specially.

It was an idyllic three years for Joanna and Stephen in the county known as the Garden of England. But living so deep into Kent had its disadvantages when it came to Joanna's and Stephen's working lives. 'That part of Kent was so badly served by trains,' she says, 'and I'd sometimes spend up to five hours in the car going up to London to do a voice-over which took just ten minutes. So I sat down and thought about it and decided life was too short to spend that long in a car.'

When the old lilac tree in the garden produced a most glorious blossom then keeled over, it seemed like a sign that it was time to move on. Theirs was an elegantly beautiful period home and so it was with much reluctance that Joanna and Stephen put it up for sale and started looking for a new home in London. They were not hopeful of a quick buyer as the housing market had come almost to a standstill but they found a purchaser within three weeks of the house going on the market and sold it for a reported £380,000.

When the day finally came to move out, Joanna knew how much she would miss the wonderful herb garden, the heavily scented old roses, the bird sounds, the corn coming up, and enquiring whether the hop harvest had been good.

But although her love affair with the Kent countryside would never diminish, Joanna was at the same time relishing returning to London. 'I always feel now that London is my adopted city,' she says. 'I first came to London at eighteen and I feel it's my town, I understand it.' In May 1991, she and Stephen moved into a five-storey house in Stockwell in south London, big enough for them both to have separate rooms in which to work, and five years later they also bought a country cottage hideaway in the wilds of Dumfriesshire in Scotland.

When Joanna married Stephen she was fully aware that his work as a conductor would take him all over the world. In Britain he has worked with all the major orchestras, including the London Philharmonic and the English Chamber Orchestra. But his international standing has also taken him to New Zealand for two months for *Madame Butterfly*, to Brisbane for *Rigoletto*, to Vancouver, and back to England for concerts with Dame Kiri Te Kanawa at the Hampton Court Festival.

Joanna knew their respective demanding careers would often mean long separations but she also knew she would cope and she looked forward eagerly to Stephen's daily faxes written in his own hand from afar. 'We don't worry about what the other is doing or we wouldn't have got married,' she said.

While filming *Lovejoy*, Joanna took time to express the happiness she had found with Stephen during the four years they had been married. 'If you're lucky, and I guess I am, romance continues wildly after marriage because you're wildly in love,' she said. 'In other people's lives maybe they get bored stiff and go off and have an affair. Not me, babe.

'There are times when I hardly ever see Stephen. I'm here and he's there, just back from Vancouver, then off to Melbourne to do *The Magic Flute* for two and a half months, then back to Vancouver again. But it is wildly romantic. Every time we see each other it's fantastic. It's catching up on all the news and spending most of our salaries on phone calls.'

By the time she was celebrating a decade of marriage, Joanna had become used to her husband working so hard in every corner of the globe. 'We think we rush about as actors,' she told one of the authors, 'but in the music world it happens more so. But the great thing is that Stephen and I know each other's lives very well. When he's rehearsing I know there's no point in my being there because he works from 9 a.m. till 10.30 at night so there's no point my sitting in a hotel in Brisbane with him panicking about what I'm doing there.

'So what I try and do is get out to wherever he is once the performances have started. Then he's conducting every two or three days and we have a chance to see things. But it doesn't always work because films and TV projects come up for me. But I'm watchful because we as actors and musicians don't get weekends off and it's too easy to get caught up in the work thing where you actually can work every day of your life and then you find your life isn't there. You haven't got a life, you're just working. The last holiday Stephen and I had together was four days three years ago, so it's a difficulty more and more of forward planning because jobs blow up like storm clouds, whole films blow up in three weeks because suddenly the money falls into place and it's all systems go and suddenly you have to go. It's really hard to plan. Often the one job I want to do happens to be when I really want to go off and just be camp follower with my husband. So it is hard but these are luxurious grumbles. We should be so lucky.'

When she was a little girl, Joanna remembers that her grandmother used to tell her that when she married she must take as a husband someone whom she could love like a brother. Joanna could never understand what her grandmother meant. She thought it was an extraordinary thing to say because, of course, as a young and unworldly teenager, the men she went for were attractive to her because of their looks. But in her maturity with Stephen Barlow, Joanna began to understand granny's advice.

'I think marriage works if you marry your best friend,' she said. 'What you've got to do is stick with somebody who's going to be your best friend for ever, your closest ally and confidant. Someone you can trust, someone you'll do anything for and you've somehow got to sense all that through the passion. You've got to be clever enough to perceive that and not just be caught up with the handsome face.

'I think marriage has made me 180 times happier and much more confident about a lot of things. Everyone can see that. There's also an emotional security. I was unmarried for a long time – I think to say I was on my own for a long time makes me sound a little wistful.

'Second marriages are happier because the first one went wrong and I think you are doubly keen for it not to go wrong the second time. I do think marriage is terrific if you can get it right. If you can't get it right don't get married. I think there is too much emphasis on "Why don't you get married?" Nonsense. Much better to have happy solitude than a messy marriage.'

Joanna enjoyed sixteen years of largely happy solitude until she married Stephen. By any reckoning, the marriage is extraordinary given that Stephen somehow managed to make Joanna's heart thump with excitement when she was twenty-one and he was a thirteen-year-old schoolboy and they had not even met. It is little wonder that Joanna believes they were always destined to be husband and wife.

It's also one of the little ironies in the life of Joanna Lumley that millions of television viewers would have been very happy to see her become Mrs Barlow back in 1973. That was when Joanna enjoyed her short stint in *Coronation Street* playing Elaine Perkins, and Ken Barlow, played by Bill Roache, asked her to marry him. Joanna declined – but then perhaps she somehow sensed that one day she would become Mrs Barlow for real.

On the West End stage Joanna appeared in Alan Ayckbourn's *Revengers'* comedies, at Chichester in *An Ideal Husband* and at Dundee Rep in Ibsen's *The Cherry Orchard* and *Hedda Gabler*, a performance which was highly acclaimed and which Joanna still rates as probably her very best. 'I loved it,' she says. 'There's nothing to beat brilliant writing. Nothing. She was most unlike me in that I'm not a suicidal character. She was a snob, a moral coward and raging, at the end of her tether.'

In 1986 she resumed her association with Noel Coward and once again found herself acting opposite Simon Cadell, this time in London at the Vaudeville Theatre in the Strand in *Blithe Spirit*, Coward's greatest commercial success with a longevity beaten only by *The Mousetrap*.

This production had Marcia Warren as the dotty suburban spiritualist who unexpectedly calls back a wraith, Elvira, who has died young, laughing at a BBC music programme. She brings back Elvira, played by Joanna, to haunt her urbane former husband Charles, played by Cadell.

The critics had almost unanimous praise for Joanna and she collected some of the best stage reviews of her career. 'Enter Joanna Lumley like a panther on a diet and in the ultimate stages of sophistication and things begin to look up at once,' said the *Sunday Times*.

'Joanna Lumley makes a stunningly incandescent Elvira in spite of her deathly pallor,' said the *London Evening Standard*. 'Thoroughly enjoyable . . . the apparition of Joanna Lumley's svelte grey Elvira, whose elegant curvature is both exotic in itself and a skeletal intimation of mortality,' commented the *Financial Times*.

The *Observer*, too, gave some glowing descriptions of Joanna. 'Kitted out like some tall fantasy doll in white face, glittery grey chiffon and full scarlet lips ... Miss Lumley is particularly good (and even funny) in meltingly languid mime and murmured aside.'

With the warmth of the success of her marriage around her Joanna used the late 1980s to diversify. Her elegantly crafted journalism brought her an offer to write a regular column for *The Times*, which she managed to produce beautifully without ever revealing too much about the private Ms Lumley. Her enthusiasm for good causes knew no bounds as she cheerfully believed that instead of endlessly complaining about her celebrity status, like so many of her contemporaries, it was her duty to use it to benefit others.

But the broader she spread her considerable talents the more the whispers of criticism grew. They were voiced publicly by her friend, the deeply uncontroversial Irishman Terry Wogan, with whom Joanna was building an understanding. As she popped in to his thrice-weekly show the host asked her with uncharacteristic candour, 'Why don't you stick to anything for very long?'

Joanna's smile scarcely flickered, but taken off-guard she answered thoughtfully and a great deal more frankly than most of Wogan's other guests: 'One of the reasons why one tends not to come on *Wogan* is that one is abused. It isn't that I don't stick at anything for very long. It's just that I have a lot of interests and I find it terribly difficult just not to be interested in things when they crop up. I love more and more things. I just try to cram them all in, whether it's charity work, writing, acting on TV or acting on the stage.

'In fact I am in a play at the moment at Chichester. I have just travelled to Shepherd's Bush very quickly to see you, Mr Wogan. I was going to say how fast I had driven but I'd better not. I did drive quickly ... and I brought my new husband with me. Tonight he is following me around. Usually it is I who follow him. I follow him around sort of dog-like. He is a brilliant orchestral conductor. Luckily I love music. I always loved classical music but I didn't know anything about it. I was a complete amateur. And I knew very little about opera. I'm learning now and it's wonderful.

'I think that you should only really marry one person and you should only marry the right person. And this is the right person. They're not everywhere. They're hard to find. Well, not hard to find. That looks as though you are looking for them. It's just that if you meet somebody who you must marry, you must marry them. I met Stephen actually a long time before we got married. I met him and even that was a bit of a bolt from the blue. I met him at somebody else's wedding where he was playing the organ. He's a brilliant organist.

'I used to fiddle about on the piano by ear but now I've got Stephen to play the piano properly at home I don't have to do that. I just say, "I think a little Chopin", and he can play it. We kept the wedding pretty much of a secret. We both did that on purpose because the press have slightly changed their complexion, I think, over the past five years. They tend not to be just agreeable monitors of what's going on, but they like to take things in their own hands and put a slant on things. And on very important occasions you don't really want a slant.

'In the old days you had to give a lot of interviews. They always wanted to know something about your private life. So I'd say I can't really answer that but I've got a wonderful recipe for yoghurt make-up. And they'd sort of go, "Oh yes, do tell me." I'd say, "Well, you get a pot of yoghurt . . ." and come out with some awful recipe which was completely made up and they'd feel they had an answer. This went on for years. I used to lie – which was wrong. I told them I was building a four-poster bed in the garage – I didn't even have a garage. But that appeared in the cuttings for a long time. I've stopped lying now. I just avoid the press.'

Afterwards Wogan sipped his usual champagne in the hospitality room while Joanna's husband moodily tinkled the odd étude on the white pianoforte. But Joanna's remarkable flair for always being the most compelling of chat show guests earned her an offer to take over the hot seat when the ubiquitous Irishman was taking one of his frequent sunshine holidays.

She considered carefully, but although she had not the remotest ambition to be tied to a television studio three times a week for the rest of her life, she has always found it almost impossible to resist a new challenge and she agreed to sit in for two weeks. She was so much more appealing than Terry Wogan it was close to embarrassing.

She charmed giant American heavyweight boxer George Foreman. She swapped hilarious anecdotes with Bette Midler and Mary Tyler Moore and her encounters with Spike Milligan and Michael Palin gave the viewers an enthralling insight into both men. It was like getting a seat at the most sparkling dinner party in town.

Not surprisingly she was asked back. And she was delighted to get the call again. 'That was very reassuring,' said Joanna. 'Much nicer than to be told it didn't really work and that it wouldn't be happening again.' Although there were suggestions that she try her own show Joanna dismissed the idea. 'It is something that I really enjoy for a couple of weeks, it is very hard work and a great lark. But after fifty programmes I could see myself having lost that freshness completely and it all becoming too much. I realized before doing it that it is a very nerve-wracking job. You want it to be entertaining and fun for the viewers, but you have no idea how your guests will turn out.

'Everyone comes on the programme for a reason,' said Joanna pragmatically. 'Why be there if they haven't got something specific to talk about?' And she understood the reason behind choosing famous faces. 'If you have the person who is looking for the cure for AIDS or who designed the Pompidou Centre, then everyone will switch off. You have to have people the viewers know. And you have to accept that they are not going to say anything new. Most of them have a standard interview, they change a few of the stories, put on a bit of a show for ten minutes and that's it. There is nothing revealing. It's a bit like inviting them around to your house for a cup of tea.

'The people I would really like to interview are all dead. Shakespeare, Mozart, Kipling, Jane Austen, Chopin, Van Gogh, Ghengis Khan, Ned Kelly, they would make a wonderful line-up, absolutely marvellous to interview.' But the questions from Joanna would never be too intrusive. 'My yardstick is that I wouldn't ask a question that I wouldn't want to answer myself. I think interviews should be based around the kind of conversations that you might have in real life. I wouldn't ask strangers about their sex lives, or why their marriage broke up, or whether or not they used drugs, or stole things from shops. These things are too personal. What happens if the person refuses to talk about it? Then it becomes very embarrassing, the guest clams up, I am embarrassed and so is the audience, that is terrible television. Much nicer to keep it light and entertaining, I think. It was a nice experience standing in for Terry Wogan but it was not what I want to do with my life.

'I loved meeting the people. Oprah Winfrey is a very nice, hard-working, affectionate woman and she wrote me a letter after the show, as did George Foreman. The Americans were much more cautious about what they said and quick to take offence. But once they realize you are not going to savage them they open like flowers.'

As the 1980s drew to a close Joanna reflected on her life to one of the authors and noted cheerily, 'This is a terrific time of my life because all the strings are being pulled together. All the ideas of wanting to write and wanting to travel and wanting to work on stage and wanting to work in films as well as on television seem possible. But at the same time I realize that I am forty-four now and unless I am really lucky in the film world there are thirty people ahead of me for any part that comes up so I have got to be bloody lucky to get that, which is why I am enjoying stage work so much because I seem to be offered a lot of that. I am going to do the new Alan Ayckbourn play next year, which is not bad for someone who never trained in drama school, someone who came to the stage via films and television. That is terribly exciting and heart-warming. But if you make too many plans you are bound to be disappointed.

'Marriage has changed my life enormously. I was probably not ready for it before. I think it is a huge step to take, you have to have stopped changing yourself. If you are lucky enough to marry someone when you are very young who happens to be going the same way as you and changing at the same speed as you then that is wonderful. But the chances are that you might just drift apart. I am not surprised that very many second marriages are happier than first marriages. I think it is marvellous if you can be married just the once and you can be happy. But I can understand that people perceive more what marriage is when you get older. It is not just a lunatic fairy story. I think it works best when you marry your best friend. That is what happened to me.

'But I think marriage should be the start of everything, rather than an awful full stop to life. I was forty while Stephen was thirty-two, and now, as we approach our fourth wedding anniversary we could hardly be happier. I don't ever want to stop changing, growing and developing and gaining more knowledge and perception which is a lot to do with travelling. But I want to stop getting richer. I want to stop this idea that we must go on getting and getting and getting. I would like to start getting poorer, not needing so many clothes, not wanting to eat in all the best restaurants, not always wanting the best of everything, not insisting on five star treatment everywhere I go.'

Joanna's eyes shone with enthusiasm as she warmed to her personal philosophy of life: 'I hate being cut off from people so I try to travel on buses or on underground trains. I always travel second class on trains. It sounds sickening. It sounds like a sort of nostalgic slumming which it is not. What I mean is that I feel we are being threatened by the feeling that people have become dominated by this driving force of having to get more all the time. It seems to promote as much unhappiness as anything I have ever seen and at the same time it has more sinister implications in that the more it is the widespread goal of the western world, the poorer it makes the undeveloped countries who have to pay a forfeit for it. I would just like to see less of everything.'

Joanna was speaking long before 'downsizing' had been heard of, let alone become fashionable, and just after she and husband Stephen had made their decision to move to a smaller house. She said, 'At the moment we live in an enormous house in the country in Kent which we are going to sell and move back to a smaller place in London. There is a purely practical reason for that. We live nearly at Dover and it's a hell of a journey. Moving house to a smaller place is part of not wanting to live in grander and grander houses as you acquire more and more money in life. It has been in the back of my mind for a long time. I suppose I am saying I have very deep religious beliefs. I do believe profoundly that our souls have been neglected and I think there is a great spiritual hunger which is around amongst all of us and particularly in young people. If everything is geared towards money and stuff that rots away and does nobody any good there is a great deal of dissatisfaction and sourness. So I have always tried to aim for things other than money in life.

'People say, "Why didn't you go to Hollywood? Why didn't you capitalize on everything, get a house with electric gates and a Maserati?" I don't want to have better things than other people, mainly because I am lucky enough in my life coming from the bizarre worlds of modelling and acting to have worn and paraded in the finest things money can buy. But pretend gold is every bit as twinkly as real gold. *The New Avengers* never paid a fortune but the things that followed from it brought untold wealth. Money itself is not bad. You can distribute it the way you want to see it go. You can take it and hand out money to people for different projects which is what I still do. I think that is terribly important. I don't want to be better than other people and I don't want to have more than other people. I don't want to be envied for what I've got. I don't think that is a nice thing. If you have got real jewels it becomes a problem. You have to insure them and lock them away. It becomes a bore. How nice *not* to have real jewels. My mother has a very successful "diamond" ring which in fact came from Woolworth's and cost about half a crown, so she can imagine she is wearing a diamond ring and if it's stolen she wouldn't worry. It is a happier way of living. I want to keep on travelling. I don't mind wearing the same old clothes but I want to be able to travel. You can read a certain amount about countries but you really don't know until you go there and see for yourself.'

Joanna provided a real insight into her thinking when she continued, 'I don't see why I shouldn't do a variety of things. Work is an extraordinary thing, I have been running away from it all my life. I have never really had a job, not a proper job. It is very important to me to do what I can to help others less fortunate. And to make that help as good as I can possibly make it. I have got nine sacks of nice clothes all clean and pressed with buttons carefully replaced which we have packed up ready to go to Poland for poor people there, because I don't see why people who have got no clothes should be given rotten old stuff to wear. I give to a massive amount of charities and I always try to give things to do with my work. Who would want my old cup and saucer that I have had for twenty years, but a charity might and it might raise £20. The danger

Joanna as Purdey poised for action
(RONALD GRANT ARCHIVE)

Joanna with fellow *New Avengers* Patrick
Macnee and Gareth Hunt.
(SCOPE FEATURES)

...anna modelling

Joanna with long-term early love, actor Michael Kitchen.

Joanna enjoyed a two month relationship with Rod Stewa

Joanna with co-star David McCallum in ITV's *Sapphire and Steel*.

..ll in gold to play a South ..merican dictator in *Vanilla*.

Joanna with
BAFTA-winner
John Travolta.
(Above left)
(ALPHA)

Joanna proudly
collects her OBE
(Above)
(ALPHA)

*Absolutely
Fabulous* fun with
Jennifer Saunders
as the alarming
Edina and Patsy.
(SCORE FEATURES)

Mr and Mrs Stephen Barlow.

(MIRROR SYNDICATION INTERNATIONAL)

All smiles on Jamie's wedding day. Jamie is pictured here with his bride Louise, Joanna and her husband Stephen Barlow, who line up for the cameras with Jamie's father Michael Claydon (far right) and his wife Rita.

(EXPRESS NEWSPAPERS)

Joanna looks frightening in
The Tale of Sweeney Todd. (Above)
(SCOPE FEATURES)

Joanna takes a pig to parliament
to campaign for Compassion in
World Farming. *(Left)*
(ALPHA)

Celebrating Prince Charles's
fiftieth birthday. *(Below)*
(ALPHA)

is that if you give everything away tomorrow almost nobody will be better off and you will have nothing at all. So you have got to be a bit wise. But I really, really do not need to have expensive things. When I was young we lived in rented flats and had a cronky old record player. I have no longing for the best of everything. Old 45s and a Dansette are fine for me. I have never been interested in good cars or expensive gadgets. I have bought all my furniture in junk shops. I am a great collector of junk. People are really shocked when they see my car. It's an old Ford Granada. I think it's lovely and it is very comfy but they expect me to be in a Porsche or a Mercedes. But my next car will be smaller, it might even be a bike. I just want to have less of everything, we should free ourselves of all the tat. Next time we meet I'll be speaking to you from a cardboard box!'

If producers offering contracts were ever in short supply, Joanna was never short of ideas of her own and what brought her much joy and satisfaction was nurturing a pet project from its infancy as an idea into fruition as a television series and a book. She fairly sparkled with enthusiasm when explaining to one of the authors her hopes for a documentary about the Brooke family, who were known as the 'White Rajahs of Sarawak'. 'I'm co-writing and presenting and it is a terrific project for me because I have never done anything like this before. Sarawak is part of Malaysia now, part of the world I know from my youth in Malaya. The programme is to be called *In Search of The White Rajahs* and the story really begins back in 1836 when Sir Stamford Raffles, who then had a trading post in Singapore, was having tremendous problems with pirates in the South China Seas. They were preventing trade coming to Indonesia and the people of Borneo were having a very rough time because all their supplies were being robbed. So the enterprising Sir Stamford contacted his friend Vyner Brook who lived in Dorset, England and asked him to bring out a ship to fight the pirates. He took up the challenge and was so effective at ridding the high seas of these dangerous pirates that amazingly the Sultan of Brunei gave him Sarawak to rule. Brooke was known as the White Rajah and he created a dynasty which was to rule over the country, which included the fierce head-hunting Dyaks in the rain forest and orang-utans in the jungle, for more than a century.'

Joanna's beautiful eyes sparkled with life as she told her exotic tale. 'The Brookes brought in railways and the British system of policing and it was a very tranquil period for a very warlike country. The benevolent despotic regime ended in 1946 when the last White Rajah handed it over to the British Empire who in turn handed it over to Malaysia in 1956. It is a very happy story and the three last princesses, daughters of the last White Rajah are still alive, in their seventies, living in Florida. And best of all they have given their full consent to the making of this film and allowed all their family papers to be used so I shall be going out to Florida to talk to them. They were a dazzling trio, all incredibly beautiful. They were very much the darlings of 1930s society. They married eight times between them. They will be part of the film but I also want to see for myself how badly the rain forests are being destroyed and the effects of modern technology like radio and television on primitive life. Hopefully I will get a book out of it.'

Joanna was as good as her word. A year later, in September 1991, the BBC screened Joanna's dream, *In Search of the White Rajahs*, and viewers marvelled at the three sprightly daughters of Sir Charles Vyner Brooke and saw Joanna travelling up the long and tortuous straits of Sarawak by express boat and long boat and then getting in her environmental message. 'The last of the great rain forests of South-East Asia are being felled. It's an ecological disaster,' she told the viewers. The book sold well and Joanna decided her reputation as an actress was less important than her need to travel the world and discover new places or rediscover old ones. 'Hang reputation!' she snorted with nostrils elegantly flaring. 'My life is preciously short and I can't bear the thought of turning down exciting adventures because I have to say I'm a serious actress. People think you're an idiot if you have more than one interest – they don't like you changing horses and they treat you as a dilettante. Well, I couldn't care less about my reputation – I am desperately keen to travel even further afield and maybe undertake more journeys like this one.'

In the 1990s Joanna's forays into the theatre were notable for the encouraging reviews she garnered, even if the critics vented their spleen on the productions themselves. Back at Greenwich in

October 1992 for *Who Shall I Be Tomorrow?*, Joanna earned the following remarkable praise in the *Daily Express*:

> The ever-luscious Joanna Lumley has performed a miracle. She kept the audience awake during Bernard Kops' dreadful new play with a virtuoso performance as a suicidal, agoraphobic actress with stage fright. Miss Lumley is tremendous in a bedraggled silk petticoat as she totters from one domestic crisis to another. Her mimicry and timing are hilarious in this woeful comedy . . .

The reviewer added that Joanna's 'nervous energy alone sustains this maudlin evening', and went on to say, 'She is at her most irrepressible when sending up her glamorous image. She also has pathos in plenty . . .'

With Beryl Reid it was always shoes. Once she had found the right footwear she could find the character they belonged to. But with Joanna Lumley it is the hair. And Joanna had the most severe haircut of her career for her role in *Vanilla*, Jane Stanton Hitchcock's ambitious social satire which was staged at the Lyric Theatre in London's Shaftesbury Avenue in May 1990. She bravely had it cropped to an all-round length of an inch and a half and dyed jet black to play the alarming South American dictator Miralda Sumac. The play was to be directed by no less than Harold Pinter. Miralda was the frightening *femme fatale* at the centre of the piece, the man-eating wife of the ailing dictator of Vanilla, who has an obsession for gloves and a 9,000 pair, wardrobe-bursting collection to prove it.

Joanna instantly noted a difference in her private life. She learned first hand that blondes really do have more fun. 'Changing your hair like that changes your life,' she said. 'I suddenly found that men ignored me. They no longer let me push in front of them in heavy traffic. I felt invisible. It was a real shock. The play only lasted for six weeks and I had to go round like that for much longer.'

Vanilla, of course rhymes with Manila, and Miralda's passion for gloves has deafening echoes of the Philippines' former first lady Imelda Marcos's passion for shoes. Joanna had high hopes of

Vanilla and joined a strong cast which included Sian Phillips, Marjorie Bland, Niall Buggy, Charlotte Cornwell, Greg Hicks, and Gwen Humble.

The play opened with Gwen Humble as an ex-hooker carefully planning her entrance into Manhattan grand society with a dinner party. Joanna, as monstrous Miralda, was one of the guests who, for security reasons, makes her entrance in a plastic bag. An after-dinner entertainment consists of 112 poor people gathered up from city streets, one for each guest to take home as a party favour.

Joanna's character Miralda is in court on the morrow on charges of embezzlement and grand larceny. She used to sentence people to death for dressing badly and once paid for a masked ball in Venice with international aid for earthquake victims.

The play came in for some savage attention from the critics. Michael Billington in the *Guardian* said, 'Watching a host of good actors trying to make this stuff come alive is like seeing carnivores sink their teeth into blancmange.'

Jeremy Kingston in *The Times* wondered: 'What aesthetic blindness had fallen upon Mr Harold Pinter that he was persuaded – and some reports say volunteered – to direct this super-banal exposure of the super-rich?' But he was one of several critics to sit up and take notice of Joanna's performance.

'On the credit side,' he said, 'there is a glittering comic performance of ravenous, elegant vulgarity from Lumley, sheathed in gold deploying the peremptory gestures of a regal hooker and observing the proceedings with understandable distaste.'

Michael Coveney in the *Observer* was clearly taken by Joanna in her underwear: 'Miss Lumley's gold lamé wraparound has very little to wrap around,' he noted, 'but stays there until required to give way to some breathtaking underwear. One of the inert elements of the last half hour is Miss Lumley herself and one of the boring ones is the fact that she remains inert in this underwear.'

Milton Shulman in the *Evening Standard* said Joanna '. . . statuesque and stunning in gold lamé is imperiously funny as she derides the Vanilla poor for not being smart enough to make money.'

Nick Smurthwaite's review in *Midweek* read: 'For Joanna Lumley one was grateful. Not only does she look sensational but the obvious relish with which she tackles the role is the play's one saving grace.'

But while *Vanilla* melted off the stage after a few short weeks the production was to spark a transformation in the life of Joanna Lumley. As the 1990s began she was at a strange point in her highly individual career. As much-loved as ever for all her good works and her enduring beauty, her energetic support of endless worthy causes was chronicled at hundreds of carefully staged photo opportunities. She had stood in for Wogan on his late and unlamented chat show and done well enough to embarrass the regular host.

Yet when a request to return arrived Joanna noted rather more charitably, 'Being asked back to present the show was wonderful, like being given a prize. It was hectic last time, but I thoroughly enjoyed it and learned it's a lot harder than it looks. People like Terry Wogan make it look easy. But it's difficult introducing guests, putting them at their ease, getting to the point and then getting them off – all in seven minutes! I'm an actress and I enjoy pretending to be someone else. I find it tiring being myself. It's like being a guest cook. It's fun for a while but you wouldn't want to do it forever.'

Her columns in *The Times* were a model of thoughtful humour and stylish whimsy. But Joanna knew perfectly well she was becoming famous for being famous. Mel Smith and Griff Rhys Jones developed a running gag in their BBC comedy series that convulsed audiences by screaming 'I'm Joanna Lumley' and then crashing through a wall or whatever. Joanna had the image of the elegant English rose certainly but as she slid inexorably towards the second half of her forties she was in serious danger of becoming something of a joke. A visit by comedienne Ruby Wax to the Lyric Theatre and the inspiration of co-star Gwen Humble was to change all that.

First, actress Gwen thoughtfully suggested to her husband, actor Ian McShane, who was then riding high in the television ratings as BBC's rascally antique dealer Lovejoy, that he might like to go to bed with Joanna. For the sake of his series of course. Gwen and Joanna's characters in *Vanilla* had shared their own bed scene so she was at any rate advising from experience. 'Joanna and I became good friends in the play. Ian already knew her from years before and we all went away together to a house in the country. I watched them walking and I just thought to myself that they looked great together. Ian had been talking about introducing a new woman into the series and to me Joanna was the only one classy and sexy enough to do it. She is so beautiful in a cool, clever and elegant way.'

Not surprisingly McShane agreed that a romantic involvement with a stylish English lady played by Joanna would be just the sort of development that would really benefit the long-running drama. He even recalled that in a previous series Lovejoy had picked up a copy of *Tatler* and gazed longingly at photographs of elegant, aristocratic ladies with names like Melissa and Veronica. The interminably smouldering screen relationship between Lovejoy and Lady Jane, played by Phyllis Logan, was experiencing one of its cooler periods, so what could be more sensible than to bring in a bewitching friend of her ladyship, a mysterious widow from Peru called Victoria Cavero, to have a passionate affair with the hero.

'I'm afraid she rather broke his heart,' smiled Joanna on location in Suffolk. She was not at all put off the high profile role by the prospect of bedroom scenes with an old friend. 'I've known Ian since 1968. He is an old chum. But it was almost more peculiar getting into bed with an old friend than with a complete stranger. To me it is rather like your relationship with your doctor. None of us would think twice about taking our clothes off in front of our doctor. It is just the same with acting. You just do it. Not that I had to take all my clothes off for *Lovejoy*. But I think love scenes are always hard to do. It is helped a lot if you don't actually have to do anything. This is *Lovejoy*. This is not heavy sex. I would have thought those scenes are monstrously hard to do at any stage. In all kinds of acting you have to appear to be in love with people, you kiss people. It is just acting and much easier to do than it sounds.'

The bewitching Victoria completely bowled Lovejoy over, and Joanna confessed with a huge grin, 'He proposes to her and she turns him down. She is absolutely madly in love with him but I don't think that people who are madly in love necessarily get married. She is astonished when he proposes. It's a real bolt from the blue because Lovejoy is definitely not the sort of guy who gets married.'

Lovejoy lifted Joanna's spirits as well as the show's ratings. But filming came at a very difficult time for her as she and Stephen were moving into their stylish new home in London's Stockwell the week production began. She deliberately chose a comfortable home in a less fashionable district. Joanna might sound very Kensington or Chelsea but she was conscious of not wanting to flaunt her wealth. Stockwell suited her very well.

Ian McShane was duly grateful which enabled him to provide a rare demonstration of the more vulnerable side of Jack the Lad Lovejoy. 'She turned out to be a little bit more mature than he is, which was nice because he was getting a little too cool in all his relationships. He got his heart broken and he took it out on the other characters – Eric and Tinker. It was great fun and my wife didn't mind me being in bed with Joanna one little bit. How could she? It was her idea.'

In fact Joanna romped on television with two of her favourite actors in 1991. After *Lovejoy* she enjoyed a fling with Nigel Havers in London Weekend Television's £4 million wartime drama *A Perfect Hero*. Joanna played glamorous 1940s film star Loretta Stone who comforts and then beds Havers, a dashing Battle of Britain pilot who is horribly injured when his Spitfire is shot down in flames. 'Both men are utterly charming,' said Joanna diplomatically. 'They show two completely different sides of Englishmen. Havers is a suave and elegant man, the well-spoken and well-mannered one, while McShane is the rogue. But they are both terribly attractive and they are both long-standing friends of mine.'

Her role as Loretta led Joanna into rare controversy when it was made public that the fur coat that the character wore was real. As Joanna is an animal lover, vegetarian and a great campaigner for animal rights this move shocked many Lumley fans. Carol McKenna, campaign director for the anti-fur trade group Lynx, was appalled that Joanna should be seen by millions wearing a coat made of fur from ten foxes. Joanna explained her predicament to one of the authors, 'Of course I don't wear furs normally but this was a difficult situation and I had a real debate with myself. *A Perfect Hero* was set in the 1940s and they had got a 1940s fur coat for me to wear. I did not feel it was my position to say, "I, Joanna Lumley in 1990 do not want to wear this coat." But it was tremendously difficult for me. We all do our best to do the right thing and

I do not agree with killing animals for their fur. But if stuff exists already and it is fifty years old and a period costume I did not feel I could protest. I don't go around spraying paint in shops but I do lend my name to the campaigns.

'I own a huge coat that I had made out of fake fur to look like a terrifically sumptuous dark mink coat. The woman who made it for me had been a furrier and then had a Damoclean conversion and suddenly decided not to make furs any more, but to switch to fake furs. Of course they are a fraction of the price, and on each one she gives something to the World Wildlife Fund because she feels that way she is paying something back. Nowadays I would never wear a fur coat in real life, but in the 1960s they were like blue jeans, everyone had them. We all did – a fox, a racoon, or a rabbit at least. It never crossed any of our minds where they all came from. We never thought. I know we knew animals did not fall down dead peacefully allowing someone to come along and collect their pelts. In those days we didn't think. Now we do.'

The wartime theme was maintained as Joanna switched to a writing project when the shrewd directors of the Imperial War Museum invited her to prepare a collection of correspondence from men and women serving away from home in wartime to their loved ones. Joanna was delighted to accept the task, cheerfully admitting she was a romantic at heart and saying, 'I always carry a hand-written note from my husband, Stephen, in my wallet. It was a real labour of love when I spent three months in the museum with boxes of love letters on one side and a box of hankies on the other.'

The museum advertised for contributions and were overwhelmed by the quantity and quality of letters and touching personal mementoes, such as long-preserved photos, poems, love tokens, even wedding dresses, they received.

Afterwards Joanna said, 'I don't think I had the smallest idea of the joy and pain it would bring . . . reading through these personal treasures was an extraordinary privilege. I was allowed to gaze into people's lives and loves, to imagine their emotions as they opened letters or wrote them, to share in their happiness or loss. Many times I was moved to tears; often I laughed out loud. War seems to have had a hot-house effect on the flowers of love. There was a pilot who wrote, "My sweetheart, if you read this it means I'm dead but I'm quite safe, all is well, and one day we will be reunited again." I got so choked reading that.'

The book, *Forces Sweethearts*, was a best-seller, thanks to the interest sparked by Joanna and the astonishing catalogue of love stories it contained. Poignantly Joanna dedicated it to her mother and father and it included a picture of a small silver powder compact bought by her father, Captain James Rutherford Lumley, in the street called Straight in Damascus in 1942. The silversmith had imprinted 'Beatrice', written in Joanna's father's hand, on the lid. He gave it to her mother in Abbottabad when he returned to India a year later in 1943.

11

The Nineties, Absolutely

Ruby Wax was so impressed by Joanna's performance in *Vanilla* that she came backstage to congratulate Joanna and to ask her to appear on her chat show *The Full Wax*. She had in mind a comic routine which would have Ruby and her camera crew surprising Joanna at home and revealing the shocking truth that she was not quite so poised and perfectly organized as she appeared.

Joanna was instantly enthusiastic. She said, 'Rather than being a fab film star person I thought it would be nicer to be a slut. I thought it would be amusing to contrast this angelic public image with a ghastly, self-centred old bitch behaving in that rather snappy, disagreeable way at home with rotten flowers, filthy food on the floor and whisky bottles everywhere. I wanted it to be an armpit.'

The sketches were hilarious and Ruby Wax, who was to be script editor on *Absolutely Fabulous*, said to Joanna, 'You should work with Jennifer Saunders.' Saunders and producer Jon Plowman had also seen *Vanilla* and by this time become very well aware of Joanna's comedy potential. 'It all happened very quickly,' noted Joanna. 'Ruby doesn't hang around.'

The key to all really great comedy is timing and *Absolutely Fabulous* certainly arrived at exactly the right time for Joanna. Her career was strangely becalmed in one of its occasional quiet lulls in between all the well-publicized gales of success. After her talented and successful dabbling at everything from documentary-making to journalism, even considerable theatrical hits in the West End failed to raise her profile. And her growing reputation as a frivolous dilettante who never really sustained anything in the long term was beginning to irritate Joanna beyond belief.

But then Patsy Stone arrived in a flurry of deliciously bad behaviour, and thanks largely to the sublime writing skills of Jennifer Saunders and to Joanna's remarkable and hilarious gift for big-hearted self-mockery, the new show was the television highlight of the early 1990s.

Even during filming the production team began to believe they were on to something special and were determined to keep that knowledge to themselves, lest the oxygen of publicity should blow them away before they began. Joanna agreed carefully that she was delighted to be given the chance to play comedy. She felt playing such a deeply flawed yet still decorative woman could be difficult to say the least because most people could not be so outrageous all the time. She certainly knew she couldn't. It was also a delicious revenge for years of preening and posing and peeling off her clothes for male-dominated media.

Absolutely Fabulous itself actually began life as a quickly forgotten sketch in the 1990 *French and Saunders* comedy series. Jennifer played the tearaway divorced mother trying to live life in the fast lane and Dawn French was the sensible, level-headed teenager giving her batty mum the cold shoulder and attempting to find her way into further education. This was much against her single parent's wishes. 'University, darling?' said Jennifer wearing a jewelled baseball cap that looked quite sedate compared with the clothes that followed. 'Do you have to go?'

Dawn stayed mostly silent while Jennifer raved on in the witty item that was transmitted on 19 April 1990. The sketch was called 'Mother and Daughter' and the characters worked instantly. 'We should get a Philippino because they work like buggers and cost flap all. It is possible to be a socialist and have staff, darling,' Jennifer yelled.

But it was anything but an instant progression to a full-blown series. Jennifer joked at the time that the show only came about because her agent was rather concerned about a long period of unemployment while her partner Dawn French pursued her many other interests. She spent a while, 'waiting to be offered the

Michelle Pfeiffer roles', but when they failed to arrive she went back to writing. When Jennifer reluctantly offered the 'Mother and Daughter' idea, the agent's response was an instant order to write a treatment.

Jennifer shrewdly observed that truculent teenagers anxious to carve out their own identities had to behave beautifully in order to be different from hippie parents. She explained, 'It's the late 80s and 90s phenomenon of the 60s women who made good. They've seen a lot, done a lot and are still there, keeping up with every trend. For a daughter to rebel against someone that hip, she has to go the other way, pretend to be square, study and want to go to university. Then you wonder how sane she is to be so sane. Are "sane" people really sane? Or are they much madder?' Jennifer said she knew plenty of real-life Edinas: 'People who grew up in the 60s and have all these mad 60s ideas, and now they're running companies or doing quite high profile jobs but somehow they've never grown up and their children are much straighter than them.' Jennifer Saunders bravely wrote the impossibly egotistical Edina some seven years older than herself. And despite her many lunacies she admired her confident creation because, 'She lives exactly the life she wants to live. She never sees other people looking at her, never imagines what other people think of her and she's right. I love that. I'm more self-conscious and more worried about what people think.'

Even by Jennifer Saunders' high standards the first *Ab Fab* script was brilliant. Jon Plowman was producer, and when they were rehearsing the show he recalled that Jennifer said to Joanna, 'You do realize this will completely change your fan base? Whereas before it was colonels writing in to say, "I admire your work immensely, my dear," it will be drag queens saying, "Can I borrow your frock?" ' Which of course was more or less exactly what happened.

Jennifer played the appalling Edina Monsoon and Julia Sawalha was drafted in to be the angelic daughter Saffron with Joanna brought in to the show as Edina's outrageous pal Patsy Stone. The first episode was discreetly tucked away on BBC2 just after the crucial nine o'clock watershed.

The project was fortunate to have the highly experienced

comedy director Bob Spiers on board. He had directed *Fawlty Towers* after first cutting his teeth as a director on the BBC's *Seaside Special*, back in the 1970s. 'We all found ourselves on the same wavelength. That was the most important thing,' he recalled fondly to the authors years later.

The series had a freshness and a bravery about it that indicated from the start that this was very much more than just another BBC sit-com. Joanna said, 'When I read the very first script I thought, "This is going like smoke." The character was born without brakes. She doesn't know when she has gone over the top and doesn't care. I wanted to do it not least because I'd never been offered anything like it. I've always been drawn to anarchic humour, and playing elegant women gets very boring. In real-life I am not that glamorous person, so it didn't trouble me even a jot. It was rather nice to wriggle out of that kind of chrysalis. Doing Patsy is just lovely. I think what's made me happiest is that I've always fooled around and it's really nice to be paid for fooling around.'

Spiers was really given his head in the very first scene of the first episode. 'It was a two-hander between Jennifer and Julia which was an eight-minute scene, a very dangerous thing to do in a half-hour show, and we did it in one take. It was establishing that relationship between Edina and Saffy. It was amazingly dangerous. It was like a Pinter play,' said Spiers.

We saw Edina frantically trying to organize a fast-dissolving fashion show with the cheerful but counter-productive assistance of her dizzy secretary Bubble, played by Jane Horrocks. 'It is all under control. I've booked every model in the world . . .'

Clearly the enterprise inspired nothing but scorn from down-to-earth Saffron. The mother–daughter clash was funny right from the start as Saffy watched the excesses and observed acidly, 'Major motion pictures are made, huge concerts are put on in stadiums, for God's sake. Five hundred thousand troops were mobilized in the Gulf and a war fought in less time, and without everyone involved having a nervous breakdown and being sent flowers. It cannot be that difficult.'

The impossibly trendy Edina retorted, 'But darling, every troop didn't have to contain Yasmin le Bon. The generals didn't require big hugs after every manoeuvre. And the whole operation didn't have to be co-ordinated to rap and Japanese avant garde pipe music.'

That first encounter really set the scene for the yawning generation gap that was perfectly balanced by the use of the veteran June Whitfield as Edina's deliciously vague mother. Clearly it was bold and adventurous and best of all it was wonderfully funny right from the start.

Saffy was enraged by her mother's pathetic dependence on others: 'Mum, you've absolved yourself of responsibility. You live from self-induced crisis to self-induced crisis. Someone chooses what you wear. Someone does your brain. Someone tells you what to eat, and, three times a week, someone sticks a hose up your bum and flushes it all out of you.' Eddie retorted, 'It's called colonic irrigation, darling, and it's not to be sniffed at.' But Saffy was not in the mood to listen: 'Why can't you just go to the toilet like normal people?'

The use of the glamorous figure of Joanna Lumley for the crucially difficult role of chain-smoking, hard-drinking, drug-taking, sexually-aggressive ex-model Patsy Stone was the idea of comedian Ade Edmondson. Jennifer Saunders' husband had seen something in Joanna's stand-in role for Wogan that rang comic bells in his head and suggested her for the part that was to finally persuade millions of viewers that Joanna Lumley was so much more than a pretty face, a cut-glass accent and a pair of everlasting legs.

Joanna was delighted by the prospect of playing the serial nymphomaniac who had known Edina since their schooldays. Both characters fiercely refused to grow up and much of the humour came from the way they were determined to continue their youthful excesses to the grave if necessary. Always quick to recognize the ridiculous in life, Joanna saw in the script a joyous opportunity to make fun of the media and fashion worlds and their obsession with ludicrous over-indulgence. One of her first moves was to go in to see Jennifer and her production team who all knew how important it was to the brave and challenging enterprise to have precisely the right person to play the high profile role of preposterous Patsy. Spiers remembers, 'Joanna came in to see us and we spoke to her and the only note we said – I don't know who said it – was, "We don't want Joanna Lumley", because up to that point she'd been playing the love interest in various things. Our view was, "Listen, Joanna. Just go for it." From day one she went for it. She's an enormously intelligent lady and so she got the plot straight away. There wasn't any great coaching or need for some Svengali to help her. She just did it.'

Joanna was given a high degree of freedom to create her character and she began with the famous sneery facial expression that she described as, 'The kind of look they tell you to take off your face at school.' She said, 'The first time I saw the script for the pilot episode of *Absolutely Fabulous* I knew it was going to be something special. Luckily the people at the BBC had enough faith in Jennifer Saunders to agree to make the series. Believe me, I have played enough disastrous roles in my time to know that characters like Patsy only come along once in a blue moon.'

Joanna loved the outrageous attitudes of Patsy. The moments when she would burst into Edina's home smoking six cigarettes, because she had been forced to travel with a 'bloody asthmatic cab driver' or when she observed about her drinking that: 'The last mosquito that bit me had to book into the Betty Ford clinic,' were a joy to her after years of smiling sweetly in her decorative roles.

Spiers and Saunders encouraged Joanna's initial audacity, which hugely helped her confidence. 'You've got to look pleased when someone goes out on such a limb. She's very experienced and didn't need much help,' said Spiers. 'She's a game bird, as it were, and the whole show became a monument to Dame Joanna.'

Joanna and Jennifer got on really well. They became firm friends and had lunches together and went out shopping together which was inclined to terrify assistants who would instantly start looking for the cameras.

In that crucial opening episode, once the fundamental relationship between Eddie and Saffy had been established, Patsy arrived to ride in the back of Eddie's Jaguar and the audience quickly learned that the eternally inebriated ex-model was even more colourful than her friend.

As Eddie complained about her daughter's attempts to stop her drinking, soulmate Patsy thoughtfully shared her friend's horror at the very idea of abstinence: 'I tried not drinking once. I heard myself talking all night and then, worse than that, next day I had total recall. It was terrifying.'

Joanna's character was always going to be big, but Saunders was so impressed during the filming of the pilot that she began to enlarge Patsy's part. 'It was not originally seen as a double act,' said producer Plowman. 'But Joanna threw herself at it with such gusto that it would have been a shame not to develop it.' Quickly Patsy became a major player. Joanna was brilliant and Jennifer was brilliant in giving all those characters so much space in that one show – an enormously difficult thing to do.

Patsy's sexually voracious lifestyle was clear from the moment she answered Eddie's query about who she was with the night before. 'Just a windscreen washer I picked up at some traffic lights. Buns so tight he was bouncing off the walls.'

Joanna loved playing the almost permanently plastered Patsy, the model turned fashion editor. Joanna noted with relish, 'Patsy smokes like a chimney, drinks like a fish, dresses like a dream and has a fragile grasp of what work is. She goes into her office so seldom that she's forgotten where it is. I'm sort of interested in fashion in a vague way. I used to be a photographic model from eighteen to twenty-five – put on clothes which were sometimes disastrous polyester nasties disguised with a bright scarf – but I can't say my part is based on any fashion editors that I know. The character sprang fully clothed from Jennifer's head and I know she has her nose to the ground and is ever on the trawl for people to imitate or lampoon.'

The action took place mainly in Edina's house, 34 Claremont Avenue, London W11 4BX, which she insisted was Holland Park rather than Shepherd's Bush. Patsy had more lovers than she could remember. In fact she went out with the Who's anarchic drummer Keith Moon once. Or as Patsy put it: 'Well, I woke up underneath him in a hotel bedroom once.'

The scripts seemed to inspire Joanna and frequently she used her own razor sharp wit to amplify and improve and so contribute some of the funniest moments, often cheerfully making herself look even more ridiculous than required. One wonderful *Ab Fab* moment saw a totally blitzed Patsy lurch out of a taxi with her unsnapped 'body' hanging out of her trousers and blowing in the wind. That particularly feminine piece of business was her idea. Joanna knew that part of the modern nightmare of being a style-conscious woman was struggling with the more intimate fastenings. It worked because Joanna was acting from her own embarrassment awareness. She has been known more than once to approach complete strangers unfortunate enough to have a label sticking out somewhere and say, 'Excuse me, let me tuck it in. You'll hate yourself if I don't.'

The wonderful thing about Joanna's portrayal of Patsy was that however raddled and sozzled she was required to appear on screen she always remained stunningly attractive to the opposite sex. Designer Betty Jackson was responsible for many of the hilariously outlandish outfits and noted that whenever the star arrived to discuss her clothes, countless numbers of men from accounts and other never-heard-from departments suddenly appeared with dockets that needed urgently signing. Joanna brought a sense of style to a role that was often described as French, which delighted her. She once remarked that one of the things she would most like to do would be to be mistaken for a French woman. The others were to photograph a golden eagle and to find a little Toulouse Lautrec drawing in a junk shop and buy it for a few francs.

The public certainly liked what it saw. After a month on BBC2 the audiences had risen to a remarkable eight million, comfortably the minority channel's most popular programme. Not surprisingly series two went straight on to BBC1.

Unfettered by considerations of taste, Jennifer Saunders' scripts were sensational from the start, and Patsy was always at the heart of the funniest scenes. In the second programme, 'Fat', overweight Eddie was terrified at the prospect of meeting an old rival from the 1960s, Penny Caspar-Morse, then such a super slim model she was known as 'The Stick'. But when she arrived Patsy saw her first and rushed to tell her friend the good news. Patsy: 'Eddie, great news.' Eddie thought for a moment and then replied, 'She's fat!' But Patsy said, 'No, no, no. Better.' Eddie: 'She's dead.' Patsy: 'No. She's blind!! Ha, ha.' Poor Penny was played beautifully by Alexandra Bastedo who led the way for a long line of famous names more than willing to join in the fun and send themselves up.

By now all the characters were really coming into their own.

June Whitfield's perfectly pitched portrayal of Edina's unflappable mother was superb. But Jennifer Saunders gave her lines that were real gems. She thoughtfully explained to her curiously clean-living granddaughter Saffy that, 'You're not like your mother, are you Saffron? She spent most of her teenage years sitting on a large bean bag, cigarette in one hand, joss stick in the other, and with a large-lipped youth suctioned on to her face.'

Patsy and Eddie went to get away from it all to a luxury house in the sunshine near Saint Tropez. But coping with anything as remotely practical as shopping or driving or communicating with the locals completely defeated them and Saffron and Bubble hilariously flew out to the rescue. As the holiday drew to a close Bubble translated what the jabbering old local had kept saying to them throughout the week. Why had they been staying in the cottage reduced to playing table tennis when the staff had been waiting for them all in the château half a mile down the road with its own swimming pool? Patsy reacted first: 'Listen, you goat, if you repeat this to anybody, I'll kill you.'

Naturally they were stopped at Customs on their return when the contents of Patsy's bag included a white powder. But after a wait they were allowed to go as the Customs man noted, 'The white powder we found was a perfectly harmless, innocent substance.' Naturally Patsy was incandescent with rage snorting, 'I demand you retest it. I paid a huge amount of money for that. Don't you tell me it's talcum powder.' Patsy was devastated but she admitted as the sorry party finally left the airport that what was bothering her was: 'The horrible realization that I must have actually enjoyed playing ping-pong.'

In homes across the country the sheer irreverence of the humour struck a chord and ratings skyrocketed week after week. We learned a little more about Patsy and Edina's long history together in the fourth programme 'Iso Tank', which saw Edina get out of her isolation tank long enough to take Patsy along to Saffron's sixth-form college. Once there they were caught up in a hilarious flashback sequence where Patsy and a pupil called Tony were in trouble for having sex at school. Then Tony turned out to be the current headmaster and the fling started all over again. As Edina's specially ordered selection of Rumanian babies arrived for her to choose one to adopt and so upset Saffron, matters really started to get out of hand. It was wonderful.

The series really got into its stride in the fifth episode devoted to Edina's fortieth birthday. After brilliantly barbed clashes with her two ex-husbands and their new partners, Edina withdrew to the loo to smoke a joint with Patsy. 'Do you feel your age?' Edina asked her friend. 'Not really,' answered Patsy firmly. 'And I make a point of not acting it.'

Patsy really shocked Edina in the last show in the series, 'Magazine', when she went into her office, even if she did have trouble actually locating the building. As fashion director of an impossibly glossy magazine Patsy insisted she had real power. 'I decide what goes in the magazine. One snap of my fingers and I can raise hem-lines so high that the world is your gynaecologist.'

Once at work the whole ludicrous world of fashion publishing was ruthlessly parodied with Kathy Burke in irresistible form as Magda the editor: 'I've got three lunches and a tights launch to get to by two o'clock.' The ideas conference came up with the plan for Patsy to take two members of the public – a mother and daughter who were described as 'a couple of miseries in shell-suits' – on a breakfast television makeover.

But Patsy fell out with the couple: 'The repellent mother and I came to blows over a geometric bob. I told her the only thing she looked good in was a body bag. And the daughter rebelled in Yamihoto's shop. She is now in hospital having a piece of modern furniture removed from her.' Which reduced her to having to plead with Saffy to stand in. In an effort to persuade Edina's daughter, who clearly hated everything about the fashion world in general and Patsy in particular, she demonstrated her rat-like cunning by creating a sob story about her past: 'I never knew my father . . . my mother only knew him fairly briefly. She had me when she was in her forties. I nursed her through her last years. It sort of put a stopper on me finding someone for myself.' This introduced a memorable flashback with Eleanor Bron playing Patsy's eccentric bohemian mother who was eventually reduced to sitting sadly in an old folks' home with Patsy storming: 'Oh, for God's sake, just die.'

As Joanna said herself when the first series proved successful. 'I was exhumed from an early grave to get *Absolutely Fabulous*. It was as if I had been in a coffin all those years, because people tend to judge you by television, and when you work in the theatre as I did, even in the West End, they seem to see you as failing. *Ab Fab* somehow restored me.'

It restored her so comprehensively with the public that in February 1993 she was nominated for her first award, a BAFTA for Best Light Entertainment Performance, beating her co-star Jennifer Saunders, Richard Wilson and Patricia Routledge. After more than twenty years as an actress her comic ability was finally getting the recognition it deserved.

She was delighted to win and was only half-joking afterwards when she announced that she was keeping the prize in a prominent position in her London home – to impress the visitors. She took the BAFTA as well as being voted top TV comedy personality and top TV comedy actress of 1993 at the British Comedy Awards. Her reaction was astonishment. 'It was shattering to win. I never win things. This year, because of Jennifer I have a stack of awards. I love them and kiss them every night before I go to bed.' She mimicked Patsy as she added, 'I mean, darlings, after all those years as Purdey, throwing myself across E-type Jaguars, and then *Sapphire and Steel* – nothing! Make 'em laugh, sweetie, that's what you've got to do to get awards.' More seriously Joanna felt that *Absolutely Fabulous* was a very special show: 'One of the very, very few comedies where women have been laughable-at. Physically funny. In the past people have found that too threatening.' As for her sublime gift for slapstick? Joanna was dismissive: 'Lots of actors are full of all kinds of talents. It's pure luck, pure chance, when you're asked to reveal them.'

Jennifer was delighted for her new friend, describing Lumley as 'a great comedy talent'. The bond between Joanna and Jennifer was so strong by then that when the envelope was ripped open and the announcement was made that Joanna had been voted Top Comedy Personality for 1993 Jennifer suggested they had got the wrong person. In a line that could have come straight from *Absolutely Fabulous* she said, 'It can't be you, darling. You haven't got a personality.' The partnership was a very happy one and Joanna was in no doubt about her debt to writer Saunders. Why was the show such a hit? 'It's Jennifer's script that is so wonderful. That's what makes it so special.'

Absolutely Fabulous was swiftly rerun on BBC and the second series began there in January 1994. After the rave reviews for the ground-breaking comedy, Jennifer expected there would be a reaction against the second. And there was, with some critics sneering that it had become darker and even not so funny. But the viewers largely loved it. The second series opened with Patsy with a blanket covering her head trying to get away from the Press who were on her trail following an affair with a member of Parliament. Or as one tabloid headlined it: 'MP in drug-crazed sex romp shock with fash mag slag.' June Whitfield's Mother did not quite grasp that it was Patsy who was involved and commented, 'Another pig-ugly MP making a fool of himself with some scrawny old hooker, I see.' Or perhaps she did grasp it was Patsy.

Joanna was certainly firing on all cylinders as Patsy stormed against the reptiles of the Press, insisting that she would never kiss and tell, until *Hello!* magazine arrived, that is. But Edina's injured foot took the double-act into hospital where their demands for drugs and general bad behaviour created some marvellous mayhem. Patsy's views on breast implants were enormously stimulating: 'I mean, who wouldn't put up with a not entirely unpleasant trickling sensation and a slight crystallization around the lower abdomen for that amount of cleavage?' But instead of larger boobs, as Edina had treatment on her foot, Patsy went for a facelift that went gruesomely wrong, leaving her with scarcely any skin on her face and a chilling end to the episode.

The next programme was even darker, as it hinged around the death of Edina's father. Patsy tried to look on the bright side: 'He chose the right season to go . . . Harvey Nicks have got some really tasty little black numbers at the moment. And black is like "in", so you wouldn't have to wear it only the once.' The funeral scene was *Absolutely Fabulous* at its most outrageous. Edina and Patsy arrive completely plastered and, while Patsy totters headlong into a nearby open grave, Edina falls in on top of her father's coffin.

And then came the memorable trip to Morocco. By then Jennifer Saunders' imagination was really fired by the partnership. Saunders recalled afterwards, 'We had a great idea. If we had thought of it in the first series, it would have been fantastic. We suddenly thought, "Patsy was a man!"' She wrote in a fabulous flashback to the 1970s when Patsy was male which featured their hilarious interpretation of an excruciating Sonny and Cher song. But when Saffy asked, 'Mum, what was Patsy?' Edina replied, 'Oh darling, it was only for a year and then it fell off.'

At the height of its popularity *Absolutely Fabulous* was impossibly trendy and stars fell over themselves to land guest spots. The cast list has included Britt Ekland, Mo Gaffney, Lulu, Eleanor Bron, Naomi Campbell, Adrian Edmondson, Dawn French, Richard E. Grant, Germaine Greer, Kate O'Mara, Suzi Quattro, Mandy Rice-Davies, Miranda Richardson and Helena Bonham-Carter.

The success of the show also brought shoals of advertising offers dangling fees of up to £1million for Patsy and Edina to lend their names to all manner of products, but they were firmly turned down by Jennifer. An American Emmy followed and further proof of Joanna's fame arrived when Cellnet featured John Cleese and Ronnie Corbett as unlikely contestants in a Joanna Lumley look-alike competition.

Students at Oxford University's New College were so impressed by Patsy that they voted to change the name of their junior common room from the Nelson Mandela room to the Joanna Lumley room. The actress responded suitably, writing to thank the students: 'From the bottom of my very base heart.'

Patsy and Edina even became unlikely pop stars as they joined forces with the Pet Shop Boys in May 1994 to make an *Absolutely Fabulous* record for Comic Relief. Pop duo Neil Tennant and Chris Lowe admitted afterwards that the record idea was at least partly a ruse to meet the comedy stars properly. Neil said, 'Chris and I are huge fans of *Absolutely Fabulous* and we wanted to fix up a dinner date with the girls.'

The resulting video was very popular and almost as much fun to watch as it was to make. Neil Tennant said, 'Doing the video with Joanna and Jennifer was hilarious. The two of them made us laugh so much that we had to keep stopping filming because we had tears running down our faces. They were doing everything to put us off – crawling between our legs and grabbing our hats off our heads.'

Joanna had her own theory on why bad behaviour made for such good ratings. She believed people were fed up with being so terribly correct and good all the time. And she agreed with Jennifer who said, 'I don't think Patsy and Edina are nasty anyway. I think they're really nice.' Joanna smiled and added, 'Patsy does everything you are not allowed to do – and it is fun.

'So many people ask me if I'm like Patsy and when I was last drunk. And I say, "Hang on, you never asked me if I was a drunk before."

'But I don't know anyone like her. I just made her up out of the blue. I can't think of any part of her life that crosses mine, except she's a woman of my age, using my body. But it's the best fun in the world. She is so incredibly dreadful, there's something marvellous about her. I would be riveted to meet her.

'Patsy isn't me. She has more of a nasal whine than I have. I also give her a round-shouldered walk, with her cigarette going ahead of her which isn't me, but based on someone I know. Patsy has trouble getting out of cars, which I don't. The beehive hair was taken from Ivana Trump. People seem to love Patsy, which has surprised us all: her bad language, her smoking, her smudged lipstick, her what-the-hell, gutsy attitude to life. People find her endearing. I do love playing her. Patsy was a gift from God. It has freed me completely. It's a new kind of writing in which Jennifer Saunders has captured the spirit of the times.

'People will say it is wrong that she smokes and drinks and I will say, "Listen darlings, haven't you any idea of humour?" This politically correct attitude is pathetic. The aim in life is to be kind. That's the only thing.'

Patsy's eighty cigarettes a day smoking habit was always far in excess of Joanna's more modest consumption. She bridled when well-wishers saw her lighting up for real and gave her a lecture on the health dangers. Joanna said, 'I actually smoke about five a day so I feel justified in telling them to bugger off.' But it was always an affectionate relationship between actress and audience. Long after the series had finished Joanna said, I never thought viewers would take Patsy so much to heart that even now they still expect me to behave like her whenever I go out.

She thanked her lucky stars for the strength of her hair. 'It's revoltingly coarse,' she said, 'but incredibly strong, thank God, because it's sprayed and back-combed to within an inch of its life to achieve Patsy's beehive. It looks glamorous but it's too extreme for me to wear.'

Joanna was surprised and highly delighted when she realized her Patsy identity was being copied by gays who loved to wear sky-high blonde beehive wigs, stilettos and tiny leather mini-skirts as a hilarious public tribute. The Way Out club in London's West End became a regular meeting place for a highly unofficial Patsy appreciation society. The star was definitely flattered. 'The gay community is usually first to jump on to what is smart and new. They're usually ahead of the avant garde. Because the show is satirical and quite sort of catty and biting, it amuses them enormously. And the characters are very easy to imitate.

'I went to an AIDS charity show at the London Palladium and there were a lot of gay men there dressed just like Patsy. Apparently they love to imitate her. Some of them looked about seven feet tall with the hair and the shoes. They could all do Patsy's walk but they couldn't do her voice. It was dreadfully funny. I was invited to the Sydney Mardi Gras down in Australia to be on a float. They had five floats of Patsy. They sent me photos and I thought, "Thank God I didn't go." They all looked so much better than I do.

'An awful lot of series at the moment are concerned with homey, normal things, and it's just nice to see people who are obsessed with glamour and glamorous things – even if they get it wrong.

'Patsy's about the only character I've played in my long life who has become another person, who when you get dressed up as her you become her. I've never had any qualms about anything Patsy does at all. In real life I wouldn't do any of these things. The difficulty is that the work you're offered tends to be pale imitations of this. And you can't do it.

'I've been here in a different way twenty years ago with *The New Avengers*. Although it wasn't shown network over here, it was very big in about 138 countries. And whatever scripts I got were kind of Purdey, that character. And I thought, "Will I ever survive this?" The only way to do it is just to believe you will and to keep on taking different parts, turning yourself around. It takes a little bit of time.'

Joanna was endlessly asked how she became Patsy so perfectly and her favourite answer was: 'Think late Sixties. I based her make-up on when I was a model. Lots of eyelashes and the kind of make-up you keep on and apply more to the next day. It's got to be very thick, nothing subtle there. And make a lot of the mouth. Actually I chose a drag queen's tip for Patsy which is to do darker lipstick around the corner of the mouth and put light in the middle. And also big. Nothing is big enough really. So hair can be very, very big. Everything big, including shoulders. The hair was no problem. It's so simple. You get Nice 'N' Easy from Boots for a few pounds and twenty minutes later you are transformed.

'Jennifer's a very generous sort of writer. We always lose ten minutes recorded off the show. It has to be trimmed out. For instance, when we came back from New York with the photograph of the door handle and it was Saffy's birthday, we went off to her room with a little present to cheer her up. There are whole scenes that have been cut because they always run forty-five or fifty minutes for a thirty-minute show. Lots of Morocco, lots of France went.'

The famous brand names mentioned in the show seemed to love the television exposure, even if Patsy and Eddie were taking the mickey. Christian Lacroix made a guest appearance and Joanna was delighted when the makers of Patsy's favourite champagne 'extended an invitation to us to go out to Bollinger in Ay, a little town in France, and see them. We haven't managed to do it yet. But it wasn't exactly crates of Bolli, darling. Bolli did have the grace to write, "You've done more for our PR than all the PR in our history." '

Joanna thought it was highly amusing that it was considered an advantage to have modelling experience to bring to the role. She believed that the only thing Patsy knew was to try to keep her bottom in at all times.

By August 1994 Patsy had registered so strongly with the national consciousness that she was given the recognition of a waxwork model at Madame Tussaud's. Joanna obligingly arrived to be photographed alongside it and was suitably stunned by the likeness. 'My God, it's incredible. The profile is amazing.' In 1998 an Arab millionaire was so taken by the figure that he offered £25,000 for it. Madame Tussaud's refused to sell, for any price, but a suitably impressed spokesman said, 'It's the most expensive offer we've ever had.'

At the very end of the series the relationship between Patsy and Edina changed. Joanna noted, 'When Saffy moved out to get rooms in university, they turned into the odd couple. And I went off to work and she had an apron on. They hadn't realized they'd got into it until they were just about to kiss each other goodbye. And there is just that hideous moment when they've turned into a married couple.'

Thanks to her acclaim as Patsy, it seemed Joanna Lumley was firmly implanted in the public consciousness as the ultimate, ultra-sophisticated West End woman. So of course it was only natural for her to react against that unreal image and go off and live alone on a desert island. Well, alone give or take the odd BBC camera crew. Producer Clive Tulloh was the man in charge of making the documentary optimistically titled *Girl Friday: Joanna Lumley survives on a desert island*.

But at least he had an enthusiastic subject. Joanna was hugely attracted by the prospect of getting completely away from it all. She loved the idea: 'Would you have said No? Spend nine days on a desert island somewhere in the Indian Ocean; exist with a bare minimum of kit, spend much of your time alone, sleep rough, make do, get on with it?' Most actresses would be asking questions about the proximity of the nearest five-star hotel. Joanna wanted no mod cons. She wanted to do it for real and she could hardly wait. Joanna noted afterwards that 'people thought I was mad and questioned my sanity. But my husband and my family, knowing me as they do, smiled in resignation. They would have rather liked to have come too, I suspect.' It was a wonderful opportunity to show the world that there was much more to Joanna than champagne-swigging, city slicker Patsy.

Before she set off she went for two crammed days of survival training with the Irish Guards. Joanna learned quickly how to purify water, make a fire, build a shelter, and at all times keep her spirits up.

Tulloh certainly had his work cut out. Finding the right island was anything but simple. It had to have a real Robinson Crusoe look to it with beautiful beaches, a hill, water and food to eat. But as Joanna refused to compromise on her simple vegetarian princi- ple: 'Never eat anything with a face', it could not be an isle where the main source of food was fish. Eventually Tsarabaina, which translates as Beautiful Sands, in the Indian Ocean some thirty miles off the north-west coast of Madagascar, was selected. A survival expert checked out the wildlife in advance and declared the island free of poisonous snakes. The idea was for Robinson Lumley to spend nine days on the exotic location, for the crew to film Joanna during the day and retreat to the comparative luxury of the BBC boat at night, leaving her sleeping alone with nature. It is hard to imagine any other actress even contemplating, let alone accepting such a tough challenge.

Joanna kept a diary of her time on Tsarabaina and typically threw herself wholeheartedly into the adventure. On day one she insisted she felt as though she was on a blind date and wanted to love her island and be part of it. But once dropped off by helicopter she felt nervous and alone as she waited for her rendezvous with the crew. She had spent so much time being typically enthusiastic that the reality of being left alone on a desert island was daunting. Joanna had slept under the stars before but she had never had to make her own shelter. She'd usually had sleeping bags and tents and clocks and Thermos flasks full of nourishing drinks to keep her company.

Joanna's essential supplies were basic indeed. She was left alone at night with two knives and a sharpening stone, two empty bean tins to cook in, an army mug, a piece of sacking the size of a large carpet, 1lb of rice, mosquito repellent and 25-factor sun cream. Her wardrobe was more empty than bare: a pair of socks, one pair of pants, one bra, one bathing dress, shorts, short-sleeved shirt, trousers, three sarongs and army issue ladies trainers. She also had a drawing book, a diary, pencils and pens, needles, string, fishing hooks and nylon line, flint and striker, four matches, three vegetable stock cubes, water purifying tablets, a button compass and a video camera with which she recorded her remarkable expe- riences for our screens. And the BBC wisely insisted she also had a walkie-talkie so in an emergency she could call for help. Joanna didn't really want to have the lifeline with the boat. She said, 'I know I won't use it unless I'm made to . . . if I fell over and snapped a limb, the jig would be up, no film and maybe a drifting corpse for the BBC, so it is a sensible plan. It's just that being sensible is sometimes a bore, a dampener on the spiky edges of fright and excitement.'

As the crew left her at the end of the first day spent filming her arrival, Joanna was still struggling to build her shelter, and get her bearings. She decided to construct an A-frame shelter as described in the SAS survival handbooks, using some long poles left by visiting fishermen. It was a desperately difficult task. As Joanna recorded, 'In my handbook it says it takes two men to make the A-frame and now the sun is going and I haven't got firewood, or done the lashings properly or put up the mosquito net.' Joanna's confidence was at a low ebb as she struggled to record her crucial video verdict as darkness fell. At least the mosquito net gave her some cheer. She recalled, 'As children my sister and I slept under them in the Far East; to me they symbolize security and happiness and make the dullest bedroll into a Turkish palace.'

On the second day rain fell in buckets which at least solved Joanna's concerns about finding a supply of fresh water, even if it did make the island paradise look 'like Aldershot'. She found a huge habitable cave, which she christened the Albert Hall, that soon seemed a safer, drier and more sensible place to sleep than her flimsy shelter on the beach.

There was a long list of things Girl Friday was not allowed, which would have floored less intrepid explorers. No books to read, no soap or brush and comb, no toothbrush, no mirror, no music, no hand cream, towel or nail-file, no scissors, no alcohol and no cigarettes. It was quite an undertaking and Joanna relied heavily on her two days with the Irish Guards constantly rerunning in her head the jumble of information from her survival course. To Joanna it was desperately important not to let them down and as she put it 'not to behave in a manner ill-fitting to the daughter of a Chindit. My father became one of Wingate's famous force in 1943 and spent six months behind Japanese lines in Burma. Their movements were directed by wireless and they were supplied and supported by air. The conditions were unspeakable. I can hardly be defeated by a spot of rain and not much food for just over a week.'

The third day began with a scare. Joanna awoke early and waited for the BBC boat to arrive. The waves looked threateningly high so after a while she radioed them to be told they had endured a choppy night and the sea was still too rough for them to be able to land. Joanna used the time to explore her new empire, and to make herself some shoes out of her bra. Her feet never seemed to dry out in the uncomfortable army trainers, and she described the thought to convert her bra into more luxurious footwear as 'an idea the size of the Ritz'. And to prove she was doing it herself she switched on the video camera from the start of the delicate operation. She bent the cups of her bra around the toes of the insoles from her trainers and stitched them in place with her sewing kit. It was always very important to Joanna to play the game by the rules. As she explained in her official record of the trip, 'Why am I so anxious to prove that I am doing these things myself? I suppose because before I left everyone said, "Oh well, you'll have food and sleep on the boat with the crew and use the telephone and wash your hair." But it's so remarkable and tough here that I couldn't bear it if people thought I was skiving. The crew offered me food yesterday, but of course I didn't take it, nor shall I. I've got to do this thing properly, even if I'm the only one who knows.'

It was still a very depressing time for Joanna. She was bitten all over by insects and weak from hunger, and a relentless tropical downpour threatened to turn the programme into a rain-soaked flop. Joanna was dejected. Afterwards she said, 'It hit me like an axe. I was quite weak due to lack of food and I had been bitten all over by sandflies and mosquitoes. All I could think was, "How am I going to get out of this?"' She passed out twice due to hunger and dehydration but she hung on because of her father. 'He would have been so ashamed of me if I had packed it in. I just had to talk myself through my black mood. I kept saying, "Pull yourself together." I felt terribly low, really depressed. In the end I slept for a while, woke up and gave myself a good talking to. I convinced myself I was just being a wimp and managed to pull myself together. Then the sun came out and it was like a different world. Suddenly I was in paradise.'

The bra shoes were a great success and lifted Joanna's spirits considerably. Her *Ab Fab* co-star Jennifer Saunders was so impressed she suggested Joanna should put the shoes in a museum. Much of the charm of the eventual programme was the frank and revealing openness with which she described her moods and feelings. In a moment of damp sleepless despair at night she reflected on day four: 'I can't believe that this is what was intended when the idea of this film came up: an angry middle-aged bagwoman in a dark cave doing nothing and complaining. I shall have to pull myself together.'

A flask of coffee next day lifted the Lumley morale and she set to digging up sweet potatoes which she noted made an interesting contrast from casually selecting them at Sainsbury's. She did bend some of the rules just a little. The crew gave her the odd apple and mango and knocked down a coconut for her to crack open. She even cadged some life-saving cigarettes and had her own small secret supply of booze. Afterwards Joanna beamed: 'I had a honey pot filled with Scotch that I smuggled off my flight from London. I couldn't have faced nine whole days without a taste of alcohol.' Patsy would surely have approved.

Her most relaxing times were in the evening when she would often take off her bathing dress and wander naked round her cave to dry off. These scenes did not make it to the screen but in her most private moments Joanna was delighted to feel 'a great tranquillity suddenly overcomes me'. Early one morning she was entranced to witness scores of baby turtles trundling down to the sea. 'Brave little creatures,' she cheered.

In spite of the lack of home comforts, Joanna immensely enjoyed the solitary feel of life on the island and with it the need for neatness. Her small collection of precious possessions recalled for her the early days at Mickledene School where in an area under the dark fir trees the young boarders swept the earth and marked out separate properties with pebbles. When everything was 'tickety-boo' they would invite each other in to have nettle tea. As she said in her remarkable record of the experience: 'The happiness of man lies in the fewness of his wants.'

The seventh day was perhaps the most difficult. The heat was overwhelming, peaking at around 110° F. Joanna found the sandflies insufferable: 'I've lived and travelled all over the world but never come across such awful insects as the sandflies here. They swarm all over me and I'm covered in bites, which itch constantly. But if you scratch, you risk infection. I'm also covered in blisters the size of ping-pong balls which burst then scab. Again, every instinct is to scratch, but I've no antiseptic so they could turn nasty.'

After her eight nights on the island Joanna reflected on the experience. She had survived certainly but there was never going to be any doubt about that. The BBC would hardly put her on an island and leave her to die. But would anyone want to spend their life quite alone? She thought, 'Not I. I love people and I love all the complicated and sophisticated things people achieve, like piano concertos, the Sistine Chapel, Indian take-aways, gardening catalogues. But what I have been allowed here is something more precious than platinum and that is solitude. It took a very short time to let go of the world outside, but when it had gone I felt completely at peace with myself.'

Absolutely Fabulous was such a ground-breaking landmark of a show that the whole television world sat up and took notice. Privately Joanna believed that the show was so hilariously anarchic it unlocked even the stiffest reserve among its viewers. Publicly she was delighted with the reaction. 'After *Ab Fab* came out,' she said, 'people would come up to me and generously say how much the show made them laugh and how good it was to be laughing again. I think people were just grateful to be holding their sides again. I remember feeling the same way when *Fawlty Towers* came on. You had been longing to laugh and then suddenly you were sobbing with laughter.'

After two hit series of *Ab Fab* Joanna started work on her starring role in ITV's *Class Act* as Kate Swift, an aristocratic Englishwoman down on her luck. It begins with Kate being sent to prison. She has to carry the can when her husband dies leaving her in a financial mess.

Writer Michael Aitkens had already enjoyed comedy success with the ground-breaking BBC sit-com *Waiting for God*, and he and *Class Act* producer Verity Lambert agreed that Joanna Lumley would be perfect to play their leading lady when they met at the

BBC Christmas party in 1992 just as *Absolutely Fabulous* was flavour of the moment.

Joanna was sent the script and observed afterwards: 'It made me laugh out loud, which I thought was a good sign.' She knew even then it was going to be virtually impossible to follow Patsy but felt that: 'The danger is to overreact and go off immediately and play something completely different like Lady Macbeth. In the end it's the writing, you feel the part is yours, you can hear your voice saying the lines. Also you can only do what you're offered. I've never been in a position where I can stand around snapping my fingers saying: "I want to do this, I want to do that." '

Kate Swift was an upper-crust woman with massive problems caused by her late husband's dirty dealings. She found herself in jail for six months after seedy journalist Jack Booker, played by John Bowe, tipped off the police that she was involved in her husband's tax-dodging deals.

Despite the unpromising start of their relationship Kate and the cowardly reporter formed an alliance to uncover the real mystery of the late Mr Swift and his missing fortune. They teamed up with Gloria O'Grady, an Australian burglar played by actress Nadine Gardner, in a cheerful comedy drama that ran for two undemanding series.

At the outset Joanna said, 'I'd like to think I have something in common with Kate Swift. She is a born fighter, a lot of fun and very witty. It was magic to play her.' But she was rightly apprehensive about taking on any new role after such an outstanding success as Patsy. 'I just hope viewers will forget me as Patsy for a little while because Kate is a completely different person, and such a big switch is always difficult for viewers to accept. She is incredibly bossy and an unbearable snob but she will try anything. She was great fun to play, but very different from Patsy.'

It was a perfectly adequate show and attracted audiences of well over ten million viewers, but with *Absolutely Fabulous* still running and still sky high in audience affections Joanna never really had a chance to register as strongly as kindly, accident-prone Kate as she had as pulsating Patsy. But it certainly gave her some memorable moments. For Joanna perhaps the most unforgettable scene was recorded with her dangling from a cable from Battersea Power

Station hundreds of feet from the ground. Joanna had to scale the heights for a story which had Kate, and her dubious chums, rushing to the rescue of the future husband of her cousin Tilly, played by Trevyn McDowell, who was threatening to throw himself off the huge structure. Joanna said afterwards that she had been trembling with fear: 'I am absolutely terrified of heights. But it was not actually as dangerous a thing to do as it looked. We were all on safety ropes, but I couldn't bring myself to look down. I would have been sick.'

Joanna faced a different sort of high jump when her older sister Ælene Frey took great offence when Joanna's character in *Class Act* used the name 'Lainie', the name family and friends use for her, to play a high-class prostitute. The sisters had not been as close as they once were and Ælene and her husband Martin Frey were so enraged they took the unusual step of airing their grievances in the newspapers.

Ælene said, 'You might describe me as being a hurt older sister. I can't remember a word of that episode after hearing my name given to a prostitute. I just don't know why she has done this. I have always thought she was fantastically friendly and loyal.'

Joanna was quick to apologize and insisted the script was 'completely inoffensive'. But Ælene's husband disagreed. Martin Frey retorted angrily, 'This programme has been used for the purposes of a vendetta. Lainie is what absolutely everyone calls my wife. My wife is in black despair.'

The rift widened when Joanna reportedly asked media psychiatrist Dr Anthony Clare to examine Ælene. Joanna made an appearance in Clare's radio programme *In the Psychiatrist's Chair*, and Ælene was incensed when it was suggested she might need help. Ælene said, 'I feel insulted and degraded. Jo thinks I need help and tries to get her celebrity friends to provide it. We were close and once lived together in London but everything has changed.' She clearly felt stardom had changed her sister for the worse. 'She is beautiful, talented and we are proud of her. But fame hardens the heart and casts a shadow across those nearby.'

Ælene went on to give long interviews detailing her sadness that the sisters were no longer close. She recalled that during their schooldays, 'Jo got away with murder because she had such a forceful personality. I was always seen as the boring little prig. I was filled with admiration for her but it could be infuriating.' Ælene said that when *Absolutely Fabulous* became a huge hit Joanna turned very grand. Joanna slammed the phone down on her sister and Ælene said, 'She didn't want to hear what I was saying. She was so famous. I was trying to say that I never saw her any more and that fame was separating us, but she said she loved fame and slammed the phone down. It was awful. I was just trying to say I wanted to see more of her ... she seemed to lose her sense of humour. She talked to us in a stage voice as if we were fans rather than family.' Joanna firmly refuses to discuss the relationship with her sister. In May 1997 the sisters' mother Beatrice collapsed with a heart attack and a newspaper contacted Ælene's home where husband Martin was reported as saying, 'We didn't know about this. We are not in contact with Lainie's mother.'

Friends say the sisters have now agreed not to speak publicly about their feelings for each other again. They are concerned that any sort of negative publicity could upset their elderly parents.

As the second series of *Class Act* was launched on television Joanna was facing the hairdressers again for another serious haircut to play upper-crust Leslie Crosbie in Somerset Maugham's play *The Letter*. She considered a wig but admitted, 'I had one at home and I pinned it to my head but it looked as though I had slapped on a dead dog. I knew the exact look I wanted to get by studying pictures from the original production in 1927 starring Gladys Cooper.' When six inches were scissored off the length Joanna was shocked. She peered in a mirror at the hairdresser's and cried, 'Lord, who are you?' But then she smiled in approval though she observed, 'The first thing I'll do is scratch my neck with the hair-brush because I'm so used to tugging it through my helmet-like hair. And when I wash it there'll be nothing there.' When it was blowdried Joanna announced, 'Perfect. It's just what I want. I look like a Roaring Twenties tennis star. When I turned forty, people told me to only have short hair, but I said "Bollocks" and grew it even longer. But I love it like this, even if I do have a face like a hammer-headed shark.'

The Letter is a tense melodrama set in Malaya about a planter's wife who shoots her lover when she discovers that he prefers his

Chinese mistress to her. It was based on a real life incident that happened in 1911 and is set on just the sort of steamy colonial verandas which Joanna recalled from the three years she spent in Kuala Lumpur as a child. 'I am a great admirer of Maugham's work,' she said. 'He can pick up an incident and observe it through a microscope like a scientist. There's the density of his writing in that opaque and terribly claustrophobic temperature of his time, not just in the climate. Seething passions under formality is always quite interesting. I spent three of the most formative years of my life there from 1951. It was the time of the emergency and travel was restricted and when we went somewhere else it was in armoured convoy because it was quite dangerous with communist and terrorist uprisings and shootings and things, though to a child it meant nothing. It was normal. I always thought that with my background I would be cast in *Jewel in the Crown* because I was born in India, but I was not even looked at. I thought they would call me for *Tenko*, but I was not mentioned.'

Joanna took advice from old friend Simon Callow before accepting the role at Hammersmith's Lyric Theatre. Her character was an elegant vision in linen, a stylish pillar of the Empire, first seen holding a smoking revolver. In this version the director, Neil Bartlett, returned to the author's original ending which required a demanding monologue with a distinct absence of Patsy-style laughs. Joanna warmed to the challenge: 'Leslie is like an iceberg. Only the very top can show, until the very end. But then it should be rather like the bit in *Fantasia – A Night on the Bare Mountain* – where the devil opens his wings and gives a glimpse of hell. Suddenly, you see her life stretching before her, in bare weariness.' She refused to accept that the drama was dated: 'I don't think it is at all dated. It is about passion, jealousy, guilt – things that happen any time anywhere. The main thing you have to do is get round the way they spoke, so clear and precise. We have tried to weld present-speak and past-speak, until it becomes so natural that we almost think in those structured sentences.' She loved the play because it took her back 'to that proper, enclosed, formal world. A world of ceiling fans and rickshaws and bicycles. A placid, ordered way of life. Now the cities are huge and elegant and you play tennis on a cooled court. It is completely westernized. I remember Kuala

Lumpur as it was when I went shopping with mummy. The smelly river and the beautiful stuccoed houses. You always spoke of England as "home", even if you had never been there. The planters' houses in Malaya were like the stockbroker belt in Surrey, all chintz and gables.'

The Letter certainly arrived for critic Jack Tinker who gave Joanna one of his most generous reviews: 'Joanna Lumley, as the object of all these tangled emotions, gives a performance of luminous credibility. Her steely charm in the early scenes invites awe and admiration.'

Joanna was awarded the OBE in 1995 and was thrilled by the honour. 'I don't think anyone thinks their name is going to be pulled out of a hat. But, when it happens, it is a great honour. I feel deeply humbled by it.'

The American attitude to *Absolutely Fabulous* was almost as funny as the show itself. The political incorrectness which is at the very heart of the comedy's appeal frightened the networks to their core. The show was an instant hit when shown in the United States on the Comedy Central cable channel in 1994. But even on cable most of the stronger language was 'bleeped' to avoid offending American ears. Patsy's shrieks of 'bollocks' escaped the ban however. The censors did not know what the word meant.

Warner Brothers saw the appeal in producing an American version and millionaire actress–producer Roseanne Barr who loved the show was brought in, and Carrie Fisher and Barbara Carrera were tentatively lined up to play Edina and Patsy but the idea was doomed from the start. The Americans were wary of upsetting either advertisers or viewers. And as they planned to show it coast to coast, Patsy's endless supply of Bollinger champagne was drastically reduced and her cocaine snorting habit was axed altogether. Even cigarette smoking was cut and the level of outrageous behaviour became a huge problem. Warner Brothers Television President, Leslie Moonves, insisted they were trying to keep the compromises to a minimum and that Roseanne Barr was pushing the writers to keep in as much of the 'danger' as possible. But he admitted there would be significant changes. In a masterpiece of understatement he said, 'Irony is not something that we Americans do well. But we are going to try to be as faithful as we possibly can, while still appealing to our audience.'

The original *Absolutely Fabulous* was clearly much too strong for the networks to contemplate for their audience. Moonves said, 'Although there has been a reduction in the restrictions on American television programming, we still have to sell our shows to advertisers. In terms of language and the use of drugs, the original was quite extreme. The use of amphetamines and cocaine will be toned down. The sexual references in your current version will also be tempered somewhat.'

Roseanne loved the show and even considered using its British stars. Joanna was flattered to be asked to America to work on the show but she said, 'No thanks – I belong here. I suppose there were vast amounts of money on offer but that didn't really come into it for me.'

Joanna was concerned that she would see even less of her busy conductor husband if she headed for Hollywood. Even when based in the same country the two found their busy schedules meant long periods apart. 'He is here and that is where I want to be,' she said simply. In 1995 Stephen Barlow travelled to New Zealand, Australia and Florida before taking up a position in Belfast in 1996. Joanna frequently flew thousands of miles to be able to spend just a few days with him. 'I think it's essential for us to be together whenever we can,' she said. 'Otherwise I end up looking at his photograph. I would much rather have the real thing. But unfortunately we are apart a lot and we spend an awful lot of the time on the telephone or sending faxes. Or writing each other long letters.'

But the show remained very popular on cable and built up a cult audience in the States. Roseanne even considered using stars like Sharon Stone and Kirstie Alley as Patsy and Edina but Roseanne's enthusiasm was hardly helped by endless interminable meetings with executives who all shook their heads when they examined the content of the shows. The frustrating thing was that they almost all said how much they personally had enjoyed the show with its vigour and uncompromising aggression, but they didn't believe their audience was ready for such honesty yet. In the end, as the original shows gathered larger and larger cable audiences and the CBS sit-com *Cybill* followed some *Ab Fab* themes, the idea was scrapped. British producer Jon Plowman agreed with the decision. He knew that the delicious meanness of the leading characters was an integral part of the charm of the show. He said the show could never have started in America because the US has a cosier tradition for situation comedies. And he noted, 'I mean, it would have had to end with a scene where they all hug and Patsy goes off to the Betty Ford Clinic.' But Roseanne featured Jennifer and Joanna as Edina and Patsy in a wonderful Hallowe'en edition of her own show in 1996. Jennifer Saunders remained a firm fan of Roseanne Barr: 'I was flattered that Roseanne wanted to do it. I think she's a genius.'

The top-rating American news programme *60 Minutes* did a semi-serious investigation into how such irreverence could be so popular. The Americans appeared astonished that *Absolutely Fabulous* could make fun out of subjects like foreign adoptions, environmentalists or even the starving homeless and build up a cult audience. Joanna's voice certainly registered on the other side of the Atlantic, however, and she was chosen to be the online personality of the computer service America Online.

By 1995 as the third series hit the screens Jennifer Saunders had had enough. The second series had attracted some muted criticism for not quite living up to the wonderful opening and in any case Jennifer wanted to move on. She said writing series three was sheer torture. 'I knew people would hate the second series because they had seen it all before. I had to try to give a different feel to it because of that. It's more manic, slightly blacker. This final series is different again. It takes the two of them twenty-five years into the future, after they have both failed to break away and lead independent lives. The pair of them remind you of Steptoe and Son, or Basil and Sybil Fawlty. They may not get on, but they can't live without each other.'

The third series opened with a hilarious dream sequence with Edina in bed wearing her 'Nothing Special' T-shirt, and moved quickly on as Edina and Patsy hit New York. They revealed a wonderful new method of high-speed shopping using a divining rod to select clothes faster than the human eye could manage. But Patsy, who had moved to a US magazine, was rather less than a roaring success in the Big Apple. 'Is your hair on purpose?'

demanded the magazine's marketing chief as Patsy failed in her usual job security ploy of sleeping with the publisher. The devastating duo flew out, on Concorde of course, on an afternoon shopping trip when Edina was in search of the perfect door handle to complete her kitchen. By the end of the series Edina declared herself 'orphaned' because Saffy had moved out of the house to live on campus and she told Patsy that she desperately needed to find herself because as she brilliantly put it: 'Sweetie, I've been to paradise but I've never been to me.' The outrageous formula worked beautifully. This time the role reversal between mother and daughter Edina and Saffy was back on top form. Saffy flushed her mother's stash of drugs down the toilet and demanded the kitchen was made more workable, after Patsy had destroyed it in a previous episode. Edina of course was much more concerned with the shape of the door knobs or her next chemically assisted high.

The third series was studded with inventive highlights. In the second show, 'Happy New Year', Edina and Patsy were planning to go to the most fabulous club on the planet when news comes of the imminent arrival of Patsy's long-lost sister, Jackie.

'Sex' featured Saffy planning a lecture on genetics and ethics, while Patsy persuades Edina that they should throw an orgy. In 'Jealous', it was awards time in PR land. Edina seemed set to sweep the board, especially as she had paid for the awards – but arch-rival Claudia Bing has other ideas. Meanwhile, Saffy received extra special tuition from her psychology lecturer. 'Fear' saw Patsy move in to live with Edina when Saffy moved out. However, it proves to be a turbulent arrangement, especially when they can't find the tin opener. Further trouble erupted when Lulu arrived at Edina's office to terminate her contract and sign with a high-powered American agency. Patsy loses her job when her magazine folds, leaving the high-living pair contemplating old age and a crossroads in their lives.

Finally in 'The End', first screened on 11 May 1995, Patsy and Edina went their separate ways, but could they live without each other? Of course not. After the credits rolled the viewers were given a wonderful glimpse of the bizarre pair twenty-five years down the road.

Joanna took the best comedy actress award at the 1995 BAFTAs, and remained enchanted with the role of permanently plastered Patsy. 'She was just wonderful for me,' said Joanna. 'Because she gave me the chance to be funny. I just can't do beautiful acting any more. Whenever I see a script that says, "Door opens, in comes Petunia, she's gorgeous, long legs, cool blonde," I turn it down.'

But the end was not quite the end. Jennifer Saunders was prevailed upon to provide a finale in the shape of the two-part film *The Last Shout*, which was transmitted in November 1996. It began with Patsy and Edina's skiing trip to Val d'Isère in France and closed with high drama surrounding Saffy's wedding.

Joanna spent her fiftieth birthday in Val d'Isère in a blizzard on a mountain top shooting *Ab Fab The Last Shout*. 'It was memorable in every way except for having no party at all. Since *Ab Fab* and Patsy I've been offered 1,000 drunken women parts, all badly written, I might add. All of them hadn't picked up on what Patsy was which was someone more complex than that.'

The grand finale opened memorably with Edina lolling in her bedroom porpoise pool, languidly singing the theme from *Flipper* and wishing her fat away. Patsy had passed out with a cigarette in her mouth in her flat which was conveniently-located in an off licence. When Edina is publicly criticized for keeping a porpoise in captivity she is warned that Greenpeace can intervene. But she snorts back: 'They owe me. I bumper-stickered the organization into existence.' Patsy had her own problems, struggling to hang on to her job as fashion editor. She is told it must be tough facing talent that is so much younger. 'Not younger,' she yells back. 'It's the gay Mafia.'

Happily the quality of insults was still sky high. Strait-laced Saffy sneers to promiscuous Patsy: 'Sleeping with you must be akin to necrophilia.' But Patsy hits back, 'You're a virgin in a world where men will turn to soft fruit for pleasure.' When they arrived at the snooty resort they were in for a disappointment: 'No Cher, no Ivana, no minor royalty, no crowned heads.' But they still managed to get into trouble. Edina got lost on the slopes while Patsy flaked out on the ski lift. The endlessly single Saffy finally met Mr Right in the shape of passionate Paolo played by Tom Hollander. When Edina met his parents and found out they were wealthy she was seriously impressed. As she characteristically put it, 'These people are so mega-conglomerate, one small withdrawal and Switzerland goes Third World. These people could order China as a takeaway.' So she goes overboard on the arrangements. 'For flowers,' she instructs at the top of her voice, 'just mow the Netherlands.'

Naturally the wedding does not go precisely to plan but the guest list was dazzling as celebrities queued up to be part of the fun. Best of all Marianne Faithful played God and sang a new version of 'Wheels on Fire'. Producer Jon Plowman reflected on the 'phenomenal success of the show. It was much bigger than we dared to hope.'

He also inquired if this really was the end of *Absolutely Fabulous*. As the closing studio scenes were recorded in front of 500 people he asked Jennifer Saunders if 'The Last Shout' really was the grand finale. Saunders replied cryptically, 'Well, maybe one for the Millennium.' But sadly as 1999 drifted towards its over-publicized close there was no sign of a last stand from Patsy. Joanna rather agreed with the decision to go out at the top. She said, "Someone once said you should always leave your audience want-ing more and I agree with that. Patsy was *Absolutely Fabulous* but she is over.'

Joanna's exotic family background provided the inspiration for another major journey and another book and television programme in 1997 when the dream of *In The Kingdom of the Thunder Dragon* became a remarkable reality. Joanna had nurtured an ambition to retrace the steps of one of her more remarkable ancestors for many years. In 1931 her maternal grandfather, the British Political Officer Colonel Leslie J. Weir was dispatched to the remote country of Bhutan to invest the second King of Bhutan, one Jigme Wangchuck, with the Order of Knight Commander of the Indian Empire. Landlocked in the eastern Himalayas by its powerful neighbours India and China, Bhutan has rigorously protected its traditional way of life and tourists were limited to some 2,500 a year.

Joanna decided to travel with her cousin Myfanwy 'Maybe' Jehu, whose illness years before had been one of the sparks for her grim breakdown. Joanna is very proud of her family history. She said, 'My grandmother Thyra Weir was the first European woman ever to be allowed into Lhasa, the capital of Tibet, so of course my interest in this whole project is very strong.' Joanna was inspired by the discovery of some creaking old black and white footage of her grandfather's journey. She and Maybe packed some essentials for the trip in the shape of cosmetics and bottles of drink and BBC cameras recorded as they retraced the arduous trip on the backs of ponies. It made fascinating television as Joanna was entranced by a native people with enormous charm and affection for Britain. They even spoke English and played Bingo. It was so cold at night Joanna and Maybe slept in their clothes. Joanna said, 'My only concession to getting undressed was to take off my bra!'

Joanna kept all her underwear safely in place for her more conventional role in two long Rosamunde Pilcher adaptations, *Coming Home* and its sequel *Nancherrow* in 1998 and 1999. Her role as the glamorous and sophisticated Diana Carey-Lewis, mother of the accident-prone Loveday was perhaps not one of her more demanding parts.

Joanna said charitably, 'This is a very different part for me. *Coming Home* was the first time I had played the mother of grown-up children in period costume. When I read the script, I thought to myself that here was something I would certainly stay in and watch, which is always a good guideline. I love things that have long rolling stories.'

Exactly twenty years after *The New Avengers* had finished, Joanna, who has maintained the firm friendships she formed with Gareth Hunt and Patrick Macnee, once more found herself acting opposite Macnee in *Nancherrow*. 'It was the first time we had done anything together since *The New Avengers*,' explains Joanna. 'It was so long ago, but it seems like yesterday every time I see him again. We have always kept in touch over the years.'

Poignantly Joanna and Macnee shared key scenes together, just the two of them, when Joanna as aristocratic but increasingly hard-up Diana Carey-Lewis, calls on Macnee, her wealthy cousin Lord Awliscombe, and uses all her considerable charm to persuade him to part with some of his money.

Since Macnee had made his home in California he and Joanna had not seen each other for many years. It was a chance for them to talk over old times, and the genuine respect and affection they felt for each other was apparent to all. Several of Macnee's scenes were filmed at 5.30 on bitterly cold mornings outside one of the largest stately homes in England where Macnee, as Lord Awliscombe, was supposed to live alone with only a butler and a basset hound for company. Anticipating that Macnee, by now seventy-six years old, would find the freezing cold difficult to bear, Joanna took the trouble personally to fill up her own small hot water bottle and lent it to him to put under his coat. Once filming was over, Joanna even insisted on hearing news from Macnee that he had safely returned to the more temperate weather of Palm Springs.

More substantially Joanna had a wonderful role alongside Albert Finney and Tom Courtenay in the award-winning BBC film, *A Rather English Marriage*. It was a gem of a part as gold-digging divorcee Liz who sees old RAF hero Reggie, played by Albert Finney, as the way out of her financial difficulties. This time when Joanna read the script she just knew she had to play the part, even if it most definitely did mean taking her clothes off.

'Nudity isn't daunting if it's right,' insisted Joanna. 'What is nerve-wracking when you do love scenes is when there is some element of prurience about it and you have to try to look attractive. That is the bad bit when you know people in the audience are saying, "She looks like a dog." But when Liz climbed into bed with wheezing Reggie it was so beautifully played and so movingly well written that viewers almost felt like cheering the old boy, even if he did finish up in hospital with a stroke.'

Joanna did find it strange but then she said, 'It's always strange kissing somebody passionately who is not your husband. But if you are acting somebody it isn't strange because you jump into different people who do these things – it's not embarrassing.' Joanna loved working with the two senior British stars. ' When you play tennis with Tim Henman your game goes up and if you're working with Finney and Courtenay the same thing happens. They were almost the reason I went into the business. You watch Albert in *Tom Jones* or Tom in *The Loneliness of the Long Distance Runner* and think, "If only." You think you'll never meet, let alone work with these people.'

Her co-stars seemed to enjoy the experience just as much. Albert Finney said, 'I have admired Joanna's work for ages, but I had no idea what to expect from working with her. In the event she was delightful, great fun and larky. I felt immediately relaxed and easy working with her – what more can you ask for?' And Tom Courtenay agreed: 'Joanna is a good egg.' Which seems to sum up Britain's loveliest leading lady rather well.

Of all her many varied productions Joanna is by a considerable margin most proud of her strapping 6ft 2in son Jamie. She refused to allow the lonely trauma of his birth ever for a second to put her off the joys of being a mother and she fiercely protected her son from his earliest days. She has never regretted the decision to bring Jamie up alone or to withhold the identity of the father from the public gaze as he was growing up. The secrecy was an exercise in damage limitation: 'I did what I thought was best at the time. I wanted to protect my family,' said Joanna. 'I was afraid that when Jamie was young the press would have made something of it and I didn't want his school life disturbed.'

But although their love affair was over Joanna remained friends with photographer Michael Claydon. 'Michael and I have always been very close,' said Joanna. 'He came to Jamie's confirmation, and our families have always been in touch. We were like a normal divorced family. All my friends, everybody knew – except the Press.' The information was widely known but in 1997 it became official, when the announcement of Jamie's engagement to girl-friend Louise Griffin appeared in *The Times* naming both parents.

Jamie was delighted and said, 'I have always known who my dad is and he has always known I am his son. We are very close, even though his identity has been kept secret from the public. Now he will be at my wedding and I'm thrilled. It will be a special day for us all. Dad has met Louise and they get on well.' Jamie was never drawn to a showbusiness career and now earns a living teaching remedial English to prisoners.

Michael Claydon appeared relieved that the secret was out. He laughed, 'It's obvious he's my son when you see us together as we look so alike – he's a good-looking boy.' Joanna was very proud as dashing twenty-year-old Jamie married office worker Louise at St

David's Roman Catholic Church in East Cowes on the Isle of Wight. The family lined up for an historic photograph as Jamie, Louise, Joanna, her husband Stephen, former lover Michael and his wife of three years Rita were snapped together for the first time.

As Jamie escorted his beautiful bride, wearing a full-length ivory gown and carrying white lilies, to their wedding car, he said, 'It's my wedding day and I'm naturally very happy that my whole family are here.' Joanna was beaming as she said, 'It's all out now and I'm deliriously happy. Weddings are magic and it's a magical one today. The sun is shining, everyone's happy and it couldn't be more perfect.' Afterwards she noted, 'The service started with "My Eyes Have Seen The Glory of the Coming of the Lord". Stephen was playing the organ. It was terribly moving. I did get choked up but I didn't blub.'

Sadly, the blissful happiness generated by her son Jamie's wedding in July 1997 was all too brief. As Jamie and Louise settled down to married life on the Isle of Wight, where her mother Julie was the island's former High Sheriff, the couple experienced problems finding peace together after the headline-hitting excitement of their wedding.

Within a year Jamie was booked into the exclusive Priory hospital in Roehampton in south-west London, in what was described as a state of severe distress. A fellow patient revealed that Jamie was troubled by difficulties in his marriage and had developed a serious alcohol problem. Far from shunning her son, as other celebrity parents have been known to do, Joanna was incredibly supportive. She paid £12,000 for the month's treatment that Jamie received and took an active part in the regular Thursday family sessions. Another patient in the hospital's addiction unit said, 'His mum was absolutely fantastic. She visited him a lot, and didn't try to distance herself, or disown him or anything like that. There was the obvious irony of her playing such a lush on telly as Patsy, who makes fun of her drinking problem and there was her son having treatment in an addiction unit – but that was not important. Joanna took Jamie's condition very seriously and did everything she possibly could to help him.'

Jamie impressed the other patients as a thoroughly nice chap, determined not to be affected by his mother's celebrity. 'He wanted to be treated the same as everyone else,' said the fellow patient. 'But with patients like Paul Gascoigne, Ruby Wax and Eric Clapton, it was not at all a special event to see a famous face around the place anyway.'

After his initial treatment Jamie had his own small room in the block of thirty on the west wing, which is reserved for men and women with alcohol and other addictions. Like the other patients his day began with fifteen minutes of meditation, and the treatment moved on to the group therapy that the Priory sets such store by. One patient explained, 'Along with the rest of us Jamie had to get himself over to Galsworthy Lodge, the building in the grounds used as a daytime addiction unit. The whole idea is that you are a group together and you work together to help each other get better. You have a meeting at eight thirty and meditation to start the day and at nine o'clock you have your first group therapy. There is no one-to-one counselling, it is all group therapy.'

The patients sit in a circle and announce their names and the nature of their addiction and then with two counsellors present they talk about their problems.

Whilst at the Priory Jamie was visited by his wife, Louise. A fellow patient recalls, 'She was very supportive and very nice. She was lovely, a real rosy-cheeked country girl, but then we heard that the marriage was in trouble while he was in there and we were all very sad. You become very close in the Priory.'

Like the others Jamie had to write his 'life story', which consisted of several thousand revealing words about his deepest feelings and insecurities in an attempt to discover the source of his alcohol dependence. Jamie's was a sad tale of a lack of self-esteem. The shadow of his upbringing certainly seemed to hang heavily over his life, said the patient.

Joanna was devastated when her only son's life collapsed. Privately she was wracked with anxieties that all her years of determined protection had conspired to undermine her son. A friend said, 'When Jamie was taken ill it was like all of her nightmares had come true at once. She loves him very much and she will always feel responsible for him. Joanna was trying to protect her son and her family from the publicity that her fame carries with it. Suddenly she felt full of guilt and remorse that perhaps Jamie had suffered from the very acts which were intended to support him.'

But in any case Jamie's marriage was sadly over and his mother swept back into maternal mode. She took him back to Stockwell and set about helping him to find a suitable flat from where he could start to rebuild his life. But through the agonizing process mother and son became closer than ever to each other. She would gladly forsake all her fame and fortune tomorrow in exchange for her only child's happiness.

Epilogue

Joanna Lumley certainly has many fine qualities: her shining integrity and tireless efforts on behalf of so many charities and good causes attract deserved tributes from far and wide. Family and friends rush to recognize her steadfast support during their most difficult times, and all agree that her devotion to her son and to her husband comes before all other considerations. People who know Joanna well insist that she is warm and witty, kind and caring. In a profession not renowned for self-effacement and generosity she is quite simply a one-off

Joanna could earn well over £1 million a year if she accepted half of the offers that she receives, but she prefers to be more selective as well as shrinking from any show of affluence. She would look so wonderfully right in the driving seat of the latest extravagant convertible, but she wouldn't thank you for one. She prefers her cars to be elderly and ordinary. 'I think high performance cars are for low performance people,' she is memorably quoted as saying.

Joanna hates waste and has been known to make a bar of soap last a whole year by storing it in the airing cupboard before use. In her opinion, real riches have nothing to do with bank balances and lavish possessions. 'People are the great thing for me,' said Joanna, who values humanity above all else. 'I am so fanatically interested in how people operate around the world, but I couldn't give sixpence for the next coloured lipstick or whether I'm thin or fat. What does interest me is the way that people think and the way that they hurt each other.' Joanna's ferocious honesty is happily coupled with a sharp sense of humour and she is often at her most entertaining when pointing out her own terribly English attitudes.

'If someone drives their shopping trolley over my heel in Sainsbury's I say "Sorry". We come from a bunch of people who say "Sorry".'

Joanna strives to make the world a better place. The authors have spoken to scores of people whose lives have been enriched by contact with her, but one simple encounter serves as an example. While making *A Class Act* for Carlton Television Joanna happened to learn that the programme's Press Officer, the usually sunny Sarah Sherwin, was under a cloud because the busy schedule decreed that she had to work on her thirtieth birthday. Joanna instantly arranged for a large bunch of flowers to be sent from the cast to brighten up Sarah's day. 'She was really busy, but she took the time to cheer me up and tell me that thirty had been a fantastic birthday for her,' said a delighted Sarah. 'She was so kind, I'll never forget it.'

Not surprisingly ITV have again turned to Joanna to spearhead their crucial schedule battle with the BBC, by giving her the title role of their flagship comedy series, *Dr Willoughby*. Joanna relished her role as actress Donna Sinclair who stars in a low-budget afternoon medical soap. Dedicated Dr Willoughby might be a saint on screen, but once the cameras stop rolling demanding Donna becomes a neurotic, ageing actress who will tread on anyone to get her own way. The irony is that dreadful Donna is the complete opposite of kind-hearted Joanna.

Joanna is calmer now, yet still driven to cram as much as possible into her busy life. Age has brought with it the experience and wisdom to avoid confrontations – something that she hates. 'She explained, 'I have lost my temper once or twice and I don't like losing my temper, so I try to avoid anything that will get me into that sort of situation. I loathe heated arguments ... I can't bear rowing. People say, "A good row clears the air", but I think it does the exact opposite.'

Only half jokingly, Joanna describes herself as a 'furnace of friendliness' and she defiantly insists, 'I would give my coat to the first person that asked me and they [the public] know that.' Joanna's relationship with her public goes far beyond mere popularity. Having seen her graduating from Purdey to Patsy without ever taking herself too seriously, many people feel a special bond with Joanna. Her charity work, her stylish good looks, her sense of humour and her English regard for decency and tradition have combined to form a unique personality. Typically Joanna says dismissively, 'I find it irritating to see myself, because I only ever wanted to look like Brigitte Bardot and Marilyn Monroe. Every time I see myself I think, "Oh damn, I look like me again."'

There are better actresses working – as Joanna would be the first to admit. There are certainly more beautiful women around in the looks-obsessed world of showbusiness. But there is surely no better-loved performer on our screens today. Joanna Lumley really is the first lady of entertainment.

Major TV Roles and TV Appearances

IT'S AWFULLY BAD FOR YOUR EYES, DARLING (BBC)
First broadcast as a BBC Comedy Playhouse 15 April 1971
Series (6 episodes) first broadcast 18 November 1971

The flat-sharing adventures of four men-obsessed girls. A series followed a pilot screened in Comedy Playhouse. The girls were Gillian Page-Wood, the sensible one, played by Jane Carr, Virginia Walker, the posh one, played by Jennifer Croxton (Anna Palk in the pilot), Clover Mason, the scatty one, played by Elizabeth Knight, Samantha Ryder-Ross, the sexy one, played by Joanna Lumley. Jeremy Lloyd played boyfriend Bobby Dutton.

STEPTOE AND SON (BBC)
One episode in 1972
Loathe Story

In the classic sit-com about rag-and-bone man Harold Steptoe (Harry H. Corbett) and his dirty old man father Albert (Wilfred Brambell), Joanna played Bunty, Harold Steptoe's posh, glamorous girlfriend. Harold brings Bunty and her mother (Georgina Cookson) home to their squalid house and they both leave infested with fleas.

CALL MY BLUFF (BBC)
Regular panellist from 1972 on the word game programme chaired by Robert Robinson.

ARE YOU BEING SERVED? (BBC)
Series 1
His and Hers (11 April 1973)

Joanna Lumley causes agitation among the Grace Brothers staff as a perfume retailer giving away free ties and knickers with each sale. The sales staff worry that she will reduce their sales. Captain Peacock tries to chat her up. After she spurns him she is driven off by staff when they discover from Mr Rumbold that she works for Grace Brothers.

Series 3
German Week (3 April 1975)

The staff of Grace Brothers try to promote the sale of German goods by dressing up in German fashion and performing a dance. Mrs Slocombe gets drunk and ends up fighting Captain Peacock during their dance. Joanna played a customer.

CORONATION STREET (Granada TV)
Eight episodes in July 1973

Joanna joined the soap as Elaine Perkins, graduate daughter of Wilfred Perkins, head of Bessie Street School. She went out with Ken Barlow (Bill Roache) but dropped him when he became too serious, proposing marriage.

GENERAL HOSPITAL (ATV)
Six episodes in 1975

Joanna played a flirty patient injured in a hotel fire in this medical drama about surgery, romance and problem-solving among the doctors, nurses and patients at a Midlands hospital.

THE CUCKOO WALTZ (Granada TV)
First broadcast July 1976

Sit-com starring Diane Keen and David Roper as newlyweds, Fliss and Chris, young parents of twins, who took in a lodger, Gavin, played by Lewis Collins. Joanna was in one episode playing a baby-sitter.

THE NEW AVENGERS (Avengers Film and TV Enterprises Ltd and IDTV Productions, Paris)
First broadcast 1976

The action-packed adventures of dandified Secret Service agent Steed (Patrick Macnee) and his sidekicks Mike Gambit (Gareth Hunt) and Purdey (Joanna Lumley) as they wage war on terrorists, criminals and enemies of the State.

Series 1 (13 episodes)
The Eagle's Nest
House of Cards
The Last of the Cybernauts. . . ?
The Midas Touch
Cat Amongst the Pigeons
Target
To Catch a Rat
Tale of the Big Why
Faces
Sleeper
The Three-Handed Game
Dirtier by the Dozen
Gnaws

Series 2 (13 episodes)
Dead Men are Dangerous
Angels of Death
Medium Rare
The Lion and the Unicorn
Obsession
Trap
Hostage
K is for Kill: Part 1. The Tiger Awakes
K is for Kill: Part 2. Tiger by the Tail
Complex
The Gladiators
Emily
Forward Base

SAPPHIRE AND STEEL (ATV)
First broadcast 10 July 1979

Sci-fi thriller serial created by P.J. Hammond, who wrote twenty-eight of the thirty-four episodes, in which angel-agents Sapphire (Joanna Lumley), Steel (David McCallum) and Silver (David Collings) roam through time and space to lay ghosts and rectify ancient wrongs.

Series 1: 10 July–22 November 1979 (14 episodes)
Series 2: 6 January–5 February 1981 (10 episodes)
Series 3: 11–26 August 1981 (6 episodes)
Series 4: 19–31 August 1982 (4 episodes)

THE MORECAMBE AND WISE SHOW (Thames TV)
First broadcast 18 May 1982

Joanna guest-starred in a show by top comedy duo Eric Morecambe and Ernie Wise. Joanna played Elizabeth Barratt in Ernie's play 'The Barrats of Wimpole Street' and also took part in a 'Thoroughly Modern Millie' routine.

THAT WAS TORY (BBC)
First broadcast 1984

One of a series of seven plays under the title *Oxbridge Blues* by Frederic Raphael in which Joanna played a classy, rich, elegant French woman Gigi married to a smugly successful Old Harrovian wine merchant Clive, played by John Bird. But dark forces are afoot under the veneer of success.

MISTRAL'S DAUGHTER (CBS)
First broadcast 24 September 1984

American eight-hour mini-series based on the Judith Krantz novel about the life of a selfish, womanizing Parisian painter from the mid-1920s to the mid-1960s starring Stefanie Powers, Lee Remick, Stacey Keach, Robert Ulrich, Timothy Dalton, Angela Thorne and Ian Richardson, with Joanna Lumley as Lally Longbridge.

THE GLORY BOYS (Yorkshire TV)
First broadcast 1 October 1984

Spy drama adapted by Gerald Seymour from his best-selling novel about a British hitman with a drink problem, played by Anthony Perkins, who has an affair with dowdy Helen, secretary to MI5's British Security Chief, played by Joanna Lumley. Rod Steiger also starred as an Israeli nuclear physicist.

WOGAN (BBC)
Two stints as guest host on Terry Wogan's chat show 1989 and 1991.

IN SEARCH OF THE WHITE RAJAHS (BBC)
First broadcast 25 September 1991

Joanna Lumley's first documentary about the English adventurer James Brooke who in 1841 defeated a pirate fleet which had plagued the north coast of Borneo and in return was given the kingdom of Sarawak by the Sultan of Brunei. Brooke and his family and descendants ruled until 1946.

LOVEJOY (BBC)
Three episodes in Series 3

Friends in High Places (12 January 1992)
Out To Lunch (19 January 1992)
No Strings (26 January 1992)

In the popular series about an antique dealer starring Ian McShane, Joanna played Victoria Cavero, Lovejoy's recently widowed girlfriend. They meet when he is asked to help her sell an ancient Inca ring and after their romance develops Lovejoy proposes to her. But she breaks his heart by turning him down and returning to South America where she had lived with her late husband for many years.

ABSOLUTELY FABULOUS (BBC)
First broadcast 12 November 1992

The outrageous adventures of neurotic PR executive Edina

Monsoon and her best friend Patsy Stone, a domineering, ultra-bitchy magazine editor. Caught in Edina's and Patsy's excesses were Edina's prim daughter Saffron (Julia Sawalha), nice mother (June Whitfield) and Edina's scatty PA, Bubble (Jane Horrocks).

Series 1 (6 episodes) 12 November–17 December 1992
1. Fashion
2. Fat
3. France
4. Iso Tank
5. Birthday
6. Magazine

Series 2 (6 episodes) 27 January–10 March 1994
1. Hospital
2. Death
3. Morocco
4. New Best Friend
5. Poor
6. Birth

Series 3 (6 episodes) 30 March–11 May 1995
1. Door Handle
2. Happy New Year
3. Sex
4. Jealous
5. Fear
6. The End

The Last Shout, November 1996

A PERFECT HERO (London Weekend Television)
1992

Drama series based on *The Long-Haired Boy* by Christopher Matthew, a fictional book inspired by the story of RAF pilot Richard Hillary who, despite terrible burns, embarked on an affair with actress Merle Oberon. Joanna Lumley played glamorous film star Loretta Stone visiting burned and scarred Battle of Britain pilots in hospital. Among them she discovers a former boyfriend, pilot Hugh Fleming (Nigel Havers) and romance is renewed.

CLUEDO (Granada TV)
1993

Television version of the famous whodunnit board game. Joanna played Mrs Peacock.

GIRL FRIDAY (BBC)
First broadcast 1994

Joanna volunteered to be cast away on a deserted island thirty miles off the coast of Madagascar in the Indian Ocean. Using a mixture of ingenuity and stoicism Joanna did more than survive on the island called Tsarabaina – Tsara meaning good or beautiful and Baina meaning sands.

CLASS ACT (ITV)
First broadcast 7 April 1994

The adventures of classy Kate Swift (Joanna Lumley), left penniless by her charming crook of a husband, who teams up with a journalist (John Bowe) to uncover the mystery of her missing spouse.

COLD COMFORT FARM
1994

Flora (Kate Beckinsale), a newly orphaned socialite in 1930s London, arrives in Sussex to stay with the Starkadders at Cold Comfort Farm and transforms their lives. Joanna played Flora's London confidante Mrs Smiling. With Eileen Atkins, Kate Beckinsale and Ian McKellern. Directed by John Schlesinger.

ROSEANNE
First broadcast 29 October 1996

A special Hallowe'en episode of the US sit-com starring Roseanne Barr in which Joanna Lumley and Jennifer Saunders recreated their

Absolutely Fabulous roles as Patsy and Edina. They meet Roseanne at a charity function after Roseanne's working-class TV character has won millions of dollars in a lottery. Insults are exchanged, Patsy is mistaken for a drag queen, and during a marathon champagne-drinking session, Edina tries to persuade Roseanne to back a theme park dedicated to the late Jackie Onassis.

JOANNA LUMLEY IN THE KINGDOM OF THE THUNDER DRAGON (BBC)
First broadcast 25 November 1997

Joanna retraced a journey made by her grandparents in 1931 through the mysterious kingdom of Bhutan, one of the most isolated countries in the world. Inspired by the discovery of original black and white film footage of her relatives' journey, Joanna, with her cousin Myfanwy, embarked on a personal adventure across the Land of the Thunder Dragon which lies in the Himalayas between India and China.

COMING HOME (London Weekend Television)
First broadcast 12 April 1998

Based on Rosamunde Pilcher's novel about two young girls growing up on a country estate during the war. Joanna played aristocratic Diana Carey-Lewis with Peter O'Toole as her husband. Also starring George Asprey, Patrick Ryecart, Paul Bettany, Penelope Keith and Carol Drinkwater.

THE TALE OF SWEENEY TODD
First broadcast 30 August 1998

Classic tale about the demon barber of Fleet Street Sweeney Todd (Ben Kingsley) who shaves his customers then slits their throats. His accomplice is beastly baker Mrs Lovett (Joanna Lumley) who runs a pie shop near the barber's salon and uses the bodies of Todd's victims for her pies.

FRENCH AND SAUNDERS (BBC)
First broadcast 24 December 1998

Joanna guest-starred in the comedy duo's Christmas show which included a spoof of the hit movie *Titanic*.

A RATHER ENGLISH MARRIAGE (BBC)
First broadcast 30 December 1998

Albert Finney and Tom Courtenay starred as two bereaved Englishmen at opposite ends of the social spectrum – ex-RAF fighter pilot Reginald Conyngham-Jervis (Finney) and former milkman Roy Southgate (Courtenay) – in a touching portrait of two widowers rebuilding their lives. Their 'odd couple' relationship is disrupted by Liz Franks (Joanna Lumley), a down-on-her-luck boutique owner who sees salvation in the seduction of a rich widower. Written by Andrew Davies, adapted from the novel by Angela Lambert.

NANCHERROW (Portman Entertainment for ITV)
First broadcast 4 April 1999

Joanna Lumley was given top billing in this two-part sequel to Rosamunde Pilcher's *Coming Home*, continuing the epic tale of the Carey-Lewis clan into the new-found peace of the late 1940s and early 1950s. Recently widowed Diana Carey-Lewis (Joanna Lumley) becomes romantically involved with a German businessman (Christian Kohlund) as the upkeep of the Nancherrow estate threatens to bankrupt her. With Donald Sinden, Senta Berger, Katie Ryder Richardson, Robert Hardy, Patrick Macnee, Robert Lang, Susan Hampshire, Patrick Ryecart, George Asprey, Emily Hamilton, Lynda Baron and Samantha Beckinsale.

WILLOUGHBY MD (Pearson Television)
Made in 1999

Series about a fictitious medical soap opera with Joanna Lumley as an ageing actress called Donna Sinclair. In the soap opera she is a caring doctor but off-screen she is a bitch, worried about her fading looks and about keeping her star billing in the series.

Films

SOME GIRLS DO 1969

Bulldog Drummond traces the sabotage of a supersonic airliner to a gang of murderous women. Stars Richard Johnson, Dahlia Lavi, Bebi Loncar, James Villiers, Sydne Rome, Robert Morley and Maurice Denham. Joanna had a bit part uncredited with one line: 'Yes Mr Robinson.'
Director Ralph Thomas

ON HER MAJESTY'S SECRET SERVICE 1969

Secret agent James Bond (George Lazenby) continues his search for his elusive arch enemy Blofeld (Telly Savalas). He finds the head of SPECTRE holed up in a fortress in the Swiss Alps plotting germ warfare against the agricultural and livestock producers of the world. His agents are twelve beautiful girls (including Joanna Lumley) who have been brainwashed into believing that Blofeld is a famous allergist. Blofeld plans to equip each of them with a deadly atomizer in their make-up kit and send them back to their respective countries where they will receive radio communications from Blofeld ordering them to spread their cargo of disease throughout the world.
Director Peter Hunt

TAM LIN 1971

Also known as *The Devil's Widow: The Ballad of Tam Lin*. Based on a sixteenth-century Scottish folk ballad but re-set in England in the Swinging Sixties, it starred Ava Gardner as a sinister, beautiful, middle-aged widow who has a diabolic influence on the bright

242

young people she gathers around her. They included Ian McShane, Cyril Cusack, Stephanie Beacham, Fabia Drake, Sinead Cusack, Joanna Lumley as Georgia, Madeleine Smith and Jenny Hanley.
Director Roddy McDowall

GAMES THAT LOVERS PLAY 1971

Sex comedy with Richard Wattis, Penny Brahms, Jeremy Lloyd, Nan Munro, George Belbin and Diane Hart.
Director Malcolm Leigh

THE BREAKING OF BUMBO 1972

Richard Warwick starred in the screen version of Andrew Sinclair's best-seller about Bumbo Bailey, an officer in the elite British Brigade of Guards, whose life and career are plunged into turmoil when he falls helplessly under the alluring spell of a rich model girl Susie, played by Joanna Lumley, who turns out to be a revolutionary. With Jeremy Child, John Bird, Natasha Pyne, Donald Pickering, Simon Williams and Edward Fox.
Director Andrew Sinclair

DON'T JUST LIE THERE, SAY SOMETHING 1973

Film of the successful Brian Rix stage farce about a British government minister putting forward a Morality Bill but secretly having an affair with not only his secretary Miss Parkyn (Joanna Lumley) but also the wife of a reporter. With Brian Rix, Leslie Phillips, and Joan Sims.
Director Bob Kellett

THE SATANIC RITES OF DRACULA 1973

Professor Van Helsing (Peter Cushing) investigates a sinister Black Magic circle of government ministers and uncovers a deadly experiment with a plague virus. The Secret Service in the form of agent Torrence (William Franklyn) and Scotland Yard's Inspector Murray (Michael Coles) join in the search for Dracula (Christopher Lee)

who is property tycoon D.D. Denham before Van Helsing unmasks him and his cellarful of chained nubile vampires. The vengeance-crazed Dracula wants to create the perfect world for himself and his mate, Van Helsing's granddaughter (Joanna Lumley). She narrowly escapes becoming one of the count's victims as Van Helsing sets out to stop him from wiping out mankind.
Director Alan Gibson

TRAIL OF THE PINK PANTHER 1983

Stitched together two years after the death of its star Peter Sellers. Famous bumbling French detective Inspector Clouseau (Peter Sellers) is reported to be on a plane missing at sea. Marie Jouvet (Joanna Lumley), a French television reporter, sets out to interview people from earlier Pink Panther films who had known Clouseau.
Director Blake Edwards

CURSE OF THE PINK PANTHER 1983

Interpol's computer is secretly programmed by Inspector Clouseau's boss (Herbert Lom) to select the world's worst detective to search for Clouseau. A New York cop (Ted Wass) is the man chosen for the job. Guest stars included David Niven in his last film, Roger Moore, Capucine, Leslie Ash and Joanna Lumley as Countess Chandra.
Director Blake Edwards

SHIRLEY VALENTINE 1988

Romantic comedy starring Pauline Collins in the title role as a bored middle-aged Liverpool housewife who goes on holiday to Greece to find freedom, romance, and herself. With Tom Conti, Alison Steadman, Julia McKenzie, Bernard Hill and Joanna Lumley as a high-class call girl called Marjorie.
Director Lewis Gilbert

A GHOST IN MONTE CARLO 1990

Set in 1875 and based on a book by Barbara Cartland about an ageing Parisian (Sarah Miles) who fetches her eighteen-year-old niece (Lysette Anthony) from a convent and takes her to Monte Carlo, where she becomes the belle of the Riviera. But her mother has a secret past as a notorious Paris brothel-keeper. With Oliver Reed, Christopher Plummer, Marcus Gilbert and Joanna Lumley as Lady Drayton.

Director John Hough

INNOCENT LIES 1995

The story of Jeremy and Celia Graves, a brother and sister bound by the tragic events of their childhood, and a detective who allows himself to be drawn into their private world of sexual obsession, forbidden passion, betrayal and murder. Starring Adrian Dunbar, Gabrielle Anwar, Stephen Dorff and Joanna as Lady Helena Graves.

Director Patrick DeWolf

JAMES AND THE GIANT PEACH 1996

Part-animated film based on the Roald Dahl tale of a little boy's adventures and his travels with his friends in a giant overgrown peach. Joanna Lumley played James's wicked spinster Aunt Spiker.

PRINCE VALIANT 1998

Sword and sorcery adventure adapted from Harold Foster's Arthurian comic strip. In a blurring of myth and history, cross-bow-wielding Viking warriors steal the sword Excalibur but cunningly leave a kilt behind at the scene to try and blame the Scots. With Edward Fox as King Arthur, Stephen Moyer, Udo Kier, Thomas Ketschmann, Katherine Heigl, and Joanna Lumley as Arthur's wicked half-sister, the leather-clad sorceress Morgan Le Fey, who comes to a sticky end in a jacuzzi.

Director Anthony Kickox

PARTING SHOTS 1999

A wedding photographer (Chris Rea) dying of cancer with just a few weeks to live seeks revenge on those who have harmed him.

With John Cleese, Bob Hoskins, Ben Kingsley, Joanna Lumley as a hippie barmaid called Fred still stuck in the 1970s, Diana Rigg and Felicity Kendall.
Director Michael Winner

MAD COWS 1999

Comic adventures of Anna Friel as Maddy, an unwed, lippy Aussie having a difficult time adjusting to motherhood. After a failed reconciliation with Alex (Greg Wise), father of her baby, she turns for help to her best friend Gillian (Joanna Lumley), who prides herself on looking fabulous for her age, using rich men's credit cards and getting by without working.